Trump and Mussolini

The Fairleigh Dickinson University Press
Series in Italian Studies

General Editor: Dr. Anthony Julian Tamburri, Dean of the John
D. Calandra Italian American Institute

The Fairleigh Dickinson University Press Series in Italian Studies is devoted to the publication of scholarly works on Italian literature, film, history, biography, art, and culture, as
well as on intercultural connections, such as Italian-American Studies.
On the Web at www.fdu.edu/fdupress

Recent Titles

Anna Camaiti Hostert and Enzo Antonio Cicchino, *Trump and Mussolini: Images, Fake
News, and Mass Media as Weapons in the Hands of Two Populists* (2022)

Raymond Angelo Belliotti, *Heroism and Wisdom, Italian Style* (2022)

Joseph Francese, *The Unpopular Realism of Vincenzo Padula:* Il Bruzio *and Mariuzza
Sbriffiti* (2021)

Marie Orton, Graziella Parati, and Ron Kubati (eds.), *Contemporary Italian Diversity in
Critical and Fictional Narratives* (2021)

Giorgio Linguaglossa, *Alfredo de Palchi: The Missing Link in Late Twentieth-Century
Italian Poetry* (2020)

Daniela Bini, *Portrait of the Artist and His Mother in Twentieth-Century Italian Culture*
(2020)

Cinzia Russi, *Sicilian Elements in Andrea Camilleri's Narrative Language: A Linguistic
Analysis* (2020)

Raymond Angelo Belliotti, *Values, Virtues, and Vices, Italian Style: Caesar, Dante,
Machiavelli, and Garibaldi* (2020)

Elio Attilio Baldi, *The Author in Criticism: Italo Calvino's Authorial Image in Italy, the
United States, and the United Kingdom* (2020)

Patrizia Sambuco, *Transmissions of Memory: Echoes, Traumas, and Nostalgia in Post-
World War II Italian Culture* (2018)

Thomas Cragin and Laura A. Salsini (eds.), *Resistance, Heroism, Loss: World War II in
Italian Film and Literature* (2018)

Catherine Ramsey-Portolano, *Performing Bodies: Female Illness in Italian Literature and
Cinema (1860–1920)* (2018)

Ryan Calabretta-Sajder, *Pasolini's Lasting Impressions: Death, Eros, and Literary
Enterprise in the Opus of Pier Paolo Pasolini* (2018)

Robert Pirro, *Motherhood, Fatherland, and Primo Levi: The Hidden Groundwork of
Agency in His Auschwitz Writings* (2017)

Theodora D. Patrona, *Return Narratives: Ethnic Space in Late-Twentieth-Century Greek
American and Italian American Literature* (2017)

Ursula Fanning, *Italian Women's Autobiographical Writings in the Twentieth Century:
Constructing Subjects* (2017)

Gabriella Romani and Jennifer Burns (eds.), *The Formation of a National Audience in
Italy, 1750–1890: Readers and Spectators of Italian Culture* (2017)

Lisa Sarti and Michael Subialka (eds.), *Pirandello's Visual Philosophy: Imagination and*

Thought across Media (2017)

Elena Borelli, *Giovanni Pascoli, Gabriele D'Annunzio, and the Ethics of Desire: Between Action and Contemplation* (2017)

Gregory M. Pell, *Davide Rondoni: Art in the Movement of Creation* (2016)

Sharon Wood and Erica Moretti (eds.), *Annie Chartres Vivanti: Transnational Politics, Identity, and Culture* (2016)

Flavio G. Conti and Alan R. Perry, *Italian Prisoners of War in Pennsylvania: Allies on the Home Front, 1944–1945* (2016)

Graziella Parati (ed.), *Italy and the Cultural Politics of World War I* (2016)

Susan Amatangelo (ed.), *Italian Women at War: Sisters in Arms from the Unification to the Twentieth Century* (2016)

Alberica Bazzoni, Emma Bond, and Katrin Wehling-Giorgi (eds.), *Goliarda Sapienza in Context: Intertextual Relationships with Italian and European Culture* (2016)

Trump and Mussolini

Images, Fake News, and Mass Media as Weapons in the Hands of Two Populists

By
Anna Camaiti Hostert
and Enzo Antonio Cicchino

Preface by
Anthony Julian Tamburri

Translation by
Christine Marciasini

Fairleigh Dickinson

FAIRLEIGH DICKINSON UNIVERSITY PRESS
Vancouver • Madison • Teaneck • Wroxton

Published by Fairleigh Dickinson University Press
Copublished by The Rowman & Littlefield Publishing Group, Inc.
4501 Forbes Boulevard, Suite 200, Lanham, Maryland 20706
www.rowman.com

86-90 Paul Street, London EC2A 4NE, United Kingdom

Fairleigh Dickinson University Press gratefully acknowledges the support received for scholarly publishing from the Friends of FDU Press.

British Library Cataloguing in Publication Information Available

Library of Congress Cataloging-in-Publication Data Available

ISBN 9781683933663 (cloth) | ISBN 9781683933687 (paperback) | ISBN 9781683933670 (epub)

Contents

Preface

Anthony Julian Tamburri

As a scholar of Italian and Italian diaspora studies, I feel a certain compulsion to engage with this book. Since the 1970s I have dedicated my intellectual life to studying Italy, its language and culture, and the culture of Italians in the United States. Often over the past four-plus decades many of us have pondered the relationship between and the commonalities among these two countries. In a most auspicious time, Anna Camaiti Hostert and Enzo Antonio Cicchino have penned a most significant study that compares two very controversial figures who, despite the difference in time, mirror each other in a patently uncanny manner.

This book was published in October 2020, before three momentous events affected the fate of democracy in the United States and the world. First, it came out before Covid-19 became a pandemic; second, it predates January 6, 2021, the attempt at insurrection on Capitol Hill by Trump's followers; and third, it appeared before the war in Ukraine. All three of these epochal events marked a point of no return from where we were before their respective onslaughts hither and yon.

The Italian edition of this book had yet another quality; even before these three calamitous events, it had predicted that American democracy was in great danger under the presidency of Donald Trump. September 11, the wars in Iraq and Afghanistan; and the 2008 crisis had already hinted at major cracks in the compactness of democracy's fabric. But only the advent of Donald Trump highlighted the great state of danger in which democracy has come to find itself.

The comparison that the authors make between Donald Trump and Benito Mussolini, in fact, illustrates that in spite of the 100 years that separate them—a century that saw World War II, millions of deaths, the atomic bomb, the Cold War, the Internet, and increasing globalization—there has been no possibility to shelter humanity from the dangers that led to the ferocious dictatorships of those years and the disastrous conflict that they caused. The authors write:

> 1922. 2016. Extremely far and extremely near. Mussolini and Trump. Tied by history. Both men of beginnings. . . . Both are engines of violence, one of direct bloodshed, the other of an indirect verbal incitement to violence. Mussolini had staggered rows of marchers . . .; stadiums filled to overflowing adoring crowds for Trump. . . . The first marched against the entire Italian liberal and socialist class held responsible for the *vittoria mutilata* (*mutilated victory*) of World War I. The latter against the democratic establishment of a nation in crisis that had undermined the interests of the American people. In Italy, it is the survivors of World War I. In the US, those who lived through the tragedy of September 11, 2001, an irreversible *vulnus* that has been said to be even deeper than that of World War II. (11)

And that, as Anna Camaiti Hostert writes in her *Trump non è una fiction. La nuova America raccontata attraverso le serie televisive*, sanctions a moment of no return "in which the first important restrictions on citizens and, in general, on the democratic fabric of the United States were enacted with the motivation of ensuring their security" (26; my translation).

The two authors split the required tasks: Anna Camaiti Hostert narrates Donald Trump, while Enzo Antonio Cicchino chronicles Mussolini. The book offers a close analysis in which these two seemingly different leaders are reflected in each other—indeed, as if they were carbon copies. In each chapter the authors compare the various elements that unite these two men. They begin with their respective manipulation of information and move on to the narrative each man used to both gain and maintain power. Camaiti Hostert and Cicchino compare their leadership styles that, from the beginning, figure as extremely ductile, malleable, or, as the authors define them, "protean," both men able to adapt and move in every and any direction with agility and unscrupulousness within the maze of politics in order to achieve their desired goals.

This comparison also demonstrates how the tools of consensus in a democracy are bent to the personal objectives of these two politicians, and how this operation is presented in the end as a common feeling. They mock the progressive ruling classes that, in their vulgate, constitute the *establishment* responsible for all the evils; they try to influence information by manipulating its flow and content.

Mussolini and Trump well understood the discontent that stirred in the belly of their respective countries and used it for personal gain: often wielding violence, in the case of Fascism; encouraging it, as we also heard after November 3, 2020; or, when plausible, ascribing it as part of political normality.

Their relationship with ideology is also very similar. Neither of them was attached to any specific system of ideas. Initially cultivating a closeness to progressive forces (the Socialists for Mussolini; the Democrats for Trump), they eventually situate themselves within the more conservative sector of politics, while creating their own ties with dangerous anti-democratic ideologies. The internal consensus can only be based on the sharing of a widespread skepticism toward democratic governments, on a mistrust that they claim permeates both the popular and middle classes, on the objective weakening of a pluralistic dialectic, and on the independence of the information world that they want dedicated to their very specific objectives.

In addition, the small circle of their collaborators draws from family members who are given positions and responsibilities for which they have little to none of the requisite skills for such roles. Friends and associates are also invited into the circle of collaborators because of absolute personal loyalty; and should any one of them deviate from the feelings and wishes of the leader, they are summarily removed.

In their geopolitical conception, dictators and autocrats occupy a place of honor: for Mussolini it is Hitler; for Trump it is Putin. They grant to such dictators and autocrats benefits and credibility that they would otherwise deny to other leaders in the democratic universe. In those propitious moments they seemed overwhelmed by their autocratic tendencies; in the first case, Mussolini enacts the racial laws; in the second case, Trump defends Putin on the world's stage against accusations of interference in the American elections.

* * *

At the center of this book is the state of the health of democracy, especially the American one, which—weakened exponentially with the presidency of Donald Trump—had its momentary collapse with the insurrection of January 6, 2021. Therefore, the choice of comparing Donald Trump with Benito Mussolini in particular, and not with other ancient, modern, and/or contemporary autocrats, has the merit of underlining the fact that both inaugurate a historical period in which they introduce new characteristics and peculiarities that seem, for now, unfortunately destined to last. If Mussolini well understood what the advent of mass society meant, Trump made the most of the world of social networks. Respectively, both understood very well in advance the novelty that these elements represented and used them for their purposes. Oratory, gestures, and body language have also been used as weapons to impose their will on the crowds, whose mechanisms of identification with leaders they have well understood. Indeed, even with regard to their relationships they have with women, as our authors tell us:

> Both Trump and Mussolini are often called "serial predators." Despite their differences in personal history and time periods, they have a relationship with women based on the use and consumption of their bodies. Women are disposable trophies to display in the living room of their personal egos. (98)

And that, according to Camaiti Hostert and Cicchino, is a hallmark of how, even on a metaphorical level, they lived and wielded power.

Trump's similarity to Mussolini stems not only from the comparison of parallel personal experiences, but also from the times in which they lived. In fact, the authors at the beginning of this book quote the words of CNN and *Washington Post* columnist Fared Zakaria, who in a November 2018 editorial titled "We Once Trusted Too Much in Inevitable Progress. We Got World War I," wrote:

> If you compare the world today, it does feel less like the 1930s than it does the 1920s. Economic growth and technological progress were accelerating then, as now. We are also seeing a surge in nationalism and the breakdown of cooperation, which were hallmarks of the 1920s. New great powers were ascending, as they are now. Democracies were under strain from demagogues, such as in Italy, where Mussolini destroyed liberal institutions and established control. And amid all this was the growth of populism, racism and anti-Semitism, which were used to divide countries and exclude various minorities as outside of the 'real nation'. Of course, because of the pressures of the 1920s, we got the 1930s.
>
> Today's trends are all connected. Economic growth, globalization, and technology have given rise to new centers of power, within nations and in the world at large. This is an age of big winners and big losers. The pace of change makes people anxious that their countries and cultures are changing—throughout the world. And they find comfort in strongmen who promise to protect them.

Of overriding interest today is understanding the impact of Donald Trump's presidency on American society and on the global chessboard. We know how it turned out for Mussolini, and we harbor heartfelt hopes that our fate today is better than it was then. But there are well-founded reasons to believe that the risks that appeared on the horizon then have not disappeared. Timothy W. Luke speaks to the ever-present challenges to preserve democracy:

> Perhaps nothing underscores how changed, if not corrupted, the conditions of the public sphere in the United States have become in 2021 than the weeks of chaos between the national elections of November 3, 2020, and Inauguration

Day on January 20, 2021. Desperate to attain victory at almost any cost, President Trump openly challenged the legality of electoral outcomes in six key swing states, while claiming that widespread voter fraud, election tampering, and media misrepresentation had all been directed at his campaign to rob him of a second term in the White House. Millions of Republican voters did not question his wild assertions as they followed him on social media. Most backed president Trump no matter what he did, remaining defiantly ignorant about the ignorant processes of American electoral democracy, including the constitutional provisions for its conduct that have been taught to all citizens for over 230 years. (141)[1]

It was not entirely apparent before the attack on Capitol Hill that American democracy was in existential danger even though there had been plenty of signs.[2] But it became immediately clear that day, January 6, 2020, that what had happened in the 1920s with Mussolini could happen again. "I could have made of this deaf and gray Chamber a bivouac of maniples. . . . I could: but I did not, at least at this early stage, want to," stated Mussolini in his first speech as Prime Minister on November 16, 1922, to the Chamber of Deputies.

Such danger is by no means gone; especially today, considering the recent war in Ukraine. One marked example is Trump's soft spot for Putin; we saw as much in his above-mentioned defense of Putin in Helsinki. That even today, in 2022, Trump considers Putin a great leader, and whom he recently called "a genius" (Gedeon) on the eve of the invasion of Ukraine, should give us great pause precisely because Trump still exhibits notable influence. But it is more than just Trump, as Luke reminds us in his collection of essays on Trumpification:

One must not doubt how real a threat Trump with his Republican, Democratic, and independent supporters remains today, as 2022 and 2024 draw closer. Even if Trump himself is sidelined by criminal investigations, civil suits, or political prohibitions by those in government bold enough to pursue them, like enforcing the ban in Section 3 of the Fourteenth Amendment (enforceable against any person "who, having previously taken an oath, as a member of Congress, or as an officer of the United States, . . . to support the Constitution of the United States, shall have engaged in insurrection or rebellion against the same, or given aid or comfort to the enemies thereof"), his close allies and eager imitators in the GOP are preparing vigorously to carry on the project of Trumpification for what they regard as the "MAGA Nation." (2021b, ix–x)

In citing Luke at this juncture, I shall do what we are told not to do, end my introduction with a quote, sort of. Luke is clearly not alone in his prognosis of what the future holds regarding Trump and his control over his many acolytes and sycophants: innumerable reams of paper and countless hours of airtime have spoken to what the future may hold. Indeed, as most depend on the various infotainment programs of TV and the Internet, Luke concludes his essay collection with the thought that "too many citizens become stranded by the distractions of their chosen electronic amusements, which tighten the halters of imprecise information making them at once smarter and more stupid in the contemporary public sphere as they suffer the travails of Trumpification" (2021b, 163). This is, in fact, the danger: that too many "close allies and eager imitators in the GOP are preparing vigorously to carry on the project of . . . the 'MAGA Nation'" (2021b, x).

NOTES

1. In addition to Luke, see also Jay A. Gupta and Mark G. E. Kelly. The three scholars each have concise essays that speak to the "Changing Character of the Public Sphere," the name of a special section in *Telos* (Summer 2021).

2. Luke, in fact, wants to revert to the 1980s to understand more fully the travails of Trumpification (2021b, vii passim).

WORKS CITED

Camaiti Hostert, Anna. *Trump non è una fiction: La nuova America raccontata attraverso le serie televisive.* Milan: Mimesis, 2017.

Gedeon, Joseph. "Trump calls Putin 'genius' and 'savvy' for Ukraine invasion." *Politico*, February 23, 2022. Accessed March 1. https://www.politico.com/news /2022/02/23/trump-putin-ukraine-invasion-00010923.

Gupta, Jay A. "Speaking B.S. to Truth: The Public Sphere in the Age of Trump." *Telos* (Summer 2021): 151–156.

Kelly, Mark G. E. "The Closing of the American Public Sphere." *Telos* (Summer 2021): 157–164.

Luke, Tomothy W. "The Changing Public Sphere in America: The Fragility of Civic Awareness, Common Community, and Electoral Democracy Today." *Telos* 195 (Summer 2021a): 141–150.

Luke, Tomothy W. *The Travails of Trumpification*. New York: Telos Press Publishing, 2021b.

Zakaria, Fareed. "We Once Trusted Too Much in Inevitable Progress: We Got World War I." *The Washington Post*, 2018. November 8. Accessed March 1, 2021. https:// www.washingtonpost.com/opinions/history-teaches-us-that-things-dont-always -work-themselves-out/2018/11/08/1baaa3e6-e3a0-11e8-ab2c-b31dcd53ca6b_story .html.

Acknowledgments

We are indebted first and foremost to U.S. Ambassador Robert J. Callahan and to Prof. Franco Ferrarotti for their availability and for agreeing to be interviewed; these interviews are essential parts of this book. We are also grateful to Prof. Laura Ferrarotti Battino and to Dr. Roberta Prevosti, respectively for speeding up the process and for editing Prof. Ferrarotti's interview. Finally, we thank Milos Fascetti for providing precious guidance in this respect.

Along with these two important contributors, we would have liked to have had a woman's point of view, but unfortunately, though we contacted several Italian women journalists and politicians, we had no luck. They all said they did not have the time or did not feel up to the job due to the state of affairs in America in the last few years. We truly regret the lack of a female perspective as we believe that such a contribution would have been invaluable, especially in a book such this one where the analysis of power goes hand in hand with the consideration of the female body to which chapter 8 is dedicated.

Special thanks goes to Nicola Fano, a leading figure in Italian theater and director of the web magazine *Succedeoggi* for which Anna Camaiti Hostert is a columnist. We are indebted to him for the amusing and provocative title of the Italian edition. It comes from a very famous Fascist slogan *Libro e moschetto fascista perfetto* (A book and a musket: a perfect Fascist). The main Italian title is in fact *Trump e moschetto* (Trump and a musket) in reference to that slogan.

Our deepest thanks to Gianluca Sacco who helped us solve several challenging questions.

Our gratitude also goes to the entire editorial staff of *La grande Storia*, of which Enzo Antonio Cicchino was author/director, for the research of the cinematographic material and the cross-checking of the many texts that formed the framework of this book with respect to Mussolini. Finally, we would like to thank Loredana Pietri, director of the Arturo Chiari Library in Rome, for loaning us many rare books.

We would like to thank Roberto Revello, director of *Mimesis,* our Italian publisher for having chosen this book. And with him the entire editorial staff of *Mimesis:* Valentina Achilli, Francesca Adamo and in particular Elena Gritti who with patience, great love and professionalism, proofread the text, guiding us step by step in that process. Special thanks also goes to the graphic designer Nicolò Ciccarone who always finds original and appropriate images to illustrate the characteristics of the texts submitted to him and which, especially in our case, were fundamental. A further thanks goes to the young American graphic designer Matthew Daniel.

Last but not least, we would like to express our deepest gratitude to George Hostert, Anna Camaiti Hostert's husband. He often joined us in our conversations, giving us precious observations that helped us to better focus on the comparison between Trump and Mussolini. This book is dedicated to him.

Introduction

Similarities in the Trump and Mussolini Eras

This book was just being completed as the coronavirus, which irreversibly changed the world and our lives, began ravaging humanity. Conceived as a comparison between two historical figures roughly a 100 years apart, we certainly could not foresee this event, but we incidentally made reference to it. There are similarities between the time of the Coronavirus pandemic and that of the devastating *Spanish flu*, which from its onset in 1918 to its disappearance in 1925, killed millions worldwide.

In Italy, there were roughly 500,000 victims. This was almost as many as died on the Karst Plateau[1] and the Piave[2] during World War I. The disgraceful conditions in the trenches and the overcrowded barracks had already caused outbreaks of typhus, scabies, cerebrospinal meningitis, and other deadly diseases. The *Spanish flu* also grafted itself onto an already precarious national situation caused by malaria (6,000,000 cases in the years of World War I and 10,000 in 1918), tuberculosis (over 2,000,000 cases, 7,000 of which in 1918), and outbreaks of other diseases that seemed to be under control, such as pellagra, measles, and diphtheria.

The Americans were also hard hit by the *Spanish flu*. The United States recorded approximately 675,000 deaths with more soldiers dying from the epidemic than in World War I. The outbreak was further exacerbated by a severe shortage of medical personnel, many of whom were on the front lines. At one point, the city of Philadelphia found itself without cemetery space, without coffins, or without gravediggers. Trenches had to be dug with excavators to make room for the massive number of bodies, as Catherine Arnold tells us in her 2018 book, *Pandemic 1918: Eyewitness Accounts from the Greatest Medical Holocaust in Modern History* (St. Martin's Griffin, New York, 2018).

Looking at the events of our time, we can say that today there have been profound changes in the international geopolitical order also due to the Coronavirus. In particular, the relationship between the United States and China has been deeply modified, as the two countries are engaged in a sort of cold war. In addition, Trump had a gigantic plan to inject aid into the American economy, brought to its knees by the virus, while accusing China of spreading the pandemic. At the same time China was glorifying its ability to quickly defeat the virus, unlike the Americans and the other Western democracies. Within this context, the image of both these powers pitted one against the other is diminishing their standing displaying a weakness before the entire world thereby creating an unprecedented sense of insecurity.

CNN contributor and columnist Fareed Zakaria, in commemorating the centennial anniversary of the end of World War I, defined as the "the greatest and bloodiest conflict ever seen," wrote in his opinion piece "We Trusted too much in inevitable progress. We got World War I" published on November 8, 2018, in the *Washington Post*: "World War I marked a turning point in human history—the end of four massive European empires, the rise of Soviet communism and the entry of the United States into global-power politics. But perhaps its most significant intellectual legacy was the end of the idea of inevitable progress."

He continued by writing that when the war began, people were living in a period similar to our own, defined by rapid economic growth, technological revolutions, and increasing globalization. As a result, people believed that the ugly trend lines were temporary and would be overwhelmed by the inexorable march of progress. In 1909 the famous best seller by Norman Angell (he was later awarded the Nobel Peace Prize), *The Great Illusion*, was published. Shortly after the publication of the book, which stated that a war between the great powers would be so costly as to be unimaginable, "a generation of Europeans was destroyed by the carnage of the World War I." And so, the columnist asks whether we are not in the same situation today and are too distracted to clearly see the facts before us. He answers:

> If you compare the world today, it does feel less like the 1930s than it does the 1920s. Economic growth and technological progress were accelerating then, as now. We are also seeing a surge in nationalism and the breakdown of cooperation, which were hallmarks of the 1920s. New great powers were ascending, as they are now. Democracies were under strain from demagogues, such as in Italy, where Mussolini destroyed liberal institutions and established control. And amid all this was the growth of populism, racism and anti-Semitism, which were used to divide countries and exclude various minorities as outside of the "real nation." Of course, because of the pressures of the 1920s, we got the 1930s.
>
> Today's trends are all connected. Economic growth, globalization and technology have given rise to new centers of power, within nations and in the world

at large. This is an age of big winners and big losers. The pace of change makes people anxious that their countries and cultures are changing—throughout the world. And they find comfort in strongmen who promise to protect them. (Zakaria 2018)

The goal of our book is not only to compare the two politicians, Benito Mussolini and Donald Trump, but also to consider the similarities of their eras. Although in many instances the similarities have a different origin, the differences will show that it is possible to escape the inevitability of history that cyclically presents comparable situations essential to timely identify an exit strategy. In the long run it will ensure avoiding a catastrophe of unimaginable proportions, as happened with the descent into hell that began in the 1920s. It is well known that history is not made of *ifs* or *buts*. It is self-evident and perhaps even redundant to reiterate that reasoning about one's own past helps to avoid repeating it. Nevertheless, the opportunity to reflect on historical similarities does permit studying such situations that emphasize differences, as well as provide potential solutions to current-day problems. Above all, it allows us to understand that the degeneration of certain historical conditions derives from a malaise to which answers need to be provided, without believing that these problems will be simply resolved, through the inevitability of progress, or through the possibility of stopping them by force or violence.

Popular sentiment can be likened to a river in the Alps that appears and disappears into a mountain side, almost as if it were a warning to heed its course even when invisible. Because, when it reappears (and it always reappears), it does so with an unusual unstoppable virulence. Thus, like the river popular sentiment cannot be ignored.

In a small but significant volume *Trump or Democratic Fascism* (Meltemi, Milan 2019), Alan Badiou argued that Trump's election was the result of the dialectic of the present historical moment. He identified several reasons that define this moment: the globalized absolutism of capitalism, the irreversible crisis of the politics of the bourgeois elites, the general disoriented and frustrated state in which people live, and the lack of an alternative strategy which includes the other reasons. All of this can be condensed in the simple phrase: *there is no alternative. There is no alternative* to the fact that wealth is concentrated in the hands of the few. *There is no alternative* to the fact that capitalism is unable to ensure the survival of billions of men and women wandering the world. *There is also no alternative* to the fact that the domination of globalized capitalism carries within itself the seeds of its destruction. As a result, political elites are irreparably compromised and lose control. Thus, within Western democracies, there is a proliferation of politicians who constitute what he calls an "internal exteriority." They use violent, inflammatory, and contradictory language with the aim of creating emotional flows that coagulate into artificial solutions. People in moments of crisis are magnetized by irrational and often unattainable promises that are sometimes based on a mythical past impossible to regain. Thus, is born what Badiou calls "democratic Fascism," which sneaks in those old ideas such as nationalism, racism, colonialism, and sexism, and fuses them into a pastiche where old and new coexist without any rational criteria. Unlike true Fascism, this new one does not have a physical antagonist like communism and does not even have specific organizations built around its leader. However, it is a phenomenon within the dominant system that for Badiou focuses on the sacredness of private property.

In addition, in the first twenty years of this millennium the United States underwent a period of unprecedented upheaval. Three events in particular have shaken its core. The first was the trauma of September 11, 2001, from which it has never recovered. It was an aggression aimed at the heart of America. The second was the Great Recession of 2008, which was comparable to the Great Depression that began with the stock market crash of 1929. The third was the election of Barack Obama, the first African American President in its history. All three events, for different reasons, brought out the dark side of America's soul: the first showed the loss of an innocence that never really existed; the second showed that capitalism was not the best of all possible worlds; and the third that the DNA of the country harbors a racial prejudice, that has never really been overcome. Despite all this, the great merit of this country is its ability to continuously regenerate and to be reborn like a phoenix, thanks to its pitiless ability to skin itself to the bone, without any sugarcoating, while seeking alternative solutions. All this, however, not before having hit bottom as it has done in this period.

This book has analyzed Trump and Mussolini, with tools that belong to the two authors who have different, but complementary backgrounds. Our *outillage* is the one of images, information, and mass media. One of us, a philosopher has worked for years to deconstruct and reassemble the images through the theoretical devices of Visual Studies (Metix. *Cinema globale e cultura visuale*, [*Global Cinema and Visual Culture*] Meltemi, Rome 2004). She was instrumental in having translated into Italian, the work of the creator of Visual Studies, Nicholas Mirzoeff, *Introduction to Visual Culture* and wrote the Introduction for the Italian edition. The other author worked for the Italian national broadcaster, RAI, and is a Mussolini scholar. He is long familiar with images having used them from cinema and television, on the program *La Grande Storia*, and in his essays on Fascism.

October 30, 1922, Italy. November 8, 2016, United States. Europe, America. Two continents and an ocean of history separated by ninety-four years. Similarities?! On the one hand Benito Mussolini, the son of a blacksmith and a film *A noi!* (*Leave it to Us!*), with scenes that mark the various stages of his March on Rome. On the other hand, Donald Trump, real estate developer, son of a millionaire real estate developer made a TV celebrity by the program *The Apprentice*. He is one of the richest men in America, running for the leadership of the most powerful democratic empire in the world.

However, there is something amiss with the man aspiring to live in the White House. He is accused of having an unpresentable role model: Benito Mussolini, precisely! On December 9, 2015, Dana Milbank wrote in the *Washington Post* an article entitled: "Donald Trump, America's modern Mussolini." Milbank was baffled by the billionaire's harsh, populist tone that sought to erect walls, create divisions, and exclude certain groups from entering the nation. He expressed his concern about the "strong-willed jaw and broad right-handed gestures" he displayed. Trump wanted to create a sense of fear, make his followers feel like victims of his opponents. He hunted for scapegoats and asserted that he was the only one who could solve these crises. He altered reality, truth, and common sense, and spoke to the gut of the country especially to that of Republicans, moving them all further toward an extreme conservatism. And then on February 2016 he tweeted: "It is better to live one day as a lion than one hundred years as a sheep." This is a famous phrase of the Italian *Duce*[3] and taken from the account @ ilduce2016: the profile picture is the one of Mussolini with blond hair like Trump.

1922. 2016. Extremely far and extremely near. Mussolini and Trump. Tied by history. Both men of beginnings. Early twentieth-century Rome. Early 2000s Washington DC. Both are engines of violence, one of direct bloodshed, the other of an indirect verbal incitement to violence. Mussolini had staggered rows of marchers as shown in the 1922 film mentioned above *A noi!* Stadiums filled to overflowing adoring crowds for Trump. Faces, smiles, eyes, hands trying to reach him, screaming bodies. Are these people or just pawns in a gigantic chess game? The first marched against the entire Italian liberal and socialist class held responsible for the *vittoria mutilata* (*mutilated victory*)[4] of World War I. The latter against the democratic establishment of a nation in crisis that had undermined the interests of the American people. In Italy, the survivors of the World War I. In the United States, those who lived through the tragedy of September 11, 2001, an irreversible *vulnus* that is considered to be even deeper than that of World War II. In the United States it was a date that marked:

> a point of no return for the country and which was the moment when the first important restrictions on its citizens' freedom and in general on the democratic fabric of the United States were enacted on the grounds of guaranteeing their security. After that, Americans discovered that the US was not an oasis of innocent and *super partes* democracy they had believed up to that moment, but that

in many parts of the world hatred towards it was a widespread reality." (Camaiti
Hostert, p. 26)

How is this possible? Why this double advent? The beginning must be from
afar: Mussolini.

"We are decidedly against all forms of dictatorship, from that of the saber
to that of the tricorn, from that of money to that of numbers." These words
would have been words without effect if they had not been pronounced by the
man seated in Rome's Palazzo Venezia, the man who sided with Adolf Hitler,
the man of the declaration of war, and the man of the racial laws. Today they
sound curious, but on March 23, 1919, the day the *Fasci di Combattimento*
(Fasces of Combat, also known as Fighting Leagues)[5] were founded in Piazza
San Sepolcro in Milan, those words were persuasive to all who were present
to hear them. Moreover, he even managed to embarrass the industrialists present in the meager audience, because he added: "We therefore must accept the
demands of the working classes. Do they want to work eight hours? Do they
want disability and old age pensions? Do they want control over industry?
We will support these demands. If the trade unions' *credo* asserts that heads
of factories can be drawn from the masses we will not stand in the way."

Mussolini could not have imagined in those early days that just three years
later, as the head of government he could have achieved those goals, but he
chose not to do so. In fact, there was an 8 percent regression in the value of
wages compared to those before World War I. The quality of workers' lives
had become evermore spartan. Moreover, the Fascist unions had relinquished
their right to strike in order to place controversies with their employers in the
hands of the government. The state monopoly on life insurance was eliminated. A hiring decline in the Railways was underway with a reduction of
36,000 positions. The Telephone Service was returned to the private sector.

In any event, the containment of public spending, the increase in industrial
production, and the tightening of wage restraints would lead, by the end of
1925, to a balanced budget and the return of Italy's accounts to parity. Mussolini thus enjoyed a stable twenty years to subsequently lead Italy, in 1940,
to the catastrophe of war, the effects of which Italians are still suffering today.
Moreover, during that time the lives of Italians had consistently deteriorated.

There is often a contradictory relationship between "easier said than
done." Between the vision of one's own political universe and that of the
people, or rather of what one wants the people to believe. Thus, Trump in a
tweet of October 17, 2016, after a rally in Green Bay, Wisconsin, where he
had already reiterated this concept, a few weeks before the election, wrote:
"The election is absolutely being rigged by the dishonest and distorted
media pushing Crooked Hillary but also at many polling places—SAD."
And in a later one, "Of course there is large scale voter fraud happening on

and before election day. Why are Republicans denying what is happening? So naive!" questioning not only the ability of his own party to control the election, but also the veracity of the results and the democratic process, and then having his Vice President reiterate that "we will absolutely accept the results of the election. Elections, you know, by nature are not subtle, they are hard, but they have always been held in the tradition of a peaceful transfer of power," said Mike Pence immediately after the remarks of the President.

In March 2016, candidate Donald Trump was forced to cancel a gathering in Chicago due to heavy unrest in the streets. After complaining in an interview with MSNBC's Chris Matthews that the country was divided and shaken by unusual and dangerous anger, Trump said such phenomena should not occur in a democratic country:

> What happened to freedom of speech? You can't have a rally in a major city in this country anymore. What happened to the right to get together and discuss? It was very sad to have to cancel this peaceful initiative, but after I met with law enforcement, I made the decision in conjunction with law enforcement that it was not the case and democratically postponed the event. (Matthews 2016)

Asked by the interviewer to define the reasons for the discontent of these largely African Americans and Hispanic minorities, Trump replied that more jobs were needed as unemployment plagued 55 percent of these minority groups, citing as the reason for this unemployment the fact that many jobs had been moved out of the United States. "This is what these people are missing and this is what we're going to give them." After he was elected, he would claim that he was responsible for the drop in unemployment, knowing full well that he was contradicting reality. "Unemployment among African-Americans, Hispanic-Americans and Asian-Americans reached an all-time low"—Trump said in February 2019. And if it was true that during his term of office in May 2019, African American unemployment was 5.95 percent, the lowest since 1972, it immediately rose again to 6.8 percent in August of the same year. It is also true that fundamentally this increase in employment was the product of Obama's economic policy, which had caused that unemployment rate to fall from 16.8 percent in March 2010 to 7.8 percent in January 2017. Regarding the unemployment rate of Hispanic Americans and Asian Americans which was respectively at 4.4 percent in October 2018 and at 2.2 percent in May 2019, it subsequently increased again due to the shutdown of the government. The Trump presidency generally speaking brought a growth in unemployment levels among these minorities nationwide.

NOTES

1. Part of the Italian front in World War I, the Karst Plateau or the Karst region (in Italian it is called the *Carso*), is a rocky plateau region extending across the border of southwestern Slovenia and northeastern Italy. It lies between the Vipava Valley, the low hills surrounding the valley, the westernmost part of the Brkini Hills, northern Istria, and the Gulf of Trieste. The western edge of the plateau also marks the traditional ethnic border between the Italians and the Slovenes.

2. The Piave, an important river in Northern Italy, was also part of the Italian front in World War I. It begins in the Alps and flows southeast for roughly 140 miles into the Adriatic Sea near the city of Venice. It was the site of numerous battles in World War I; it is often remembered for the Second Battle of the Piave River which was a decisive victory of the Italian army in June 1918 against the Austro-Hungarian army.

3. This is the Italian title, derived from the Latin word *dux*, meaning leader, given to Benito Mussolini as leader of the Fascist movement and later of the *Partito Nazionale Fascista* (PNF, National Fascist Party).

4. The mutilated victory was what the Italian nationalists and Italian irredentists used to describe their disappointment over the territory assigned to Italy at the end of World War I. Italy did gain Trentino, part of Slovene-speaking Gorizia, Trieste, the German-speaking South Tirol, and partly Croatian-speaking Istria. However, Dalmatia was excluded, as was Fiume (today Rijeka, Croatia), a Yugoslav port largely inhabited by Italian speakers as were any colonial territories in Africa or Asia and any claim on Albania. The rhetoric of *mutilated victory* was taken up by Benito Mussolini and was among the factors that led to the rise of Italian Fascism, becoming a key point of Fascist propaganda in Italy.

5. This was an Italian Fascist organization that Mussolini created in 1919. The name of it was inspired by the *fasci*, or the fasces carried by Roman lictors, which were symbols of ancient Roman authority. These leagues were to be groups of fighters bound together so tightly that they resembled these *fasci*. The *Fasci di Combattimento* were the forerunners of the *National Fascist Party* and were transformed into it in 1921.

Chapter 1

Manipulating Information

On August 24, 2015, Donald Trump was more than a year away from election day. He was in Mobile, Alabama, where he was busy exciting the crowd with provocative and controversial jokes laced with sexist and racist undertones. He could ignore the contempt of those who called him unpresentable, of the media that snubbed him, and of the TV channels that refused to broadcast his campaign. He was totally euphoric, totally free: he was not yet the Republican nominee for President. He actually came from a past as a Democrat, a supporter of the Clinton Foundation to which he had donated hundreds of thousands of dollars. In 2005, he had also invited former President Clinton and his family to his Florida wedding to the then Melania Knaus. At that moment no one in the world was betting on him. He had zero odds. His colorful language, however, made his campaign lively. The great favorite to win the election, Hillary Clinton, was a woman (and he is a misogynist), the wife of Bill Clinton, *crooked Hillary*, as Trump called her. He represented an unprecedented element when compared to candidates who usually run for the White House.

Mussolini had a similar turncoat attitude. Moreover, politically he was a nobody. He was only famous for betraying the Socialist Party. Everyone remembered him as an untrustworthy journalist when on October 18, 1914, while editor of the pacifist *Avanti!*, he tried to make it a bellicose publication by publishing the well-known article "Dalla neutralità assoluta alla neutralità attiva ed operante" (From absolute neutrality to active and operational neutrality). In that article he tried to lead the entire nation to the hell that was World War I. He was kicked out of the *Partito Socialista Italiano* (PSI, the Italian Socialist Party) and became an outcast. He was also viewed as a traitor for having received covert funding from France and England to start his own newspaper: *Il Popolo d'Italia*. The price of that newspaper was the life of the Italians who would go to war.

Mussolini took money not only from the belligerent countries, but also from his mistress, Ida Dalser. By the end of the war the political climate in Italy was red-hot; the country was on the brink of a civil war. Nationalist sentiments against the so-called "mutilated victory" had been ignited, and these created sparks of revolt. Workers and peasants were urging the government to honor promises made by members of parliament to soldiers in the trenches to encourage them to willingly face Austrian machine guns. Idle words which, with the east wind of the Soviet revolution, became a weapon of the poor to demand concrete commitments: improving the quality of life at work, encouraging joint management of factories, and the distribution of land.

The workers and peasants were backed by a strong Socialist Party, and the threat of communism was genuine. Mussolini thought of proposing a compromise solution that would meet the social demands of the masses without disrupting capitalism. When he founded the *Fasci di Combattimento*, they had an ambitious program of a social nature that was also supported by many men, like him, who had left the Socialist Party, as well as many intellectuals. The truth, however, was that he did not believe in it. It was more of a journalistic exhibition to get a tally of the consensus for his newspaper, *Il Popolo d'Italia*, among the middle and upper classes, than an innovative proposal to be conducted in the *agora* of the country. He was not really interested in the quality of life of the lower classes; his concern was rather determined by the bundles of unsold copies of his newspaper. The paper's revenue was directly proportional to the consensus of his articles among readers, who had to identify both with the writer and with what they read. The idea behind the *Fasci di Combattimento* was not ideological, but economic at least in the beginning. He created them, because if he had not founded them, he knew that someone else would have done so.

The political position of the *Fasci* by necessity had to be the founder's profits. And even when two years later the movement became a party, the *Partito Nazionale Fascista* (PNF or National Fascist Party) would always be hindered from its being the emanation of an entrepreneur for whom its special status was as a "business-firm party" (*partito azienda*). To protect his paper there would be many times when Mussolini would be forced to retreat from a certain position to prevent a disastrous plummet in its circulation.

Despite having a few business failures behind him, despite being called a TV "clown," a reputation he also held in Europe, Trump was in a much better position than Mussolini even though in August 2016, when he was already the Republican Party candidate, his odds of winning in New Hampshire were still only 18 percent. He was only leading in Florida. In Alabama Trump had thrown down the gauntlet from the skies. Departing from New

York, he flew down on his Boeing 757 in front of a huge crowd waiting for him in the stadium. The effect was spectacular. Half an hour later he reached the crowd amidst delirious cheers to then deliver a harangue from the podium.

It was a performance that brings to mind a slogan of Goebbels "Hitler over Germany" when in the 1932 elections the future Führer made continuous propaganda trips by plane to German cities. This is not an isolated comparison. Michael Moore's 2018 documentary *Fahrenheit 11/9* (a play on the title of his documentary *Fahrenheit 9/11* dealing with the tragedy of 9/11) on Trump's November 9, 2016, victory, is evidence of this. In it Moore suggests a historical comparison between Trump's speeches and those of the Führer in a daring cross-over montage of the September 11, 2001, event and the Reichstag fire. We are inclined to think that perhaps his colorful expressions, his jokes, and his body language are more reminiscent of certain incitements, even gestures, of Mussolini, when in the 1930s he seemed to shake with his exaggerations, in sentences peppered with absolute superlatives broken up by continuous *Eia, eia alalà*[1] and "I don't care," rather than the words of the German dictator. Nevertheless, it must be said that more recently, with Trump's conspiracy theories and his attention and support of far-right delusional organizations such as QAnon, which has focused on plots against the President, Trump has certainly veered very close to certain positions taken by the Führer.

Trump also butters up his fans: "Hot as guns," he defines them. However instead of answering as the Italians did with *A noi!* (*Leave it to us!*), the fans respond with the more cautious "Make America Great Again." Every destabilization has its songs. The Fascists had *Giovinezza* (Youth), and Trump fans had the controversial *Sweet Home Alabama* by Lynyrd Skynyrd.

The origins of each man could not be more different. Mussolini came from *Predappio*, in the Romagna region of Italy, the child of a petit-bourgeois family. He was first an elementary school teacher, then an entrepreneur, as publisher of a newspaper. Trump was born and raised in New York, son of a millionaire real estate developer, born to wealth, accustomed to luxury from birth, and a TV jet-set star. Both, though, are connoisseurs of mass media and attentive to the use of technology.

Mussolini sensed before anyone else the advent of mass society and the importance of mass media. It is said that on his bedside table he had kept for years the bible of what has been called a before-its-time description of mass society: *La psychologie des foules* (*Psychology of Crowds*) by the French anthropologist and sociologist Gustave Le Bon who wrote it in 1895, which Mussolini read in the original language. This book also helped him to identify the importance of the new means of mass communication such as radio and film.

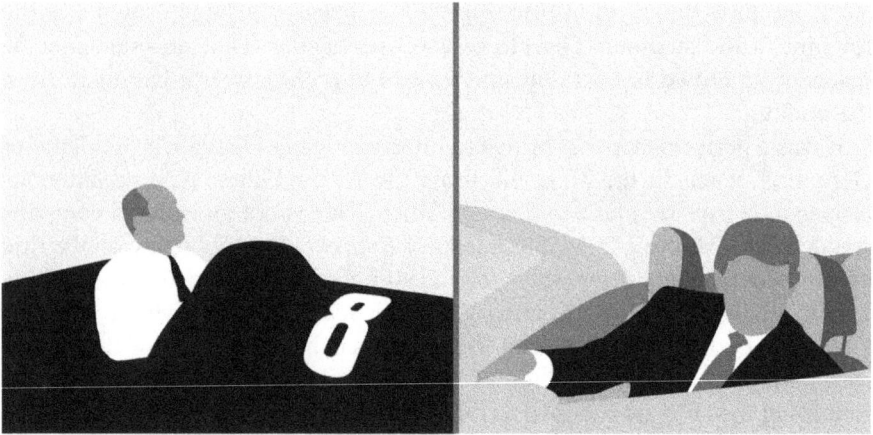

Figure 1.1   Mussolini And Trump in Sport Cars Flirt with New Technologies. By the authors.

Trump is definitely less sophisticated than Mussolini, and he definitely does not speak another language. Nevertheless, he is an avid and astute user of mass media, particularly television, as can be seen with his show *The Apprentice* which granted him a vast number of fans. He also lives in a period of great technological transformation that has made the country and the world completely connected with anyone able to be seen and heard on the internet. Social media is the master and Trump is a serial writer of tweets and messages on the net.

In a book with the explanatory title *Trump and the Media. The Election of Donald Trump and the Great Disruption in the News and Social Media* edited by Pablo J. Boczkowski and Zizi Papachirissi, there are a series of essays by experts in journalism and technology that address the unease in the current media landscape, the disconnect between voters and the media, the emergence of what has been called "fake news," and consequently of what are known as "alternative facts." They also discuss Trump's use of social media. They observe that the relationship between the news media and politics in the twenty-first century has undergone a notable metamorphosis. The television series *The Newsroom* (HBO 2012–2014) written by Aaron Sorkin (author of numerous successful television series such as *The West Wing* and films such as *The Social Network* and *Steve Jobs*) had as its theme the transformation of the manner in which communication was conducted in the United States from the late 1980s to the present day. The series illustrated that what is referred to as "fake news" is running the show. This dangerous approach to truth based on the ideology of the news channels in the last decade has changed the nature and the main purpose of the news world. A striking example can be found in the presidential debates of 2016. In many of these, especially in the last ones, the comments of several journalists from various channels reflecting on the themes that had dominated the discussion, emphasized completely different points of view based on the political position of the channels for which they worked. Those perspectives consequently influenced exit polls and the electorate. Further, the ridicule and the hostility shown by Trump toward the "liberal" press, accused of being against him simply because they asked questions he did not like and refused to answer, did the rest. Trump even went so far as to openly mock freedom of the press.

The Newsroom (HBO 2012–2014) addressed something that preceded the current situation. It pointed out that the news world had lost its independence and its principles of professional ethics that made it famous across both the United States and the world as a pillar of American democracy. Symbol of that freedom of the press was the Watergate scandal: the two famous *Washington Post* journalists, Bob Woodward and Carl Bernstein, fought for the truth and revealed a cover up by President Nixon. He was ultimately forced to resign.

In July 2016 in conjunction with the Republican convention, which nominated Donald Trump as its candidate for President of the United States, a news story emerged which was bound to make people think about the news media world in the United States. Roger Ailes, CEO and founder of Fox News, had been accused of sexual harassment by the Fox News journalist Gretchen Carlson. She alleged that he had sabotaged her career because she refused his sexual advances. Twenty other women also came forward and confirmed the misogynistic attitude of Roger Ailes. This included Megan Kelly, also a Fox News journalist, the very same journalist Trump accused of being irritated with him because she was menstruating. Kelly, who owed her career entirely to Ailes, admitted to the *Los Angeles Times* that she had been harassed by him. Roger Ailes denied all of the allegations.

But who was Roger Ailes? The beautiful 2019 television series *The Loudest Voice* broadcast on *Showtime* and based on the novel by Gabriel Sherman, *The Loudest Voice in the Room* published in 2014, tells the story of the rise and fall of this arrogant and overbearing man, played magnificently by an unidentifiable Russell Crowe. Ailes was one of the most powerful men in America who, in 1996, at the request of Rupert Murdoch, created the 24-hour television news channel Fox News as an answer to CNN, just as MSNBC, a Democratic-inspired television channel, was being launched. Ailes made Fox a clearly partisan channel that brazenly favored Republicans without hiding its partisanship. Something that was absolutely new and unknown in the United States. He built the channel from scratch, making divisiveness, aggressiveness, and quarrelsomeness its distinctive brand. Because these characteristics provided entertainment and increased ratings, especially among the over-sixty-five demographic, which was also the age group that

preferred using television for its information, Ailes hired conservative journalists like Bill O'Reilly, defended Glenn Beck in his reactionary crusades,
and made Republican politicians feel at home. Sarah Palin (John McCain's
2008 vice presidential running mate) and Newt Gingrich (Republican speaker
of the House of Representatives from 1995 to 1999) considered Fox News a
friendly platform from which to address their electorate.

When at more than eighty years of age, Rupert Murdoch took over Ailes
he told NBC in a July 21, 2016 interview:

> It is always difficult to create a channel or a publication from the ground up and
> against seemingly entrenched monopolies. His [Ailes] grasp of policy and his
> ability to make profoundly important issues accessible to a broader audience
> stand in stark contrast to the self-serving elitism that characterizes far too much
> of the media.

"Fox News has dominated not just conservative viewers but has shaped
the modern Republican Party. Ailes has played an outsized role in making
sure conservative views and viewpoints got into the mainstream. That's
his legacy" as Donna Brazile, at the time a CNN contributor and influential
Democratic Party strategist, stated in an interview included in the article "Is it
the End of Roger Ailes? The Convention crowd wonders what's next at Fox"
of the *Washington Post* on July 19, 2016. She continued,

> But the end of Ailes' career doesn't mean the end of what he created. I don't
> think you can change the brand. Many Americans view it as a conservative sta-
> tion. It will stay the voice, the face and the heart of the conservative movement.

Before he died in May 2017, Roger Ailes had a long resume to his credit.
He began his career in the late 1960s as Richard Nixon's 1968 campaign
adviser, continued during Ronald Reagan's 1984 re-election, and reached, as
supervisor of media strategy for George H.W. Bush, the apogee of information star. A true Republican, a "hawk" who enriched the Murdoch family
with 700 million dollars every year, which served to support the publications,
both printed and otherwise, of the large publisher. Because of his excessive
unscrupulousness Ailes clashed, with Murdoch's two sons, Lachlan and
James, who did not hesitate to announce his immediate resignation, without
even waiting for the conclusion of the investigation.

In recent years, the free voices of American information have not been
sufficiently alert, vigilant, or ethically equipped to combat this new attitude
created in the world of information, especially by Ailes. Denouncing the
authoritarian deviation of the American press in a long article entitled "Why
don't honest journalists take on Roger Ailes and Fox News" published in the

Washington Post on March 14, 2010, Howell Raines, editor of the *New York Times* and winner of the Pulitzer Prize in 1992 wrote:

> Why has our profession, through its general silence, helped Fox News legitimize a style of journalism that is dishonest in its intellectual processes, untrustworthy in its conclusions, and biased in its *gestalt*? [And he continued] For the first time since the yellow journalism of a century ago, the United States has a major news organization devoted to the promotion of one political party. And let no one be misled by occasional spurts of criticism of the GOP on Fox. In a bygone era of fact-based commentary typified, left to right . . . these deceptions would have been given their proper label: disinformation. Under the pretense of correcting a Democratic bias in news reporting Fox has accomplished something that seemed impossible before Ailes imported to the news studio the tricks he learned in Richard Nixon's campaign think tank: He and his video ferrets have intimidated center-right and center-left journalists into suppressing conclusions—whether on health-care reform or other issues—they once would have stated as demonstrably proven by their reporting . . . [The Fox News] news operation can, in fact, be called many things, but reporters of my generation, with memories and keyboards, dare not call it journalism.

Harsh words that, however, show a state of information that has deviated very far from those standards to which the U.S. media had accustomed the world. This deviation also weakens the foundations of American democracy. The election of Donald Trump was situated in this climate. Trump did not need to build consensus, as Mussolini did when he came to power through the creation of a myriad of newspapers under his control. With Fox News he already owned it. And it was someone else who built it for him.

Mussolini's first action was his most moderate, but also his most unscrupulous: he used formal legality and Parliament to silence the vigorous anti-Fascist press. And he did so in a Chamber of Deputies elected in 1921, that was still liberal, with all the parties still present, including the socialists and communists! The complicity of King Vittorio Emanuele III was evident in this action. During the summer of 1923, Mussolini presented a very insidious decree-law to the King for his signature. The decree empowered a Prefect[2] to order that any newspaper desist from publishing false or tendentious news capable of unsettling the action of the government. The effectiveness of the measure was such that after the Giacomo Matteotti[3] murder, on June 10, 1924, the seizure of opposition newspapers would be continuous. This was the first step in imposing a national gag order. And the first success of the *Duce*. And it was obtained legally!

The fine action of a file is followed by a second . . . that of the hammer. With the advent of the dictatorship between 1925 and 1926, the *leggi Fascistissime* (Very Fascist laws)[4] would decree the end of political dissent and with it of the parties with the consequent definitive closure of all anti-Fascist press organizations.

Mussolini knew that to increase consensus, it was not enough to silence the voice of the opposition. The void it left had to be filled by the rise of new Regime newspapers. "The newspaper is used as a club. It must strike inside the head until it conditions the formation of public opinion" (Leonardi p. 152). He invited the *gerarchi*[5] to follow this example, and invest in a regime press that, while partisan, would be authoritative, credible, and convincing. As a consummate journalist he had first-hand experience. Beginning in 1914 he was the owner of his own newspaper, and until 1922 also editor. The *gerarchi* quickly became editors. Italo Balbo[6] established in the city of Ferrara *Il Corriere Padano*, Roberto Farinacci[7] founded in the city Cremona *Il regime fascista*, Dino Grandi[8] bought *Il Resto del Carlino* in Bologna, Costanzo Ciano, father of Galeazzo Ciano,[9] *Il Telegrafo* in Livorno (Leghorn), to name just a few.

Actions cannot always be carried out with a bludgeon; sometimes a chisel and a file are needed. It was one thing to get rid of such left and center-left party dailies as *Unità*, *Avanti!* and *La voce repubblicana*; however, the relationship with authoritative historical national newspapers that were an expression of very specific economic groups was more complex. An example of this was, the *Corriere della Sera*.[10] The seizure of hundreds of copies in various Italian cities began in June 1924, coinciding with the Matteotti murder, and lasted until July 2, 1925, when the Prefect of Milan, Vincenzo Pericoli, sent the editor, Luigi Albertini, a formal warning implying the threat of suppression of the newspaper. Albertini was forced to resign and sell his shares in the newspaper. After a period of temporary management, the direction was taken over by the writer and journalist Ugo Ojetti, one of the signatories of the *Manifesto degli intellettuali fascisti e academico dell'Italia* (*Manifest of Intellectual and Academic Fascists of Italy*).

A much more serious fate awaited *La Stampa*[11] of Turin which had its publication suspended: the owner and editor, Alfredo Frassati, was forced to sell the newspaper. He was replaced by the Agnelli family who, in 1926, placed the more aligned Andrea Torre at the helm.

Nevertheless, it was not enough to remove the heads of the opposition and insert complacent editors. In order to control the press, the National Order of Journalists and the Professional Journalists Union, which also organized recreational activity, were created. Royal Decree n. 384 of 1928 provided: "Those who have carried out activities against the interests of the Nation cannot under any condition be enrolled in the registry of journalists and, if they are enrolled, must be removed!"

Mussolini decreed that the news published be in well-shaped form from a mold issued from the Stefani Agency. The Stefani Agency was founded in

1853 and had one of Mussolini's few intimates placed at the helm, the former director of *Il Popolo d'Italia*, Manlio Morgagni. Its dispatches were so faithful to the regime that they represented its true "secret weapon." Editors of newspapers were explicitly required to use the services developed by Stefani, making sure that their spirit and contents remained unchanged.

In 1929, the Stefani Agency had 30 provincial branches with 255 correspondents in Italy and 40 in Europe and America.

Stefani's indications became more and more detailed. Mussolini also supervised the crime news: "It is indispensable to reduce reporting of crime news, in particular the reporting of suicides, tragedies of passion, violence and acts of lechery committed on minors, and other facts that can exert a dangerous influence on weak or weakened spirits" (*La Grande Storia/Propoganda* Cicchino).

Mussolini would receive the Chief of the Press Office, every day around one o'clock, to give him precise orders to be sent to the Stefani Agency, to the editors, and to the chief editors of the newspapers. The orders were transcribed in multiple copies with carbon paper on top of tissue paper and then sent out with a motorcyclist. These very thin sheets of paper, called *veline* in slang, would number in the thousands during the twenty years of the Fascist regime forming the rule book for the regime's consent.

Over the years, first the Press Office of the Prime Minister's Office, then the Ministry of Popular Culture (*Ministero della Cultura popolare:Minculpop*), or rather the institutional organs of Propaganda, came to have almost physical control over every written page of newspapers. A maximum of forty-five lines for each fact. For example, a *velina* would specify that crime reports to be published in a local newspaper could be no more than a fifth of a column and no more than one column overall. The *veline* also dealt with the coverage of other types of news as well. When covering sports a *velina* about Primo Carnera, the Italian heavyweight boxing champion, would specify that photos of Carnera on the ground could not be published. It appears that showing him knocked out would have been offensive to Italians. When writing about the cyclist Gino Bartali[12] papers were to focus on him as a sportsman, and avoid unnecessary reports on him as a private citizen. Bartali was at the time so famous in France for his victories that perhaps he aroused the envy of Mussolini. And again, editors were urged not to question any authority: "We renew our invitation not to 'mock' the referees in the chronicles of soccer matches and in comments on the championship" (Cassero p. 35).

From sports on to religion: "[E]nough with the statue of the Virgin that supposedly changed color." The regime was concerned about the credulity of Italians toward disputed miraculous phenomena. "No news of alleged miracles and related phenomena, except for the traditional episode of San Gennaro in Naples"[13] (Ibid p. 61). Action was also taken on the image of women as future mothers. "Do not publish photographs and drawings of young girls depicted with the so-called 'wasp waist.' Drawings and photographs must represent healthy and flourishing broad-hipped women." And again "Do not publish photographs of women on bicycles wearing pants." Moving on from there to the climate: "Decrease news about bad weather" (Ibid.).

Newspaper editors were at the helm of a machine with very little room for maneuvering. "It is absolutely forbidden to publish any newspaper without the *Duce*'s speech on the front page and Stefani's report from Palazzo Venezia, under penalty of seizure! The text of the speech must be in bold, carefully proofread because it must not have any errors" (Ottaviani p. 21).

The *veline* often were concerned not only with the text of the articles, but also with photographs. The image of the leader could not tolerate smudges, snags, or slips. "Publish only the photos of the *Duce* with the crowd, or of the crowd alone" (Ibid p. 31).

Photographs could never show him alone, but always in the midst of a large clapping and cheering crowd. When there was a mistake in these directives seizure was the penalty. If a photographer got out of line he risked not only severe reprimands, but also arrest and detention.

It is a well-known anecdote that Mussolini would thumb through the photos of himself every morning, ready to remove those that were not to his liking. He often did this for insignificant details: even a marching step that was a little too comical: "Carefully review photos of military parades: publish only those from which impeccable alignment results." Or photos of the *Duce* in a group of *gerarchi* in which he is not in the foreground: "Do not publish any of those of the *Duce* with the authorities. But also, do not publish those with him next to disgraced men" (Sovera p. 18).

Further, the *Duce* absolutely refused to be photographed next to clergy, as he was convinced they brought bad luck. "Do not publish photographs in which the *Duce* is shown together with friars" (Ottaviani p. 18).

Even worse would be photographing him with those in unfortunate circumstances, such as among earthquake victims, flood victims, building collapses, and other unpleasant events with which he feared being associated. His own newspaper, *Il Popolo d'Italia*, even ran into serious trouble with this prohibition when on December 7, 1934, it published the *Duce* among the flood victims of Polesine (a geographic area in the Friuli Region). Beginning at end of the 1920s, the Press Office of the Presidency of the Council of Ministers and the Ministry of Popular Culture began to bestow substantial outlays of varying amounts of money depending on the talent and availability of each journalist. Some received considerable sums of money, ranging from 1,000 to 5,000 *liras* per month. In some cases, more. At that time, a worker earned between 10 and 20 *liras* a day.

Journalists were not the only ones involved in this largesse. It also involved poets, writers, musicians, filmmakers, painters, intellectuals, and actors. In his book *Gli intellettuali di Mussolini. La cultura finanziata dal fascismo.* [*Mussolini's intellectuals. Culture financed by Fascism*], Giovanni Sedita lists from page 190 to page 216,907 public figures who obtained subsidies from the Regime totaling to what corresponds to about two decades of salary at a 1,000 *liras* per month![14]

These sums were bestowed by the Fascist regime, through *Minculpop* (Ministry of Popular Culture). By 1943, the total amount it had dispensed as personal contributions to intellectuals, as well as journalists, was 28 million *liras*.

Mussolini hoped that this would put an end to any opposition. He counseled journalists that they should consider themselves "soldiers" in the most advanced and delicate sector of the Fascist front, ready to wield the most powerful and dangerous weapon of this battle.

This is just what occurred in the print sector and does not convey the full panorama of influence as even higher learning and culture came under Fascist control. The projects of new universities, new scientific institutions, and even the creation of the Italian Encyclopedia Institute must all be viewed through this lens. The purpose of this latter project was to ensure that scholars who had been forced to use the Encyclopedia Britannica, the French Encyclopedia, or even the Soviet Encyclopedia could finally turn to a similar resource in Italian. The *Enciclopedia Italiana di Scienze, Lettere ed Arti* (Italian Encyclopedia of Sciences, Letters and Arts), commonly called the *Treccani* Encyclopedia first created on the initiative of the textile magnate Giovanni Treccani and then transferred to the state, was directed by the philosopher Giovanni Gentile. The work concentrated knowledge viewed through the prism of Fascism. Mussolini was the project's most authoritative guarantor. The *Duce* actually authored the entry on Fascism with Gentile. Although there were many non-Fascist contributors, the Treccani encyclopedia did not represent all of Italian culture due to the refusal to contribute by important intellectuals such as Luigi Einaudi, Benedetto Croce, Giuseppe Lombardo Radice, who all blamed Gentile for having enslaved high culture to Fascism. The work, in thirty-six volumes, was completed in 1937.

NOTES

1. This cry was created by Gabriele D'Annunzio in 1917, by using the Greek war cry *alalà* preceded, by *Eia, Eia!*! According to tradition, it was the expression that Alexander the Great used to spur his horse Bucephalus. *Eia, eia alalà* was subsequently adopted by the Fascist movement as its greeting.

2. Prefect or *Prefetto* is a high-ranking public servant who is the Italian state's representative in a province. His office is called *Prefettura—Ufficio Territoriale del Governo* (Prefecture—Territorial government office). Prefects have political responsibility and coordinate the local head of the State Police (*Questore*), who has the technical responsibility, to enforce laws when public safety is threatened.

3. Giacomo Matteotti was an Italian Socialist who after he had accused the Fascists in Parliament of committing fraud in the recently held elections, and condemning their use of violence to secure votes, was kidnapped and murdered.

4. A series of laws, issued between 1925 and 1926, that began the process of transforming the legal system of the Kingdom of Italy into the Fascist regime. Among the first provisions was the cancellation of the freedom of the press and the right to strike, as well as the abolition of all political parties, with the exception of the PNF.

5. A *gerarca* (singular), *gerarchi* (plural), was a higher officer of the *Partito Nazionale Fascista*.

6. Italo Balbo (June 6, 1896–June 28, 1940) was an Italian Fascist politician and leader. He was Italy's Marshal of the Air Force, Governor General of Libya, and Commander-in-Chief of Italian North Africa. He was also often seen as one of the most probable successors to Mussolini. After serving in World War I, he became a Fascist organizer in Ferrara. He was one of the four principal architects (*Quadrumviri del Fascismo*) of the March on Rome 1922, along with Michele Bianchi, Emilio De Bono, and Cesare Maria De Vecchi. In 1926, he was given the task of building the Italian Royal Air Force. He was placed in charge of the government of Italian Libya, where he remained for the rest of his life. Apparently, he was not an anti-Semite and was the only leading Fascist to oppose Mussolini's alliance with Nazi Germany. He was accidentally killed by friendly fire when his plane was shot down over Tobruk by Italian anti-aircraft guns.

There is an interesting note tying Balbo to the city of Chicago. In 1933 he led a fleet of twenty-five aircraft on the first flight from Italy to Chicago. The feat, which was carried out during the Century of Progress Exhibition, held in Chicago between 1933 and 1934, was so impressive that the city decided to re-name South 7th Street "Balbo Drive." During the last few years, the name of the Drive has been the subject of an as yet unresolved controversy.

7. Roberto Farinacci (October 16, 1892–April 28, 1945) was born in the city of Isernia in the southern region of Molise. He grew up in poverty and in 1909 immigrated to Cremona in the northern region of Lombardy to work on the railway. He was an ardent supporter of Mussolini and the Fascist movement. He became a Fascist leader in Cremona and organizer of the *squadre d'azione* in that town; the Cremone *squadre* were among the most brutal in Italy terrorizing the population into submission. Once the Fascist movement became a party he rose quickly in the ranks. He represented the most radical syndicalist faction which thought that Mussolini was too cautious and moderate as a leader (Mussolini thought that Farinacci was too violent and irresponsible). Farinacci was known to be xenophobic and antisemitic. By 1925, he was the second most powerful man in the country when Mussolini appointed him secretary of the party. He was used by Mussolini to centralize the party and then to purge it of thousands of its radical members. In

1926 Mussolini removed him from that office. He disappeared from the public eye, practicing law for much of the late 1920s and early 1930s. He was called back to power in 1935. When World War II began, he sided with Nazi Germany. He frequently communicated with the Nazis and became one of Mussolini's advisors on Italy's dealings with Germany. He urged Mussolini to enter the war as a member of the Axis. When Mussolini was overthrown, Farinacci, protected by the Germans, escaped arrest. He returned to Cremona but tried to flee Italy when the Allies advanced northward. Recognized by Italian partisans, he was tried and executed by a firing squad.

8. Dino Grandi (June 4, 1895–May 21, 1988), the 1st Conte di Mordano, was an Italian Fascist politician, Minister of Justice, Minister of Foreign Affairs, and president of Parliament. He was born in the province of Bologna and joined the Fascists at the age of twenty-five. Once the Fascists took power, he became part of the new government. He subsequently served as ambassador to the United Kingdom (1932 to 1939). Grandi was an ally to the most radical and violent groups of Fascists. In his diplomatic career, he created a net of connections that were rivaled only by Mussolini's son-in-law, Galeazzo Ciano, and he used them for his own gains. He was able to convince King Victor Emmanuel III to grant him a title and he managed to retain a comfortable position until he was sent by Mussolini to the Greek Front. Grandi reportedly opposed the Italian racial laws and Italy's entry into World War II. Because of his increasingly critical stance against the war, he was removed from the Cabinet in 1943. He voted for Mussolini's ouster in the Fascist Grand Council meeting on July 24, 1943.

9. Gian Galeazzo Ciano, 2nd Count of Cortellazzo and Buccari, was an Italian diplomat and politician who served as Foreign Minister in the government of his father-in-law, Benito Mussolini, from 1936 to 1943. During this period, he was widely seen as Mussolini's most probable successor as head of government. Following a series of Axis defeats in World War II, Ciano began to urge Italy's exit. Therefore, he was removed from his position as Foreign Minister and made ambassador to the Vatican. In July 1943, he was among the members of the Grand Council of Fascism that forced Mussolini's ouster and subsequent arrest. Ciano attempted to flee to Germany but was arrested and turned over to Mussolini's new regime, the Italian Social Republic. He was tried in Verona by the Italian Social Republic for having committed the offence of voting for Mussolini's removal from power, sentenced to death and executed by firing squad with with four others: Emilio De Bono, Luciano Gottardi, Giovanni Marinelli and Carlo Pareschi.

10. *Corriere della Sera* (*Evening Courier*) is one of Italy's most important and influential dailies. It was first published on March 5, 1876. During the period between 1910 and 1920 under the direction of Luigi Albertini it was the most widely read newspaper in Italy.

11. *La Stampa* (The Press) is an Italian daily. It was founded in February 1867 by the novelist and journalist Vittorio Bersezio with the name *Gazzetta Piemontese* (Piedmont Gazette). In 1895, the newspaper was bought by Alfredo Frassati who gave it its current name. It is distributed in Italy and other European nations and is one of Italy's oldest newspapers.

12. Gino Bartali was a champion road cyclist. He was the most renowned Italian cyclist before World War II having won the *Giro d'Italia* twice, in 1936 and 1937, and the *Tour de France* in 1938.

13. San Gennaro (Saint Janarius) is the patron Saint of Naples and is famous throughout Italy for the miracle of the annual liquefaction of his blood. The feast of San Gennaro is celebrated by the Catholic Church annually on September 19. Neapolitans believe this annual liquefaction is essential to their city and its well-being. If it does not liquify, tragedy and catastrophe are thought to be on the horizon. The liquefaction ritual is still so important today that its results are broadcast on the national news.

14. This information can be accessed in the Central State Archive at EUR in Rome in the section Minculpop, Reports, Envelope 5 with the title *A Complete List of All Subsidies Given to Italian Newspapermen, Artists and Writers 1933–1943.*

Chapter 2

The Climb

A New Narrative

July 20, 2016. Cleveland. Donald Trump has won the Republican nomination. He will run for President of the United States. When compared to Mussolini in 1919, Trump had already made real progress. He had routed sixteen Republican primary candidates. Despite this fact, the *New York Times* was still predicting that he only had a 33 percent chance of winning; all the polls confirmed that Hillary Clinton was still the overwhelming favorite.

To overcome this gap, Trump needed the votes of the poorest and uneducated Whites, the "silent majority" invisible to the pollsters, as well as the lower and middle bourgeoisie classes. Trump's idea of building a wall at the border with Mexico to stop illegal immigrants and drug traffickers seemed to be fascinating. These points became the focus of his campaign rallies, as did opposing Clinton's tax plan. Taxes had to be cut to relaunch the economy. Trade treaties had to be canceled, especially NAFTA (North American Free Trade Agreement with Mexico and Canada signed by then President Bill Clinton), as these weakened not only the United States but also forced multinationals to close their factories at home. Another hope was that Clinton would continue to attract people's anger against globalization. And then would the avalanche of votes against him from the Hispanic and African American minorities in favor of Hillary really happen? And would Hillary's desire to corner Putin and the former USSR with the risk of a real East-West war be appreciated by Americans? What about Islamic terrorism? And what about China?

Who would really vote for Donald Trump? His electoral base became more protean, and it expanded at a rapid pace, to the extent that it began to worry his Democratic adversary, but unfortunately too late.

Before responding to the question of the growth in his voters, there is a crucial term that has little to do with politics that needs to be taken into consideration, as it can help answer this question. The term is *narrative* and apparently it belongs more to the realm of literature or fiction than to the one of politics.

On March 18, 2016, Clarence Page, a well-known columnist for the *Chicago Tribune*, wrote in an article entitled *What the O.J. Simpson trial and Donald Trump have in common* that there was a relationship between the airing of the FX Network television series *The People Vs. OJ. Simpson. American Crime Story* in 2016 and Donald Trump's election campaign. Page noted: "Trials like political campaigns, are contests between dueling narratives. The side with the best story wins, [as stated] by one of Simpson's defense attorneys [in the series], Johnnie Cochran."

And later, quoting the words of another lawyer on the defense team, Page wrote:

> The media, people—they want narrative too. But they want it to be entertainment. And what's out in the world osmoses back into the courtroom, sequester be damned. If there's gonna be a media circus, you better well be the ringmaster. Twenty-one years later, the era of so-called "reality TV" that the Simpson trial launched with its slow-speed white Ford Bronco chase, bloody gloves and Kardashians (the series reminds us of how Simpson hid out in the bedroom of Kim Kardashian, daughter of his since-deceased pal Robert Kardashian) has led us to Trump's surprisingly successful presidential campaign, an example of how far you can get if you're rich, famous and stubbornly resistant to any sense of embarrassment. (Ibid.)

Therefore, it is thanks to the *narrative* that elections in America are won by the candidate that the public finds the most entertaining. In fact, consensus is actually broadened through it. There are three important steps to be followed to achieve this result.

> Step One—Page writes: [s]ay something outrageous that breaks conventional rules almost every day. While people are still reacting to your last outrage, give them another. . . . Step Two: [e]ncourage your social network friends and followers to retweet messages and build communities of supporters impenetrable by any ideas or information that disagrees with the often-inaccurate pronouncements of Trump. Step Three: [e]verytime you need to get attention (in the final days before a state's primary or caucus, for example) raise your visibility, respond to an attack, or simply change the subject, say something outrageous and let the cycle start again. (Ibid.)

"The Donald," an unpredictable individual who knows no limits, followed this strategy almost literally. This is why he continued and continues to attract supporters, thereby expanding his base. His statements changed depending on the political composition of the state he was in and the event of the moment.

He kept in mind that his *narrative* appealed to an audience that changed from time to time, but was always eager to be entertained, just like in a real reality show.

Initially, the core of his electoral base was made up of only poor unsophisticated Whites with a low level of education. Among this core were citizens, especially in the South, who had lost their jobs in the Great Recession of 2008 due, according to them, to the entry of Mexicans. Trump flagellated that ethnic minority with words of fire, that were offensive and racist, blaming them for stealing jobs from Americans and being "just thieves, drug dealers and rapists." But this base expanded as it did in his home state of New York, when in April 2016 he won 61 percent of the total vote in the Republican primary. He won across the entire demographic spectrum. Further with respect to characterizing his voters as uneducated, a shift occurred there as well. Sixteen percent of his Republican voters had a high school degree and made up one-fifth of Trump voters, and he received 43 percent of the support among college graduates and post-graduates. Things began to change with respect to the income of his supporters as well. This shift deflated the initial notion that only the poor and uneducated would have voted for him. Moreover, an exit poll by the Rand Corporation showed that generally the base of Trump supporters was composed of those who considered themselves "voiceless." This can be seen in the comparison with one of his fiercest primary opponents, Ted Cruz. Trump won against him thanks to voters who believed that "immigrants threaten American customs and values," and those voters who strongly favored raising taxes on the rich. In confirmation of this, 85 percent of voters who agreed with the statement "people like me don't have any say in what the government does" preferred Trump. Thus, Derek Thompson in his article *Who Are Donald Trump's Supporters, Really?* published in *The Atlantic* on March 1, 2016, wrote "[t]his feeling of powerlessness and voicelessness was a much better predictor of Trump support than age, race, college attainment, income, attitudes towards Muslims, illegal immigrants, or Hispanic identity."

Added to this was a Republican party in upheaval. Hostage of the Tea Party and therefore divided, it continued to lose support among ethnic minority voters. It had no concept of how to deal with the phenomenon of "The Donald" and the spectacularization of his political arena. Trump both a businessman and a great communicator whose *narrative* is basically entertainment and not politics represented a huge complication for the GOP. The 1996 film *Big Night* illustrated Trump's philosophy. It tells the story of two Italian brothers who immigrated to the United States in the 1950s to bring Italian cuisine to America. They fail, cheated by an American of Italian descent who to the question "What are you?" answers describing the golden rule of business: "I am a businessman. I am anything I need to be at any time." In the case of Trump, this rule must be combined with the other that has come into vogue more recently, especially thanks to television: that of a *narrative* capable of capturing the public through forms of entertainment. Now, as never before, it applies to politics because it ensures success. And Trump knew that these were the golden rules which could guarantee him victory against Hillary Clinton.

Clinton was defeated by Bernie Sanders in West Virginia, and the polls had begun to show she was in danger in the three crucial states of Florida, Ohio, and Pennsylvania against Trump. Her way of presenting herself and telling her story, her *narrative*, began to change as well, but it was not enough to win the presidency. Her claim in the book *What Happened* that she lost only because Comey reopened the investigation on her emails is not completely persuasive. Her *narrative* appeared to many voters to be distant and disconnected from people's needs. As David Remnick in his September 13, 2017, article *Hillary Clinton Looks Back in Anger* published in the September 25, 2017 issue of the *New Yorker* beautifully explained:

> She lost because of the tactical blunders of her campaign. She lost because she could never find a language, a thematic focus, or a campaigning persona that could convince enough struggling working Americans that she, and not a cartoonish plutocrat, was their champion. She lost because of the forces of racism, misogyny, and nativism that Trump expertly aroused. And she lost because of external forces (Vladimir Putin, Julian Assange, James Comey) that were beyond her control and are not yet fully understood.

The paradox was that she was perceived as part of the establishment, untrustworthy and therefore unethical, while her adversary who was by nature, lacking in moral principles, personally and professionally, was preferred to her. Her mistake was to underestimate the importance of a narrative of genuine ethics, being straightforward and authentic. Trump to the contrary came across as sincere and candid with his blunt brutal narrative always entertaining as if ethics were no longer relevant in society. Neil Postman in 1985 wrote a prophetic book on the subject, *Amusing ourselves to death: Public Discourse in the Age of Show Business*, referring to the role of TV and generally speaking of entertainment in politics and society. All this brings to mind the beautiful and provocative speech at the beginning of the television series *The Newsroom*, in which a splendid Jeff Daniels, as the anchorman of an American national television channel, reminded everyone of the ethical rules that any profession, be it that of journalism or politics, must follow in a democratic country. These rules though, all seem far removed from entertainment which, has like the world of politics, simply incorporated the rules of personalism and corruption more than emphasizing the principle of the common good.

Between 1919 and 1920 Italy and the Italians were under the heel of the *Biennio Rosso*.[1] Factories were occupied. There were strikes. Serious threats were made to employers. But there were also those who lived and illustrated this world with the satisfying sense of irony.

First on foot because of the streetcar strike, then with long hair because of the barbers' strike, a young Florentine Fascist joked. "Then again without gas and electricity because of the gas and electricity workers strike. Railway workers stopped striking and then the milkmen went on strike, the milkmen returned and the laborers went on strike." In Ferrara about sixty thousand peasants and laborers abandon their fields and stables; in Lomellina [An area located in the Po Valley in the south-western part of the Lombardy region] another one hundred and fifty thousand men cross their arms. (Piazzesi p. 59)

This pre-revolutionary situation was supported by the Socialist Party and the anarchists and also had aspects of *squadrismo*.[2] In the countryside, the heads of the Red Leagues had absolute power over the protests.

Because of the abandonment, hundreds of cows are dying daily of hunger and thirst, while hay is rotting in the fields. Milking cows is even forbidden. In the lowlands of Ferrara, the local Red Leagues stamped the hands of the peasants with the mark of the league so that they could not squeeze the cow's teats. Every morning the head of the League would check them and the stamp had to be intact. (Piazzesi, p. 66)

In the Northern Italian regions where the Red Leagues had an ironclad organization, based on an almost military discipline, as well as a strong system of blackmail, laborers and peasants who accepted lower pay than that imposed by the Leagues in order to have year-round work, were subject to harsh punishment. League members would harass them mercilessly. The local baker might refuse to sell them bread and family members might be marginalized like lepers.

Punishment is imposed on anyone: landowners, tenant farmers, sharecroppers, peasants, and laborers. It is inflicted for a myriad of irrational reasons. For example, an individual who appears unconvinced of the imminence of the proletariat revolution would be forced to go to the local Socialist club and drink a liter of wine with his comrades for ten days in a row; naturally he would pay for the liter. The landowner who had not shown enough sympathy for the revolution would be ordered to hire ten laborers for two months. A landowner guilty of having used the threshing machine instead of threshing by hand and this for the pure purpose of impoverishing the free and working proletariat would be obliged to pay three to five thousand liras as punishment, which would naturally go into the pocket of the head of the league; otherwise, the farms and their hay-stacks could go up in flames. (Ibid.)

During the *Biennio Rosso*, landowners, small farmers, and tenants endured the strikes and the violence without reacting, in the hopes that it would soon be over. The League leaders themselves behaved paradoxically. On the one hand they were violent, on the other they sought the protection of the Socialist Party. This behavior stemmed from the fact that what they really wanted was a piece of the political pie: candidacy in local or national elections or to be placed in charge of a local administration. This ambiguous bargaining would never achieve the real results typical of a socialist state. The occupation of land often ended only with the expulsion of the owners, without the land being farmed. The violence was thus nothing more than arrogance.

In the parallel between Mussolini and Trump, the realm of political correct-ness comes to mind as something similar, even if it is only a pale copy of the violence of those years. While the intent of political correctness is to use lan-guage, policies, or measures to avoid offense to members of particular groups in society, a rigid approach in the name of the sacrosanct rights of women, LGBTQ, and ethnic minorities may simply become purely barren statements. In fact, even though the rights of those voiceless minorities were achieved after hard, and even bloody struggles, excesses of political correctness can

Figure 2.1   Mussolini and Trump Display the Same Oratory Language. By the authors.

become an impediment to action. In tone this recalls the inflexibility, though not the physical violence of the Leagues.

Trump, as all the Republican right wing, has used a rigid approach himself to accuse President Barack Obama and Hillary Clinton of ignoring the interest of those common people not a part of the minority groups who are the beneficiaries of acquired rights. The key to Trump's fabulation is his way of communicating in no uncertain terms, as hard as a punch to the stomach, simplified and unsophisticated, often offensive and without limits. He makes a mockery of political correctness which rings false and insincere to him. Exhibiting kindness is to be hypocritical and weak. He permits himself to do what no candidate has ever been able to do: he blusters. He throws out crazy and dangerous statements, such as when he asserted that if he had taken a gun and shot someone on New York's Fifth Avenue, no one would have done anything to him, and he would have been elected anyway! Addressing everyone and being understood. Trump succeeds brilliantly at this.

Trump has a simple, immediate way of speaking, without too many flights of syntax. Rich in imagery and very poor in vocabulary. He relishes repeating an opponent's mistakes, like when a year earlier he stole from right under Jeb Bush's nose the just-expired web domain Bush had forgotten to renew. He is timely and perhaps even ingenious. His way of communicating is to reach people in their niches, one at a time, the message needs to be precisely targeted and pitched, like a voice outside of the crowd, including very questionable statements. Simplification is the secret. Short phrases, no technical terms. He is often before a crowd of functional illiterates and in the United States, there are thirty-two million of them. They have difficulty understanding a newspaper article. Further, only 13 percent of those who read know how to compare data and read graphs; or possess a sufficient vocabulary to engage in a complex conversation. This is not just an American phenomenon. In Italy, functional illiteracy is at 47 percent. Thus, in political marketing campaigns, capturing the interest of this segment must be a strategic goal. Never take anything for granted. Every complex concept must be cut into segments and explained in comprehensible, almost obvious terms. All articulated reasoning must be organized into primary elements that follow one another.

Interestingly, the gay Jewish British actor and director Stephen Fry, who in his lifetime had been subjected to violence and ostracism, both swept away by political correctness, in the May 2018 Munk Debate in Toronto explained his opposition to the extremism of political correctness. He noted that its limit lies more in its obsession with always being on the right side, rather than being effective in eliminating injustice and discrimination. Sometimes that way of thinking—affirmed Fry—is so blinded by that logic that it cannot even see others suffering.

Donald Trump is a man in his seventies, the son of a real estate developer born in New York. He was a rebellious child and to set him straight his father sent him to a military academy. He graduated with a degree in economics from the Wharton School. He had a very brief experience as a bricklayer in his father's company, remaining there only three weeks! He has always lived among the New York jet set. His name is linked to one of the most famous skyscrapers in Manhattan, the Trump World Tower completed in 2001 with seventy-two floors in front of the UN Plaza. He has other luxurious buildings in New York as well. In Manhattan, he successfully remodeled an old hotel on 42nd Street. He also invested in casinos, such as the Taj Mahal in Atlantic City, which ended in bankruptcy. In fact, four of his companies have failed, but miraculously he always managed to cancel the debts. For the director, Michael Moore:

> Trump's election is going to be the biggest "fuck you" ever recorded in human history. . . . Whether Trump means it or not is kind of irrelevant because he's saying the things to people who are hurting, and that's why every beaten-down, nameless, forgotten working stiff who used to be part of what was called the middle class loves Trump. He is the human Molotov cocktail that they've been waiting for, the human hand grenade that they can legally throw into the system that stole their lives from them. (Sheffield 2016)

At the time he came to power what was known of the former socialist Benito Mussolini? One who was quite knowledgeable about Mussolini was the criminologist and police inspector Giovanni Gasti. On June 4, 1919, he wrote a report from Milan for the Ministry of the Interior. He stated that Benito Mussolini had a strong physical constitution, although he was affected by syphilis. This robustness allowed him to work continuously. Gasti included in his report, what is today common knowledge, that Mussolini was known for his sexual appetites, having had relationships with numerous women. "He is emotional, impulsive; these characteristics make his speeches suggestive and persuasive although, while speaking well, he cannot be said to be an orator."

Gasti was quite wrong in that respect. Mussolini was an orator whose style had much to teach twentieth-century politicians. He had the *narrative* of a great orator, capable of a total mastery of silences, gestures, threats, flattery; three-second pauses that riveted crowds, while he called the square to attention. Hyperboles. Each phrase became a slogan, such as the famous: "The important thing is not to live, it is to sail!" he stole from the Latin classics. And the slogan that gave the title to the Italian edition of this book "A book and a musket: a perfect Fascist!" (*Libro e moschetto: fascista perfetto*) attributed by some to Leo Longanesi.[3] Mussolini is full of paradoxes, provocations, and challenges: "If Fascism has been nothing but castor oil and billy clubs, and not a supreme passion of the best Italian youth, I am to blame! If Fascism has been a criminal association, I am the head of this criminal association," he said to the Chamber of Deputies on January 3, 1925.

He was bold and rough, but also subtle. No one noticed how studied he was: no movement, gesture, tone, nothing he did was by chance. He rehearsed in front of a mirror, analyzed his postures, mannerisms, and grimaces. Body language. Exaggerations. He possessed a torrential eloquence.

> The power of speech [Mussolini confided to the famous journalist Emil Ludwig] is invaluable to those who govern. It simply needs to be varied continuously. One must speak imperiously to the masses, reasonably before an assembly, in a familiar manner to a small group. It is the mistake of many politicians to always have the same tone. Of course, I speak differently in the Senate than in the square. (Baima Bollone p. 45)

Gasti pointed out that Mussolini was sentimental, and this attracted sympathy and friends; he was generous with money he handled, and disinterested; this created a reputation for altruism. "He is very intelligent, thoughtful, a good connoisseur of men, of their qualities and shortcomings. Close to the bourgeoisie. But also to the working class." He then concluded his report with "He is very ambitious." In the 1920s and 1930s, Gasti was treated rather well by the regime, and the *Duce* was pleased with his positive judgment. Mussolini felt at heart that he was a part of the poorer classes even though he was not. He felt their dignified pain. He had spent the first nine years of life in his family's house, growing up as an antisocial and a manic. *Un dscuréva; piciéva!* (He didn't speak, he hit), his playmates remembered. He was also a great storyteller. He loved to tell of when, as a child, he and his brother Arnaldo slept in the same room that sometimes served as a classroom for his mother who had to raise her children practically alone: "My poor mother, how she worried for her family! Sometimes she couldn't sleep, and I'd hear her get out of bed and pace on the brick floor, even ten or twenty times in one night trying to find relief from her pain. In the morning, she would get up exhausted and have to go to school!" (Mussolini p. 50).

If his teenage years with the Salesians in Faenza were rife with unhappy rebellions, as a young adult he lived even more under the banner of anarchy, spending time between Swiss construction sites and nursing grudges in squalid cellars and prisons. He talked about these days to his lover, Margherita Sarfatti, who wrote his biography *Dux*. There is an unknown anecdote Mussolini recounted to her. During one of his many expulsions from Switzerland for participating in Socialist demonstrations and violent marches he was detained in prison before being placed on a train bound for Italy. His cell mate was a seriously wounded compatriot who also was about to be removed from Switzerland. The man, expelled for committing a common crime, confided in him that he had killed two ex-convicts who were exploiting his prostitute sister. If the Swiss had discovered what he had done he would have been sentenced to death. He urgently needed to return to Italy. Mussolini felt sympathy for this man guilty of murder and tried, to the best of his ability, to heal his wound before boarding the train. Near Como the man died, making Mussolini promise to visit his mother in Turin and tell her everything, which Mussolini did. It is curious how the escape of this unknown outcast to Italy and Como seemed to represent the tragic metaphor of Mussolini's last journey in the same places when, defeated, with his government enroute to Germany, he was captured at Dongo, near lake Como, and then killed in the *De Maria* family farmhouse at *Giulino di Mezzegra*,[4] on the morning of April 28, 1945. His temperament combining humanity and complicity with a criminal provides a view of Mussolini's personality as that of a man who did not hesitate to make risky and emotional decisions depending on the moment and his feelings. Character traits that later would place the life and future of the Italian people at risk. Unscrupulousness and ambiguity are qualities he shares with Donald Trump and which are part of the parable of the danger that these two men represent.

NOTES

1. The *Biennio Rosso* (in English referred to as the Red Biennium or Two Red Years) was a two-year period, between 1919 and 1920, of intense social conflict in Italy. The violence of this period was among the causes of the ushering into power of Mussolini and his Fascist regime.

2. *Squadrismo* was the movement of the *squadre d'azione*, or action squads. These were the Fascist militias organized outside the authority of the Italian state and led by local leaders. *Squadrismo* was an important asset for the rise of the National Fascist Party, using violence to systematically eliminate any political parties opposed to the Fascists. Members of the *squadre d'azione* were known as *squadristi* (plural; singular: *squadrista*) and the leader of a *squadre d'azione*, was known as a *ras*.

3. Leopoldo (Leo) Longanesi (August 30, 1905–September 27, 1957) was an Italian journalist, publicist, screenplay writer, and publisher. He is mostly known in Italy for his satirical works on Italian society and people. During the period between 1927 and 1950, he published several magazines, including *L'Italiano* ([*The Italian*] 1927), *Omnibus* (1937), and *Il Borghese* ([The Bourgeoisie] 1950), the last of which is a cultural and satirical weekly paper with a conservative orientation. Longanesi described himself as a "cultural anarchist." After World War II he became a prominent opponent of the republican democracy that replaced Fascism, espousing conservatism, agrarian virtues, anti-democracy, and nostalgic post-Fascism.

4. *Giulino di Mezzegra* is a subdivision (*frazione*) within the Italian municipality (*comune*) of *Mezzegra*, located in the province of Como in the Lombardy region.

Chapter 3

Protean Leaderships

The Fascists burned red flags and destroyed local union offices to stop the Bolshevik danger. Trump and his "Trumpers" brandished their harsh anti-Islamic and anti-Hispanic rhetoric exclaiming that there would be a total and complete shutdown of Muslims entering the United States; that a wall would be built on the southern border to keep out immigrants and that Mexico would pay for that wall. Like Mussolini, Trump distrusts professional politicians, or "the establishment," which he claims reduced the country to its present-day disgraceful conditions. He attacked liberals, who respect political correctness, because they have obstructed the country making it unrecognizable to its own citizens. According to Trump everyone is afraid of saying or doing the wrong thing. He also treats his party no better: its members, inept! And he proclaimed, "Finally, the silent majority is back and will have its voice: me!" Can Trump voters be called Republicans? Not really. Much better to call them *Trumpers*: they were born to oppose what exists and to change it; and it is a change that is almost an end in itself.

The *Fasci di Combattimento* were created to oppose the pre-revolutionary status quo. They stood up to the Socialist Party and the Bolshevik red menace, but they were corrupted by nationalism. "Being against" is such a paradox that it does not exclude actually being against "who is being against." Proof of this fact is that, although they rose up against the red menace, when they were founded the *Fasci di Combattimento* actually had a left-leaning perspective. Further their secular nature attracted the solidarity of the Masons. Was Mussolini consistent? How consistent will Trump be in the future? The answer is beyond the scope of this book, even if a partial answer can be provided by simply observing the continuous changes in Trump's staff and his cabinet. Until they left their positions, Trump would exaggerate their abilities and sing their praises. A partial answer can also be found by observing his contradictions with respect to Putin and the invasion of Ukraine. It can also be seen with respect to his relationships with the likes of dictators such as Assad, President of Syria, guilty of massacres against his own people or Crown Prince Mohammed bin Salmad of Saudi Arabia, whose innocence he accepted even against the conclusions of the American intelligence community that claimed to have evidence of his involvement in the murder of the naturalized American journalist Jamal Khashoggi, who was dismembered, it seems, within the Saudi embassy in Istanbul. Trump's inconsistencies do not stem from ideological reasons, but purely from the business relationships he has had with all these political figures.

During the *Biennio Rosso*, between 1919 and 1920, Mussolini had to strongly water down his already cautious solidarity toward strikers' demands with winks and nods to factory owners that he did not want to antagonize. The latter were, after all, advertisers in his newspaper. He did not visit the workers at the Dalmine steelworks in the town of Bergamo until the occupation of the steelworks had ended. Addressing the workers, he expressed his praise and encouragement. He affirmed that their strike had opened new horizons and had given a voice to labor. He used the same duplicity during the labor agitations in July–August 1920. Only when it was clear that the protest would have failed did he begin to speak in favor of the unions and workers on the pages of *Il Popolo d'Italia*, as he urged them to accept the agreement that the Giolitti government was negotiating directly with the industrialists. The circumstances meanwhile had produced a great impression in Italy and in Europe because the Italians had not fallen prey to Bolshevism! The actions of the League leaders of the *Biennio Rosso* meanwhile continued. Emilio Lussu testified in his book *Marcia su Roma e dintorni*, (*The March on Rome and Surrounding Areas*) that fear was so great that, as he wrote, speaking of a friend who had become Chancellor of a prestigious Italian university, "[h]e had moments of terror and panic, obsessed by the certainty that the Bolsheviks would take away his wife. In fact, that was the moment when the European press announced that in the Soviet Union the communes had socialized the women" (Lusso p.19).

Mussolini used to say provocatively that it was indifferent to him whether the factories belonged to the workers or the industrialists. As in a game he always sought to hold all the cards. His greatest flaw. This is the reason that industrialists maintained reservations about him and never fully backed him.

Back to New York. Did Trump have an adequate staff to win? If we compare it to Hillary Clinton's it was a skeleton staff. He did not rely on polls, or even TV commercials, but placed his trust in social media and as Ali Pardo, deputy director of his campaign, told *Time Magazine* on March 27, 2020 "he's been making investments since 2015 on big data and technology infrastructure in the communications and social responsiveness sector." Trump had a small fierce team with clear roles and no misunderstandings. Financial chairman Steven Mnuchin told in the Robert Draper article "Is Trump's Campaign Too Small or Is Clinton's Too Big?" published in *the New York Times* on July 26, 2016, "I think this is a very different campaign from the others starting with the fact that Donald has a larger audience than the traditional Republican one. We don't think we need to spend as much money on commercials as Clinton does. Donald doesn't think we need to have nine hundred people on staff."

Hillary's staff was gigantic; it was slow to decide and change course, or to even adopt a plan of attack. There were many leaders and experts, such as John Podesta, spokesman; Robby Mook, campaign manager; Joel Benenson, strategist; Jennifer Palmieri, communications star; Mandy Grunwald, message expert; Jim Margolis, television commercial analyst; not to mention Minyon Moore, John Anzalone, or David Binder, all polling gurus.

When a campaign staff is large, there are certainly more ideas to create a sophisticated strategy, but everyone must be disciplined. This is a very difficult task. A large campaign staff risks creating confusion, producing internecine competitiveness, and nullifying the advantages of having that positive competition of ideas that is the product of having numerous highly skilled individuals working on the campaign. *Politico* and the *New York Times* revealed that it would have taken a new David Axelrod to hold everyone firmly in place. It has been inferred that Robby Mook and Joel Benenson did not share much of their prestigious experience. Jennifer Palmieri and Mandy Grunwald also struggled to make each other's messages count. It seems that the campaign had chaos and not strength.

Trump brought on board only a few strictly necessary individuals whom he trusted implicitly. His public debut was so bizarre and buffoonish that it was the target of great irony; Clinton's analysts did not give enough importance to Trump's absurd gimmicks. They were convinced that he was going about it all wrong. A look at his close associates tells us a lot about him and his personality. He surrounded himself mainly with family members, such as his daughter Ivanka, his personal confidante, and his son-in-law, Jared Kushner, who initially also wrote his speeches and later had a large role in Trump's administration, comprising trade and government operations, especially on Israel. Kushner is an Orthodox Jew, and his family has interests in that country. In Trump's mind this fact could play an instrumental role in Israeli-Palestinian peace talks. There was also Kellyanne Conway, his fierce and tenacious campaign manager, a veteran Republican pollster who joined the team in July 2016; the first woman in that role. She was ubiquitous on television. She would then go on to fill one of the most important female roles in the White House where, as she said, she would take on the role that the President would designate for her. At the start of his term, she was even more important than Vice President Mike Pence, the former governor of Indiana and a six-term Republican member of the House of Representatives. Given the President's inexperience with administrative matters, Pence's expertise with the inner workings of Congress and political mediation helped shape Trump's cabinet. In fact, Pence would be essential in keeping in touch with Congress. Conway was joined by David Urban, a lobbyist, who held the role of senior adviser. And then there was Davide Bossie, long-time president of the conservative group *Citizens United*, who was appointed deputy campaign manager.

Last but not least, was Steve Bannon, chairman of the conservative website Breitbart. He was the Chief Executive Officer of Trump's election campaign and beginning in January 2017 White House Chief Strategist and Senior Counselor to the White House (a position created by the President especially for him). Steve Bannon, arrested in 2020 for money laundering,[1] was really the mastermind behind Trumpian politics. He was born in 1953, has been divorced three times, and has a Bachelor of Arts from Virginia Tech University, a Master of Arts from Georgetown University, and a Master of Business Administration from Harvard University. He was a naval officer, an investment banker at Goldman Sachs, and an executive producer in the Hollywood film and media industry before being placed in charge of Donald Trump's 2016 election campaign. In August 2018, he returned to "Breitbart" after criticizing actions of Trump's staff, in particular his daughter and the President's son-in-law. In fact, in Michael Wolf's 2018 book *Fire and Fury* Bannon was quoted making critical comments of the President's son for his dealings with Russia. The President then accused Bannon of losing his mind and talking nonsense. Although Bannon left the White House neither his relationship with Trump nor their falling out appears to have been as traumatic as some made it out to be.

Bannon has been described by friends and acquaintances as an extreme conservative activist who promotes a populist agenda and fights against the Republican establishment and globalism which, in his opinion, have undermined the roots of the working class. Interviewed on *60 Minutes*, by Charlie Rose on September 10, 2017, he reiterated what was said about him. "The media's portrayal of me? It's perfectly accurate: I'm a street fighter." Bannon like Trump is not a traditional conservative and is above all against "the establishment." During the interview, he attacked even the very Catholic Cardinal Dolan of New York who spoke out against Trump repealing DACA (Deferred Action for Childhood Arrivals). There is one striking thing about Bannon: he does not pretend to be what he is not. In an age where appearance is everything, Bannon arrived for his CBS interview unshaven with tired bloodshot eyes, showing that he is clearly someone who does not care about physical appearances. For this reason, he comes across as authentic: one who believes in what he says without worrying too much about what he looks like. This strikes a chord with many people; they perceive that he is one of them. It is precisely his every man appearance and the fact that he is not attentive to every word he utters that give him an aura of genuineness and credibility. He represents an image of America built not on the welcoming and open integration that we all know, but on the idea that its citizens are mainly represented by White lower middle-class males.

But if Trump wins on the merits of a very small staff, what does Mussolini's staff consist of?

It is known that the future *Duce* is a man without friends. He is misanthropic and distrustful. The only exception is his brother Arnaldo who succeeded him at the helm of *Il Popolo d'Italia*. In the early years of his government, Mussolini would call his brother every night for a midnight report. Arnaldo died in 1931 and Mussolini remained without his sounding board to the end of his regime. However, he did have a certain rapport with some of his newspaper employees, who, like him, had come from *Avanti!* One of these was the well-known journalist and Mussolini's lover Margherita Sarfatti, his first biographer. Also, she was not only the inspiration of a new pictorial style known as *Novecento*, but a partial inspiration of the cultural development of Fascism until the racial laws were enacted.

There were also several others of note, such as the administrative director of the newspaper, Manlio Morgagni, who shot himself on July 25, 1943, when he heard of Mussolini's fall from power. Two other men were crucial to Mussolini; both were former trade unionists, present at the founding of the *Fasci di Combattimento*. The first was Cesare Rossi, Mussolini's close adviser. It was his idea that the *Fasci di Combattimento* be transformed

Figure 3.1 **Mussolini and Trump with Two of Their Sons.** By the authors.

from a left-wing movement to an expression of the right. However, the most important was, Michele Bianchi, the first Secretary of the National Fascist Party. Bianchi was the intransigent director of the March on Rome. The March was a show of strength to force the King to summon Mussolini to the Quirinal Palace, as head of government and not simply as a minister in a government headed by the conservative politician Antonio Salandra. Bianchi was one of the *quadrumviri*[2] of the March on Rome, along with Balbo, De Bono, and De Vecchi. Bianchi went on to become Minister of Public Works; he died at the age of forty-eight in 1930. Cesare Rossi, on the other hand, became Head of the Press of the Prime Minister's Office and a member of the Grand Council. Together with Giovanni Marinelli, the administrative secretary of the National Fascist Party, he organized the Fascist *Ceka*[3] (the very first Fascist political police; its name borrowed from the Soviet political police, as well as the special squad for "dirty" operations of subversive violence), which was responsible for the heinous murder of Giacomo Matteotti. It would be a stretch to include among Mussolini's staff the generals and officers of the Royal Army, the industrialists close to him, and the bankers, including the powerful *ras*[4] of the provinces better known as *gerarchi*. In reality, Grandi, Ciano, Arpinati, Farinacci, and Balbo were his competitors. Many tried to oust Mussolini through Gabriele D'Annunzio but failed. Apart from those few close to him everyone else was used by Mussolini as they were nothing more than specialized party operatives. His close friendships with Dino Grandi, Italo Balbo, and even the philosopher Giovanni Gentile in practice really came to fruition while he was Prime Minister. In essence, Mussolini's only real staff was Mussolini. This would also be his downfall. He did not listen to anyone who had a different opinion. This personality trait led him to make disastrous decisions, such as the alliance with the Hitler and the declaration of war and coupled with the violence produced by the regime ultimately brought him to Piazzale Loreto hanging in effigy.[5]

Mussolini not only erred with respect to the industrialists who financed his newspaper, he also erred with respect to the working class. Among the *Fasci di Comabttimento* were many left-leaning "subversives" ready for social revolt, but there were also many ultra-conservative members in opposition. Mussolini was a sort of weight on the scales, moving it to the right or left according to the wind, or rather, according to the needs of his "business-firm party" to sell more copies of his newspaper, when one or the other category of readers risked disappearing.

Donald Trump learned from one of his most unscrupulous mentors, that one must try to win at all costs, acting without any scruples and above all never apologizing. "Never apologize, don't explain; attack, attack, attack; when in doubt, create a diversion and accuse the press" stated Roy Cohn, one of Donald Trump's spiritual fathers, member of the New York jet set and his lawyer from 1973 to 1985, until shortly before Cohn was disbarred. Cohn began his career working on the McCarthy Commission as an assistant attorney general and was responsible, in addition to the death sentence of Ethel and Julius Rosenberg, for the persecution of many communists and homosexuals, despite being himself a closet homosexual. The fear of communism was the symbol of a strategy that used fear of a common enemy to keep an entire country under control. Cohn later became one of the most controversial and criticized figures in the American legal world. He defended the most important heads of the mafia families from Salerno to Galante to Gotti; he even asked President Reagan for favors and along with Rupert Murdoch and Roger Ailes was responsible for the creation of Fox News. He died of AIDS in 1986 denying his homosexuality to the end, declaring he had liver cancer.

In 2018, during a moment of great tension in the Trump administration, after the President had basically fired Attorney General Jeff Sessions for not acquiescing to his demands on *Russiagate*, Donald Trump was heard to exclaim "Where is my Roy Cohn?" This expression became the title of a documentary by Matt Tyrnauer that examined the life of the very controversial American lawyer that was Roy Cohn; a man who would stop at nothing or for anyone. "Trump seems exasperatingly made of Teflon," said the director of the documentary, "the student seems to have eclipsed the master."

Six weeks after he was disbarred Cohn died in solitude, abandoned by his jet set friends including that very same Donald Trump who owed him so much. Trump, as is well known, does not believe in gratitude and does not like funerals. What Cohn and his father taught him is that by taking one's first steps within the rules, one can later circumvent them to do what is most convenient for oneself, even mocking the system. All this with a few simple principles and as many slogans that simplify and condense a primitive and elementary philosophy. Thus, Trump reads off two scripts: with one he credibly "identifies" with the poorer classes through words ("we are ignorant, we understand each other") and with the other he feeds their fear, which as he learned from his mentor Cohn, is the bond that unites people once the enemy is identified. Hence, Trump dusts off the fear of communism and its Democratic Party representative in the 2016 election: Bernie Sanders.

As often happens with dictators, their first steps in the conquest of power take place within the framework of Democracy. Mussolini's rise to power occurred exactly in such a context. What Mussolini needed first was a victory in the elections of November 1919. The Fascists presented themselves within an extremely varied slate. It included candidates from the Italian Republican Party, who, by virtue of having won the war, believed they could obtain numerous votes. It also included ex-socialist interventionists and syndicalist revolutionaries, with links to the working class and peasants and radicals, attuned to the lower middle class. The results were a bitter surprise for everyone. Not even Mussolini was elected. The Fascist coalition was defeated, but the election was a great success for the Socialist Party, the Popular Party, and the liberal right.

This failure changed the movement. The future Socialist Party leader, Pietro Nenni,[6] who had been in prison with Mussolini in 1911, resigned from the Bologna section of the Fascist Party when he realized where it was headed. Indeed, with other comrades he would soon become a staunch opponent of Fascism. Shortly after Nenni's resignation, members from socialist, unionist, anarchist, and republican backgrounds also left the party. Mussolini's political aspirations seemed to be at a collapse.

This large defection actually generated a new movement. Without Mussolini even imagining it, the void was filled by an influx of former soldiers, bourgeois, D'Annunzio volunteers, nationalists of all types, and those opposed to the Socialist and Popular Parties. A whole host of people eager to lead the country, and to strike back for the humiliation suffered during the *Biennio Rosso*. The political base of Fascism had completely changed to the point that a left-wing Fascist wrote indignantly to Mussolini,

> In Ferrara, many popular and liberal people joined the Fascist Party, who (to make it even worse) brought nothing less than the support of the Agrarian Federation, which, after several compromises, became the Fascist Party's sponsor. This is monstrous and it discredits us. Thus, in Ferrara the Fascist Party is no more and no less than the bodyguard of profiteering! (Roveri, p. 105)

These new members were the first to bring money into the Fascist movement. They expected that soon their contribution would be re-paid through an exchange of favors.

Although not enthusiastic, Mussolini, by virtue of the needs of his "business-firm" party, discovered that it would be opportune to convert Fascism from a revolutionary movement to a movement "of law and order." It would be extremely useful for the Fascists to relieve him of the burden of the expense for the movement and for it to become financially independent.

It is important to understand that in his conquest for power Mussolini was at the first of those junctions that in less than three years would lead him to become the head of the Italian government.

This change in the nature of Fascism was so important that the *Prefetture* informed the Ministry of the Interior and Prime Minister Francesco Saverio Nitti that in the event of a risk of a Bolshevik revolution, the Fascist squads could be counted on to cooperate with the military.

This leads to the conclusion that despite the fact that for both Trump and Mussolini, communist ideology is presented as a bogeyman, and that their intervention is presented as the deterrent to the chaos that would result from its advent, both are far removed from any ideology and both make promises that cannot be kept, just to reassure voters who feel they have no certainties, except that they have been neglected by all the other political forces. They both presented themselves as the only possible solution to the issues created by the chaotic situation. They addressed voters through a fictitious identification process, making people believe that they were part of the common folk, although in both cases the two political leaders were men of power, belonging to an elite that had nothing to do with the downtrodden and the poor. In the case of Mussolini we had a cultured and powerful intellectual, and in the case of Donald Trump a billionaire who is part of the international jet set. However, both were capable of making their supporters feel that they were one of the people.

NOTES

1. In 2020 Steve Bannon was arrested and indicted for conspiracy to commit wire fraud and money laundering in connection with a crowdfunding campaign to raise money for building the U.S.-Mexico border wall. He has pled not guilty to the charges.

2. *Quadrumviri*, (quadrumvirs) has its origins in ancient Rome. It was a post held by four citizens who had police and juridical power and were elected by the Roman senate. During the beginning of the Fascist era the term was used to refer to the four leaders (Michele Bianchi, General Emilio De Bono, Cesare Maria De Vecchi, and Italo Balbo) who led Mussolini's March on Rome.

3. At the beginning of 1924 Mussolini created the Ceka, based on the Soviet-style secret police. The purpose of the Ceka was to frighten people into voting for the Fascists. It soon established itself as a very efficient terrorist group. It was succeeded in 1926 by the *Opera Volontaria di Repressione Antifascista*—OVRA (Organization for Vigilance and Repression of Anti-Fascism).

4. After the *Negus*, or emperor of the Ethiopian Empire, the office of *Ras* was the title of the sovereign of each of the of the various Ethiopian provinces. However, when the Italian troops attempted their colonial conquest, landing in Eritrea in 1885, the title began to take on a derogatory meaning, conveying violent and despotic exercise of power seasoned with a truncated self-awareness. After the founding of the *Fasci di Combatimento* in 1919, the Fascist leaders of the various Italian cities were referred to as *ras* laced with scorn for their violence. They accepted the epithet as a title of honor.

5. *Piazzale Loreto* is a major piazza, or square, in Milan. It was the scene of one of the worst best-known events in the modern history of Italy: the public display of the corpses of Benito Mussolini, his mistress Claretta Petacci, and many Fascist *gerarchi* on April 29, 1945. Their bodies were taken to Milan and hung upside down from the roof of an Esso gas station in Piazzale Loreto, located between Corso Buenos Aires and Viale Andrea Doria. People gathered in the *Piazzale* and their corpses were bombarded with vegetables, spat at, urinated on, shot at, and kicked. Mussolini's face was disfigured by beatings.

6. Pietro Sandro Nenni (February 9, 1891–January 1, 1980) was an important leader of the Socialist Party who became one of the founding fathers of Italian Republic which emerged after World War II. He served as the national secretary of the Italian Socialist Party (PSI) and in 1970 became a lifetime Senator of the Italian Republic.

Chapter 4

Mechanisms of Consensus
and Democracy

Between 1919 and 1920, landowners attempted to organize local volunteer squads to combat the violence of the Red Leagues. The effort was a complete failure; these volunteer squads were mercilessly defeated.

Faced with the seemingly unstoppable power of the Red Leagues, many of these often absentee and fearful landowners decided to sell their lands lock, stock, and barrel. Farmland passed from the hands of these traditionalists to individuals who suddenly found themselves rich with little cash outlay. This triggered a revolution beyond the possible imaginings of any Communist union leader. The effects of those two years completely changed the destiny of the Italians and of Italy. The smartest tenants, sharecroppers, and peasants seized the opportunity and quickly bought half of the Po Valley[1] at previously unimaginable prices. It changed the composition of a social class which then completely shifted its political orientation. This was both a typical and unique phenomenon of those years that marked an epochal transformation of the social classes in Italy and Europe.

In the Soviet Union, the Bolshevik revolution totally canceled private property, placing it in the hands of the State, completely obliterating the landowning class, deporting it to Siberia. In Italy, the red menace forced that same class to flee the countryside for the city, abandoning the land to a new emerging social class. These new landowners completely shifted the voter pool of their productive chain—the workers, sharecroppers, and laborers—from the parties on the left to the Fascist Party, foreshadowing a development that would subsequently overtake Germany and Spain.

In many instances these new owners were former soldiers. Men who had fought in the trenches and who had invested their war pensions and savings in the land. They were used to weapons. They knew how to react to aggression.

43

Above all, they were determined to defend their unexpected property by any means necessary. It was this fact that changed the rules in Italy.

This new class of landowners, tired of being harassed, acted with the clear-sighted intent of getting rid of the Red Leagues and communists at any cost. The previous landowning class was certainly richer than this new one, but it did not possess its determination. The new landowners, often the very same peasants that had voted for the socialists in 1919, began organizing against the Red Leagues. Of course, like all the *nouveau riche*, they would not be defending themselves personally. They created a militia. It was composed of men who were more like them: the Fascists. These men were often unemployed World War I veterans, who had been humiliated by the socialists one time too many, and who had been forced to fight a war, which, like good pacifists, they had opposed. The *squadristi* were given generous financing. They returned the trust placed in them by enthusiastically arming themselves and responding to Red League attacks with their own violence. A real physical clash ensued with authentic and unfortunate battles. The 1934 movie *Vecchia Guardia* (*The Old Guard*) directed by Alessandro Blasetti years later would recreate the atmosphere even though the Fascist hierarchy did not like the violence portrayed in it because it undermined the respectable image the party was at that time trying to cultivate. In the arc of three years the dead on both sides would total roughly a 1,000, with many more wounded.

The process of transforming the American electorate is more complicated. It has occurred with the opportunity of reaching it in more pervasive ways, which paradoxically fostered a reduction of the democratic dialectic. In 2015–2016, Hillary's financial and economic network raked in more money than Trump and the campaign spent it all. Would voters respond in proportion to the spending? Or would there be a performance disparity? How many times in democracies has a dark horse candidate won, even in local elections, simply because that candidate was inspired by a forceful idea? How are voters persuaded to vote for one candidate or another? Does the fascination that arises from the candidates and their messages count, or is there more to it? In 2015, a very important essay was published on the transformation of the way politicians look at the electorate. In his *Hacking the Electorate: How Campaigns Perceive Voters*, Eitan D. Hersh, a political science professor at Tufts University, observed trends in election campaigns. The transformation in recent years involved the use of Big Data (i.e., population data versus sample data) in elections. This resulted in an explosive combination of technological power and infinite detailed knowledge of never before available voter information.

Sample data provides limited elements. Big Data on the contrary allows a campaign to access information on the entire population. It can be used to understand which voters are supporters and which are opponents. For example, if you are a Democratic candidate and you have data available that allows you to know that an individual voted Democrat in the primary, or is a registered Democrat, or is African American, or Hispanic or under the age of twenty-five, you can easily surmise that they will be supporters. Now, Hersh argued, a candidate knows everything about his or her constituents. Like large corporations, campaigns know much more about individuals: what they read, what movies they watch, what shows they like, where they shop, and what products they buy. It is all public information.

What is different is that Big Data also provides the tools with which to fight a political adversary. In fact, a politician knows with increasing accuracy how people voted and how they will vote in the future and why. Candidates can now circumnavigate the entire process of persuasion. They are no longer interested in persuading people with different ideas or arguing to influence those voters who view things differently. They simply identify the social categories they are sure will vote for them and then exclude the others. This can generate errors. Among the reasons Hillary Clinton lost the election was that her campaign focused on those who had previously voted for Obama, calculating that they would surely vote for her as well. She never asked whether, or why, rural voters might switch their votes to Trump. There are two other examples of this type of error. The first is Mitt Romney's famous comment during his 2012 run for president against Obama, when he said, "there are 47% who are with him, who believe they are victims, who believe the government has a responsibility to care for them . . . they will vote for this president no matter what . . . these are people who pay no income tax." The second is another error by Hillary Clinton when in her 2016 campaign she referred to Trump voters as a "basket of deplorables." "Both of these statements are forms of representation where you dismiss the people who are not your supporters. When I think of my job as a politician, I can think of it as serving the entire population, or I can think of it as serving my people, my voters. So, I'm looking for 51 percent, not 60 or 70 percent. [Candidates] now know, with greater and greater precision, how people voted and how they're likely to vote in the future, and their campaigns reflect that," Eitan Hersch said in the interview with Sean Illing, *A Political Scientist explains how big Data is Transforming Politics*, published in *Vox* on March 16, 2017. The assumption that most voters are essentially unreachable is implicit in the Big Data approach and this assumption leads to a narrowing in the democratic process because it bypasses any discussion.

But perhaps, Hersh believes, it is the voters themselves who also determine the polarization and extreme entrenchment in their beliefs. The easiest way for the average voter to engage in politics is actually through the party or a group affiliated with it. Politicians also prefer this mindset because they immediately know who is on their side and they need not worry about defections. In theory, at least, Big Data seems to make the "convincing" process unnecessary. It also changes the way political decisions and programs are created, as these are often modeled on the wishes of voters. If candidates always speak and respond only to their constituents, this leads to strategies of closure, inflexibility, and futility of democratic dialectics.

However, in the 2016 election we learned that there is no guaranteed protection. We also discovered that inefficiency always comes with a price tag. Consequently, it seems that Congress members think that the best strategy for keeping their seats is to engage in partisan battles rather than negotiate through political mediation. It is certainly possible that Big Data on voter preferences has informed them that this is a winning strategy. However, if Big Data reduces politics to a mechanical process where algorithms become the Holy Grail and voters are of no great interest, political debate becomes unnecessary. Nevertheless, there are still variables that make this process unpredictable, albeit with a narrowing of democratic choices.

Trump's victory is an example of this unpredictability. In many ways his campaign broke the model. Clinton had a staff that implemented an incredibly sophisticated data strategy and yet she lost. Statistical tools often develop on their own before we even fully understand their implications. Consequently, is Big Data really, Hersh wonders, an example that technology outpaces politics and changes things unexpectedly and out of our control? It also makes one wonder how social classes that were taken for granted have changed and why their priorities shifted. The phenomenology of transformation is similar in intensity to that of the 1920s. We should keep in mind that any technology is a tool that can always be used for purposes other than that for which it was originally created. We do not know how online advertising targets consumers, or how use of Big Data for marketing or campaign purposes will be used or will influence results. There is a great deal of uncertainty.

The emergence of public relations in the mid-twentieth century profoundly changed the way we do politics; it turned election campaigns into marketing campaigns. Politicians became products, and the techniques used to sell cars or toothpaste were adapted to election campaigns. It may not be completely accurate to speak in such terms about Big Data as there are vast differences between commercial marketing and campaign marketing. If you get to 49 percent of the toothpaste market for example, you are really talking about a huge success for the company selling toothpaste. If you get to 49 percent in politics, you have lost the election. The incentives are different. The individual voter is more important than the individual consumer in the commercial market, and candidates are limited in terms of their ability to exclude segments of the population. The more a candidate—Hersh argues—addresses voters willing to agree with them, the less likely a politician is to make arguments and defend positions against an opposing candidate. The democratic dialectic will weaken and tend toward being more of a rhetorical exercise on the candidate's part for those who are already in agreement. When politicians are too misaligned with their voting district or sound inauthentic, the "market" will present an alternative in the next election. That fact does constitute a deterrent, but it is not strong enough.

Big Data is not necessarily evidence of good governance or lawmaking; it just simplifies the process of winning. It encourages political extremism and rigidity and diminishes the strength of democracy, because while it is true that there is always an alternative and Big Data cannot change that, it is also true that the democratic dialectic between candidates' different positions is hollowed out and reduced to a purely rhetorical non-persuasive exercise among likeminded individuals. By not allowing a real confrontation and taking positions to extremes, it encourages an inevitable clash between opposing positions.

The path to intolerance, rigidity, and violence is short, very short. Although Hersch believes that the problem of Big Data is overstated, since voters are still free to choose. However, today because of the Coronavirus, the situation does not appear so very straightforward. The Coronavirus paved the way for greater control over individuals, which they themselves requested and willingly permit. A dystopian world can be envisaged in which Big Data would have a fundamental role and in which transparency, an essential feature of democracy, is envisioned rather in terms like those described in the 1926 film project *The Glass House* by Eisenstein which was never filmed. In it, the Soviet director wanted to depict hell as a glass house, with unshaded windows, where everyone could see and be seen by everyone, with deadly consequences for a viable democracy.

Figure 4.1 **Mussolini and Trump Strongly Emphasize Their Arguments.** By the authors.

Mussolini loved neither the *squadristi* nor their supporters. He thought they were crude, reactionary, and ignorant. Regardless of what he thought, they guaranteed him readers and voters. When Mussolini founded the *Fasci di Combattimento*, Prime Minister Vittorio Emanuele Orlando's government had just extended the right to vote to all ex-soldiers of any age. Thus, honoring a promise made during World War I to expand the right to vote for soldiers that had been made after the defeat of *Caporetto*.[2] Five months later, on August 15, 1919, law no. 1401 was passed by Parliament with the approval of Prime Minister Francesco Saverio Nitti's government, changing the electoral system to proportional representation and further extending the right to vote to all male citizens who were either twenty-one years of age or had completed their military service. After the March on Rome, Mussolini's "law abiding" government was able to exploit the persistent bickering between the parties favoring a proportional system and those favoring single-member constituencies to propose an amendment to the electoral law. Thus, the *Acerbo Law* was passed on November 18, 1923. There were two very important changes. The first provided that the single national electoral district be divided into six constituencies. The second change was a hefty bonus for the coalition that attained a majority of the constituencies: two-thirds of the 535 seats of the Chamber would be reserved for the coalition winning at least 25 percent of the vote; the remaining 179 seats were to be divided among the other coalitions proportionally. The *Acerbo Law* also lowered the age for eligibility to stand for Parliament from thirty to twenty-five. This allowed several Fascist deputies elected in 1921, but disqualified for being underage, such as Farinacci, Grandi, and Bottai, to take their seats in Parliament. The paradox is that this serious decision, which was clearly freedom destroying and suicidal for democracy, was legitimized by the unfettered vote of the two branches of Parliament. It was akin to what would happen in Germany with Nazism and Hitler ten years later in 1933. The *Acerbo Law* was applied only in the election of April 6, 1924, which saw the victory of the National Coalition wanted by Mussolini, called the *Listone* ("Big List"), in which not only all Fascists but also proponents of the liberal and conservative Catholics converged. Thanks to continuous violence and abuses of power, the *Listone* obtained 65 percent of the vote. It was followed by the murder of Giacomo Matteotti and the birth of the dictatorship. But in these three years what was the electoral growth of Fascism?

Not long after the *Fasci di Combattimento* were founded, at the inception of the movement there was a flurry of socialist demonstrations in the streets of Rome and Milan, praising the Spartacist uprising[3] in Germany and Soviet bolshevism. It was also alarming that they had added to their red flag a hammer and sickle, the symbol of the Soviet October Revolution. The threat was so serious that liberals, conservatives, nationalists, hard-liners, and ex-military men took action to prevent it. This resulted in a series of conflicts and skirmishes between opposing protesters with deaths and injuries. The police charged. The Socialists, in turn, called strikes that people considered unjustified, and to which they protested by taking to the streets. It was a pre-civil war climate. Mussolini shrewdly praised those Fascists who participated, offering in *Il Popolo d'Italia* a sounding board for the anti-Bolsheviks. He gathered more and more followers that quickly transformed into votes and consensus. The fundamental point was that the first successes of the *squadristi* shattered the myth of the invincibility of the Red Leagues. The *squadristi* predominantly focused their attacks on the Railwaymen's Clubs, which were the best organized and most combative category of workers. They even went so far as to attack the homes of Socialist deputies. It was 1920. The acts of intimidation and violence did not abate. The headquarters of *Avanti!* in Milan were attacked countless times, as were the paper's various provincial editorial offices. Other newspapers and magazines were also vandalized. Neutralizing the press meant prohibiting national coordination of anti-Fascists with the consequent disintegration of their political unity.

The movie *Camicia nera* (Black Shirt), directed by Gioacchino Forzano, produced by the *Istituto Luce*[4] in 1932, written with the collaboration of Mussolini, evoked the violent climate of early Fascism, but put the blame squarely on liberal and socialist forces. According to police archives, from January 1 to April 7, 1921, the black shirts killed 77 people and wounded 280. Killing and injuring peasants, workers, trade unionists, liberals, and Socialist deputies all at the hands of the *squadristi*. The reality is that there were victims on both sides. If it is true that the forces of law and order often sided with the Fascists, it is also true that sometimes they were the ones who killed them. This was pointed out in the periodical *L'Ordine Nuovo* when on the front page on September 27, 1921, the editor of the periodical, Antonio Gramsci,[5] wrote "Serious massacre in Modena: the royal guards shoot Fascists and kill five." On July 21, 1921, one of the most tragic episodes took place in the small town of Sarzana.[6] A squad of 600 black shirts attempted to enter the city to free the future president of the *Opera Nazionale Balilla*,[7] Renato Ricci, and nine other Fascists from prison. The squad was led by Amerigo Dùmini, a U.S.-born Italian citizen whose mother was American. He would be one of Giacomo Matteotti's murderers.

A heroic rhetoric existed among the *squadristi*. Their organization was modeled on the Roman military, including its terminology. The *prìncipi* were the young *squadristi* destined for action and the *triari* were the older Fascists, the reserve. The basic unit, the squad, was formed by a minimum of twenty to a maximum of fifty men; four squads formed a *centuria*; four *centuria*, a *coorte*; from three to nine *coorti*, a legion. The chain of command ran from the inspectors general, at the top, to the *consuls* who commanded the legions, to the *seniores* who commanded the *coorte*. At the lowest level were the *centurions*, *decurions*, squad leaders, and their assistants.

Their uniform, a symbol of order, organization, and hierarchy, consisted of a black shirt, a black sash at the waist, a leather belt, dark military-style breeches, a black fez with a bow, and long socks or puttee. Roman eagles and five-pointed stars were placed on their lanyards along with the other decorative elements of the uniform. The inspectors of the general command were appointed by what would later be the National Fascist Party. All other ranks were elective by designation of the *squadristi* of immediately lower rank.

But how did Mussolini manage to make this monumental structure work? Propaganda and the means of mass communication were fundamental, including those means that were more complex than the printed page: radio, film news reels, and the movies. A glance at the future of the regime provides a picture of what was to occur. There is a pivotal episode that needs to be mentioned once again here. On June 10, 1924, Giacomo Matteotti was kidnapped and murdered. Mussolini was crushed by the wave of indignation that shook the country. The anti-Fascist deputies and senators' withdrawal from Parliament in opposition became known as the *Aventine Secession*[8] (*secessione dell'Aventino*). It was a critical moment for Mussolini. He needed an idea to re-shuffle the deck and to allow him to take action. Thus, National Public Radio was born. Barely three months later, the airwaves of the Italian peninsula were permeated by the first Hertzian signals aimed at the general public and no longer just the military. *URI—Unione Radiofonica Italiana—*(Italian Radio Union) began broadcasting at 9 p.m. on October 6, 1924, when the voice of Ines Viviani Donarelli, a violinist, inaugurated radio broadcasting in Italy. The day before Mussolini had given the inaugural speech in Rome at the *Teatro Costanzi*.[9] The radio materialized the new specter behind which was hidden the power of politics, as well as that of culture. The radio drew intellectuals, poets, artists, and voices of talent that immediately brought quality to the programs, transforming them into an expression of their time: capturing the turmoil, the passions, life in the balance, and the hope of imagining a better future. Inspired by the Stefani Agency, the first news reports on the stock market, shows, fashion, and travel were soon broadcast. The airwaves gave voice to the thousand desires of a bourgeoisie that, having wholeheartedly given itself over to the hope that Fascism offered, was grateful for the promise to defend it from Bolshevism. It had closed its eyes to the violence of the regime. The radio would soon be joined by the movies and information of the *Istituto Luce* newsreels.[10]

According to *Politico*, thanks to her enormous staff, Hillary Clinton established a direct relationship with 26 percent of the voters, while Trump only reached 17 percent of them. However, it is one thing to talk on the phone, another to convince a voter to cast a vote. What matters is the effectiveness of the message, as well as the qualities of the candidate in spreading and making it popular. It is slogans that win, and the ideas they express. In 2008 and 2012 Barack Obama won with *Hope* and *Yes we can.* It is suggestive narratives not numbers that stir voter imagination. Thus, Trump coined his slogan: *Make America Great Again* An unattainable achievement in the world of globalization unless the intent is to go backward reversing the course of the economy and the country's customs. The slogan, though, resonated with many American voters who felt, at best, neglected, if not abandoned by the Democratic Party establishment. Donald Trump invariably attracted media coverage, especially the opposition media with his extravagant style. His team invented strategies that had never been used before. Trump made headlines with provocative tweets; his posts, caustically offensive, set off explosive fireworks. TV and newspapers, bewildered, cried scandal. Forgetting a strategic fact: this entire media chain of incalculable value was set in motion by tools that cost practically nothing. In the meantime, press agencies and national newspapers relaunched his often-provocative phrases, creating almost radioactive viral moments. The fallacy of a tweet became a planetary fact. Trump and his unorthodox staff made people talk about them. It seems incredible that a simple controversial or offensive one-liner could attain international television coverage, yet it happened. Trump also had Fox News on his side. He received invitations to popular TV talk shows and news programs. And this often happened among Hillary Clinton's media supporters who wanted to humiliate Trump, but all they managed to accomplish was a double down effect achieving the exact opposite. Rather than humiliating him they created an even greater star. The grotesque prevailed over common sense. The world could not stop talking about him.

Trump did not use an actual club like the *squadristi* to reinforce his message; he used the strategy of shock, which delivered blows in the form of violent phrases. He used a club made of words. Extreme hyperbole about racism. Paradoxes on the economy. Exaggerations on international politics. Insults to Clinton. Threats to Mexico. He criticized the establishment. His language immediately triggered controversy along with encouraging rather dark emotional reactions. His verbal violence led to questions about the potential consequences. In a March 17, 2019 article in the *New York Times* entitled *It Isn't Complicated. Trump Encourages Violence*, David Leonhardt noted that Trump's verbal virulence was extremely dangerous as it incited physical violence. It was not enough to say "that is the way he talks" or "don't take him literally" or that finally "his speeches and tweets don't really matter," because that was not the case. Leonhardt asked political scientists with expertise in democracy and authoritarianism what they thought. Their consistent response, according to the journalist was: "No, the United States does not appear at risk of a widespread political violence anytime soon. But Trump's words are still corroding democracy and public safety."

Daniel Ziblatt, author along with Steve Levitsky of the essay *How Democracies Die*, interviewed by Leonhardt made a historical comparison with "scary echoes." Ziblatt, writes Leonhardt, "alluded to Trump's combined lies about his political opponents—Democrats who need to be investigated (for made up scandals)—with allusion to patriotic violent response by ordinary citizens. Latin American dictators including Hugo Chavez in Venezuela have used this combination. So did European Fascists of the 1930s."

Further, with respect to the use of violence Steve Levitsky adds "It slowly and inexorably makes political violence normal, transforming previously unspeakable and unmentionable speech, ideas, and facts into sayable and nameable things." Such as when Trump spoke of the "good people" in the *Ku Klux Klan* during the August 2017 riots in Charlottesville, Virginia, where a member of a racist group killed a young woman who belonged to the *Black Lives Matter* movement. The statistics on racially motivated crimes, generally not very reliable, nevertheless, showed, according to the FBI, an exponential growth. In 2019, the *Anti-Defamation League* wrote that thirty-nine of the fifty racially motivated hate murders were committed by White supremacists and another eight by killers who identified with anti-government positions. Leonhardt concluded his article by noting:

> No, Trump is not directly responsible for the exponential increase in violence but the reasoning is not complicated: the man who speaks from the world's largest pulpit continues to encourage violence and white nationalism, and it just so happens that forms of white nationalist violence are on the rise. You really have to work hard to be persuaded that it's just a big coincidence. (Leonhardt 2019)

The web was also a vector of viral epidemics; the posts and tweets that newspapers were only too happy to debunk, instead functioned as an echo chamber. The Trumpian propaganda team was brilliant at monopolizing global interest. *The Washington Post, The Huffington Post*, and *Buzzfeed* never even considered that it might be good to ignore him. Racist thoughts and quips had never before found loudspeakers and the imprudent counterattacks were extremely effective in amplifying them. How many frustrated and intolerant people would have ignored his message if all this controversy had not existed?

The *squadristi* returning in truckloads from their various assaults on newspapers, labor unions, and Red Leagues would often sing an outrageous song that went something along the following lines:

I don't give a damn is our motto
I don't care about dying

I don't care about Giolitti
Or that Socialism comes next.
A black, black flag
That wraps around us
I dont' care about the Police Commissioner
The Prefect or even the King
Dust, dust
We march with a revolver
We march with a revolver
So we can kill Lenin.
And when you were in charge
You sent us to bed
Now that we are in charge, we send you to bed
Fascists and Communists
Played cards
And the Fascist won
With the Ace of Clubs
And the electric current
Is a strong current
Who lays a hand on a Fascist
Will be in danger of death
(Piazzesi, p.202*).*

This song could also be heard in the taverns they frequented where they welcomed new members, with their blood-stained hands and drunk on wine.

The Italian political climate of 1921 was horrendous. It was rife with death and violence. One famous attack was a bombing carried out by anarchists at the Diana Theatre in Milan on the night between the March 23 and March 24, 1921. The intended victim was police inspector Giovanni Gasti, who had written the 1919 report on Mussolini. The attack left 21 dead and 150 wounded. Gasti survived. During the actual election campaign, in the period between April 8 to May 14, the violence killed 105 people and left 43 wounded.

What were Trumps clubs? *Facebook, Twitter, Instagram, YouTube, Periscope, Vine.* Their use simply requires a bit of skill, they have zero cost and need a minimal commitment. All a person needs is a cell phone. Sharp, effective thoughts count; these do not need to be right. They need to grab the attention of ABC, CNN, CBS, MSNBC, and the rest of the world's media. Trump's staff used social media to scientifically intercept voters where they really pay attention: on their cell phones. Trump launched poison pills on Instagram to inflame intolerance; would live-tweet in Twitter's Trending Topics to keep previous tweets in current view and used Periscope to create videos to provide a sort of instant gratification to his followers. Through the web, every Republican voter felt as if they were corresponding directly with their leader. This type of intimacy is impossible on TV. Trump was a new phenomenon. He is a melting pot of many elements: class aversion, desire for revenge, personal interests, yearning for payback, and a disquieting patriotism from yesteryear.

NOTES

1. The Po Valley (Italian: *Pianura Padana* or *Val Padana*) is a major geographical feature of Northern Italy. It is the vast valley around the Po River, Italy's longest river. The Po River flows eastward from the Alps for approximately 405 miles before emptying into the Adriatic Sea. The Po Valley extends approximately 400 miles in an east-west direction, with an area of approximately 18,000 square miles spanning the area from the Western Alps to the Adriatic Sea and is one of Italy's most fertile valleys.

2. The Battle of *Caporetto* was a World War I battle that took place from October 24 to November 19, 1917 on the Italian front. The Italian forces were routed by the Austro-Hungarian forces. It was a humiliating defeat for the Kingdom of Italy. The Italian Army retreated 150 kilometers to the Piave River, its effective strength declined from 1,800,000 troops down to 1,000,000.

3. The Spartacist uprising (also known as the January uprising) took place from January 5 to 12, 1919 in Berlin. It was a general strike accompanied by armed battles. The uprising was primarily a power struggle between the moderate Social Democratic Party of Germany and the radical communists of the Communist Party of Germany.

   The revolt was improvised and small scale. It was quickly crushed by the superior firepower of government troops, and daily life in Berlin was largely undisturbed. Similar uprisings occurred and were suppressed in other German cities.

4. The *Istituto Luce* located in Rome was created in 1924 for the production and distribution of films and documentaries for screening in movie theaters. It is famous for having been a powerful propaganda tool for Italy's Fascist regime. Nevertheless, it is considered the oldest public institution devoted to production and distribution of cinematographic materials for educational and informative purposes in the world. Isituto Luce in English means "Light Institute." The use of the word "luce" in the name is actually acronym for *L'Unione Cinematografica Educativa*, which means "Educational Film Union". After World War II the company continued to produce documentaries and films and in 2009 it merged with *Cinecittà Holding SpA*, becoming *Cinecittà Luce SpA*. In 2011 its name was changed to *Istituto Luce Cinecittà*.

5. Antonio Francesco Gramsci (January 2, 1891–April 27, 1937) was an Italian Marxist philosopher, journalist, linguist, writer, and politician. He wrote on philosophy, political theory, sociology, history, and linguistics. He was a founding member and one-time leader of the Communist Party of Italy and was imprisoned by the Italian Fascist regime. Gramsci wrote more than 30 notebooks and 3,000 pages of history and analysis during his imprisonment. His *Prison Notebooks* are considered a highly original contribution to twentieth-century political theory. He spent eleven years in

prison and, and although scheduled for release on April 21, 1937, he was too ill to be moved. As a result, he died in prison.

6. Sarzana is a town in the southern part of the Ligurian region.

7. The *Opera Nazionale Balilla* was an Italian Fascist youth organization that existed between 1926 and 1937, when it was absorbed into the *Gioventù Italiana del Littorio*, a youth section of the Fascist Party.

8. This secession was named after the Aventine Secession of ancient Rome, which occurred between 495 and 493 BCE. That incident involved a dispute between the patrician ruling class and the plebeian class over the burden of debt placed on the Plebian class. The patrician ruling class and the senate refused to agree to debt reform. It was actually one of a number of plebian secessions and part of a broader political conflict known as the "conflict of the orders." The senate's refusal to reform caused a general alarm over plebeian rights. This resulted in the plebeians seceding and abandoning the Aventine hill for the nearby *Mons Sacer* (Monte Sacro, another one of Rome's seven hills). A reconciliation was eventually negotiated and the plebeians were given political representation by the creation of the office of the Tribune of the Plebs.

9. On January 26, 1936, on *Via Tuscolana* on the outskirts of Rome, the foundations of Italy's "Hollywood on the Tiber" were laid. It was a complex project which included three neighboring structures in reciprocal symbiosis: the *Istituto Luce* which had its own development and printing plants and laboratories, the *Centro Sperimentale di Cinematografia* (Experimental Film Centre or Italian National film school is the most prestigious film school in Italy), and the brand new *Cinecittà* with its numerous ultra-modern soundstages. *Cinecittà* was inaugurated on April 21, 1937. To recoup the money invested, it engaged in an aggressive contracting program abroad. However, a short time later neither American nor English movies would be screened. It would be cinematic autarky.

10. In 1928 URI was transformed into the *Ente Italian Audizioni Radiofonico*, EIAR, a name inspired by the greeting of the Fascists *Eia! Eia*! In addition to broadcasts for the young, broadcasts and radio plays were also created for children. The information on the programs was included in the weekly magazine *Radiorario* which then became *Radiocorriere*. It should not be forgotten that today's *Rai (Radio Audizioni Italiane* since 1954) the national public broadcasting company of Italy, owned by the Ministry of Economy and Finance, stems from EIAR. Receivers were very expensive. Only a small elite group could afford one; roughly about 10,000 families. In fact, in 1937 there were still only a few hundred thousand subscribers out of forty million inhabitants. Mussolini then required companies to build a device at an affordable price. The *Balilla* model was born; it cost of 430 lire payable in eighteen monthly installments. And in a few months the EIAR reached one million subscribers. As with the radio Mussolini made sure to have his say on cinema newsreels as well. Placed directly under Mussolini's control in 1925 the Educational Cinematographic Union was born. However, the production of state newsreels to be screened in theaters before each film did not begin until 1927 with the collaboration of Metro Goldwin Mayer. It was a weekly broadcast that provided a view of the national and international news from the Fascist point of view. It created an image repertoire imposed

on the young by the regime. It touched all aspects of their lives at whose center was always Fascism. Where there were no movie theaters to reach all potential viewers, there was the *Cinemobile*, a complicated bit of machinery that allowed the *Duce's* newsreels to be projected in town squares and in the countryside so that farmers who had never seen him in person were able to see him for the first time on screen. Despite Mussolini's claims that cinema was the young art of the fascist century, for fifteen years Rome did not have a structured mechanism for production or for state aid to the private sector.

Chapter 5

Ideology as a Prop

It quickly became clear that the rural *squadrismo* that developed in the mid-1920s was different from the urban *Fasci di Combattimento*. Beyond being anti-Bolshevik the rural *squadristi* basically had no labor or union connection.

This difference accounted for the change in the nature of Fascist violence. It began to occur on a vaster scale and with assaults that bordered on civil war, such as massacres in Bologna and Ferrara. Many more such incidents followed with the mobilization of Fascists *en masse* streaming in mainly from the countryside.

The anarchists, socialists, and the Red Leagues quickly lost control of the territory. Mussolini took advantage of this situation. The violence of the *squadristi* became the instrument of political pressure and blackmail that he used to bring Parliament to its knees. The country was at the mercy of disorder and strife. It was a very difficult period for Socialist Party leaders, such as Filippo Turati, Claudio Treves, and Giuseppe Emanuele Modigliani as well as for the Popular Party (The Catholic party).

Nevertheless, as Aurelio Lepre in *Mussolini l'Italiano: Il Duce nel mito e nella realtà*, *Mussolini the Italian* (*The Duce in Myth and in Reality*) wrote, it was due to rural Fascism that the Fascist Party went from a movement composed of the *Fasci di Combattimento* to a national party. It went from 20,615 members at the end of 1920 to 249,036 at the end of 1921. A ten-fold growth. An enormous voter pool that tempted all the leaders of the conservative liberal classes sitting in Parliament. On June 15, 1920, the liberal government of Prime Minister Francesco Saverio Nitti resigned and the legendary leader of Italian *Trasformismo*[1] Giovanni Giolitti had become Prime Minister. Given the outcome of the local elections he immediately had to face the issue of how to deal with the young political movement based on *squadrista* violence. He

decided to legitimize Fascism making it presentable to the electorate. Giolitti brought Fascism into the special coalitions called "national blocs." He
asserted that the rural variant of Fascism was no longer a real threat to the
political system and that it would be useful to bring them into alliances with
an anti-socialist bent. This decision had an immediate tangible impact. In the
administrative elections of the fall of 1920, the Fascists were allied with Giolitti in many local slates. Many Fascists were elected. It was the third great
winning move. A difficult political situation was resolved for Mussolini and
Giolitti did it for him.

Having reaped electoral gains with Mussolini as his ally, Giolitti sought
Mussolini's assistance in resolving a particularly thorny problem: the continued occupation of the city of Fiume. Despite the exasperation of half of
Europe and the United States, for almost a year the poet Gabriele D'Annunzio
and his Legionnaires had occupied the city and showed no intention of ending
the occupation.

After the Treaty of Rapallo of 1920,[2] the League of Nations insisted that
the issue be resolved. Military action was necessary. It had to be an action that
carried a minimum of political harm. The Italian press considered Mussolini
to be D'Annunzio's close friend. The Fascists were also the only ones that
had armed squads capable of assisting in the endeavor. However, their use
would have created serious difficulties in the government. Therefore, Giolitti
had to deprive D'Annunzio of his most important support in Italy. Mussolini
was not enamored of Giolitti. He did not care for D'Annunzio either. He also
did not want to be responsible for a civil war. Mussolini chose to remain
on the sidelines as the Italian Navy bombed the city and the Italian troops
invaded Fiume. Fiume fell in what is known as the "Christmas of Blood"
of 1920. There were few deaths, but they remained on the country's collective conscience. D'Annunzio and his Legionnaires were expelled. Mussolini
pretended to be horrified, but he was pleased. D'Annunzio was the political
opponent he feared most.

Trump saved on costs. His investment in television was negligible. In his
primary campaign Jeb Bush, spent 99 percent more of his funds on television
ads than Trump. NBC News surveys showed Bush spent as much as $28.9
million, and yet those thirty-second spots did not win him the Republican
Party nomination. Up until a few weeks before election day, the predictions
of Hillary Clinton's winning the election were so conclusive that they seemed
to shred any chance of Trump's winning. What was the strategy that Trump
used to win over voters?

Republicans were not enamored of Trump, and Trump was not particularly
enamored of them either. He had never ideologically sided with the Republican Party in its political battles. He did not share the goals of the Tea Party,
which had been holding the GOP hostage, with its extremely conservative

principles, and its anti-abortion and religious crusades, moving it increasingly to the right. As a result, the Republican Party had rejected during the Obama years any kind of bipartisan position, even when Obama sponsored legislation that Republicans themselves had initially proposed. Trump was not a career politician. He was a showman, a businessman, unscrupulous and unrestrained. He is extremely egocentric, and his personal gain always came first. According to a March 2015 *Wall Street Journal* exit poll when Trump announced his candidacy in the 2016 presidential election three-quarters of Republican voters said they would not support him.

"Ever since their bitter 2012 presidential loss," Janet Hook and Monica Langley wrote in the article *How trump Won and the GOP Let Him* published in the *Wall Street Journal* on May 5, 2016, in which they also interviewed Donald Trump, "Republican leaders and the party's grassroots have been at odds, with the rank-and-file voters angry with the failure of the elites to deliver and at odds over the issue of immigration. Mr. Trump found opportunity in the rupture."

His Republican opponents underestimated his power. They mistakenly believed his campaign would be a failure. Instead, his unconventional campaigning and ubiquitous television and newspaper presence overcame any possible negative impact of his outrageous claims. "This election isn't about the Republican Party, it's about me," Mr. Trump said in that interview. "I'm very proud I proved an outsider can win by massive victories from the people, not from party elites or the state delegates" (Hook and Langley 2016).

Trump implicitly stated that his goal was not to change the Republican Party, nor to have, as is usually the case for a presidential candidate, the total support of the party when he stated: "I'd rather have a unified Republican Party, but I'm not sure it's as necessary to the voters to see people getting along. . . . They are voting for the person not a party."

He personalized the election by focusing on himself rather than a program. While the Republican Party failed to hear what the voters wanted, Trump listened to them. As of June 2016, his campaign was based on the explosive premise that whatever the risk to the party, he would immediately voice voters' economic fears and their hostility to illegal immigration. In June 2016, in Las Vegas in his announcement, he stated that he would be the official Republican candidate for president, as we said earlier, he repeated his usual litany of accusations against the Mexican government. He talked about the wall for which Mexico would pay. He pledged to dismantle existing trade agreements approved by the Republican Party. He spoke harshly against international terrorism but said he would have practiced an anti-interventionist policy contrary to all the beliefs of the Republican Party hawks. He questioned the war hero reputation of the Republican party icon and respected member of the Senate John McCain. He vulgarly insulted women and his political rivals, and he never denied that he supported White supremacists. Instead of creating a negative backlash, his support among voters increased. Further those that opposed Trump within the Republican Party suffered from a lack of coordination and Trump surged forward.

May 1921. New Parliamentary elections were expected. Mussolini had no intention of suffering another defeat like that of 1919, or to be subsumed by Giolitti. He needed all the *squadristi*, both the rural and the national ones, to vote compactly for the Fascist candidates on the national slates proposed by Giolitti. To obtain this unanimity, he had to settle all remaining political grudges among the Fascists. One of the most pressing issues was Gabriele D'Annunzio and his Legionnaires.

On April 5, 1921, Mussolini met with D'Annunzio at Villa Cargnacco[3] on Lake Garda for a friendly rapprochement, and they reached an agreement. D'Annunzio leaked it to the newspapers through a game of secret subtexts indirectly forcing *La Stampa* of Turin in the article *"D'Annunzio e i legionari"* ("D'Annunzio and his Legionnaires") published on April 13, 1921, to cryptically report:

> We hereby announce that Gabriele D'Annunzio had the opportunity recently to deliver to a trusted friend his instructions to be followed by the entire core of the Fiume Legionnaires. There are two types of instructions. The first will be known by all and will form the political action of the group; they will contain the general instructions on voter participation and the basic premises to be supported in public rallies. The second, which is strictly confidential, will be personally sent to those individuals closely trusted by the commander and will provide for the negotiations to be carried out with the candidates. (Frassati 1921)

As for D'Annunzio's candidacy *La Stampa* reported: "No explicit acceptance has been announced, and there are those who assure that D'Annunzio is prepared to relinquish such an honor in a letter of political content" (Ibid.).

D'Annunzio's consent to refrain from running was the key point of the agreement with Mussolini. With this move Mussolini was able to gain the support of the Fiume Legionnaires and those who had sympathized with D'Annunzio's Fiume occupation. Many *gerarchi* and future Fascist Party leaders were former Fiume Legionnaires. Among them were Giovanni Giuriati, future secretary of the Party and Minister of Public Works, and Giovanni Host Venturi, the future Minister of Communications. The list also includes the writer Giovanni Comisso, the painter Filippo De Pisis, the sculptor Arturo Martini, and the founder of Futurism Filippo Tommaso Marinetti. There were also the *illustrious* visitors to Fiume. These included Arturo Toscanini who arrived in Fiume with his entire orchestra on November 20, 1920 to hold a grand concert in honor of D'Annunzio and the city's inhabitants. He performed music by Beethoven, Vivaldi, and Wagner. Prior to

Toscanini, Guglielmo Marconi came to Fiume on September 22 with his family aboard his laboratory ship, the *Elettra*. It was not a spur-of-the-moment voyage; he was sent by, Giolitti, to convince D'Annunzio to abandon his occupation of Fiume and avoid military aggression. Marconi, however, was so charmed by D'Annunzio that he made available, against all of Giolitti's directives, his radio station so he could broadcast the next day, at 2 p.m., a heartfelt message in favor of the occupation and the Italianess of Fiume.

Marconi was appointed President of the famous Academy of Italy and remained there until his death. Mussolini's peace with D'Annunzio was essential to gaining a strategic slice of the country's new cultural elite. It gave him a certain polish and access to ideas. Arturo Toscanini in 1919 was a candidate with the *Fasci di Combattimento*, but not elected. In 1931, after an altercation with the Fascists at the *Teatro Comunale* (Municipal Theater) of Bologna, he decided to make a change, and left Italy for fifteen years. He would return only after the fall of Mussolini.

Everyone knows that to win, a candidate must be popular; it cannot be a fleeting popularity, but a lasting one that resonates profoundly with voters. How many searches have Americans done on Google with the search words "Donald Trump" and "Hillary Clinton"?

Mention.com data which analyzed positive sentiment for Donald Trump found that it was greater than that of Hillary Clinton. This was despite the fact 62.3 percent of undecided voters leaned toward Trump while 69.5 percent leaned toward Clinton. It was a 7 percent difference. The reason for this can be traced to Hillary's less than incisive Internet strategy. In addition, since Trump maintained a constant dialogue with the denizens of the net this meant that there were a greater number of positive comments for "the Donald" than for Hillary. Trump's effectiveness in communication was also demonstrated by the tremendous increase in followers he had on Twitter. Before the start of the campaign, the Democratic Party documented only 9,817 tweets in favor of Hillary Clinton compared to a whopping 34,000 for Donald Trump. Hillary had 9,401,000 followers which was blown away by Trump's 12,127,000. Trump was almost twice as popular on Facebook as well. He also had more followers on *Instagram* and *Snapchat*, where he caught the attention of millennials, the youngest voters. Hillary Clinton lost on every social network and the algorithms showed no mercy. Meanwhile, Trump consolidated his position as an outsider marching against party ranks and moving the ideological bar even further to the right by continuing to fuel racial hatred against Hispanic minorities and African Americans, as well as hatred against all his political opponents. He combined this ideological shift with the encouragement of violence.

In 2019 he criticized Paul Ryan, at the time speaker of the House of Representatives, for not investigating individuals on the political left with these words:

The left plays a tougher game [Trump stated on March 13, 2019, in a *"Breit-bart"* interview given at the White House] It's very funny. I actually think that the people on the right are tougher, but they don't play it tougher. Okay? I can tell you I have the support of the police, the support of the military, the support of the Bikers for Trump—I have the tough people, but they don't play it tough—until they go to a certain point, and then it would be very bad, very bad.

Words that sounded like a threat and some interpreted them as such.

Returning to the Italian election of May 1921, Mussolini was among the thirty-four newly elected Fascists. The March to power was still a year and a half away. Mussolini addressed the Chamber for the first time on June 25, 1921. He took his place in the last right-hand bench, where no one had ever dared to sit. He was detached from the other deputies and, very high up "he looks like a vulture squatting on a cliff" wrote Emilio Lussu (Lussu p. 25). "I declare to you at once that mine will be a right-wing speech. It will be a reactionary speech because I am anti-parliament, anti-Democratic, anti-Socialist" (*ibidem.*). The Socialists reminded him that he had been a socialist for twenty years. Mussolini looked at them with contempt. Then he continued: "And being anti-socialist, I am resolutely anti-Giolitti" (Ibid.). At this point protest was heard from the Honorable Giolitti. The old parliamentarian looked at him in surprise and seemed to want to ask him: What game are we playing? Were we not on the same slate just until a few days ago?

Mussolini's tone and political focus moved further to the right. He was aggressive to garner the support of the reactionary and nationalist leaders; he did not hesitate to support acts of terror against the pro-Austrians in Alto Adige.[4] In his June 21, 1921, speech to the Chamber of Deputies, he bluntly stated that the Fascist bomb attack of April 24 of that same year had been justifiable retaliation. He even claimed a share of the moral responsibility for the bomb because it marked a limit beyond which Fascism had no intention of allowing the German element to go (Susmel and Susmel p. 64).

He had no scruples. Wherever he sensed tension or fear in voters, he shrewdly exploited those fears by amplifying them. Whether these were interest groups, factions, parties, or warring countries, it did not matter to him. He knew quite well that fear was the best tool to achieve power and to keep it; throughout the *Ventennio*[5] he would use it and abuse it to do just that. But returning to the speech of 1921, when he had exhausted using aggression as his tool, he turned it upside down and resorted to mockery. He irritated Gramsci's deputies, calling them choirmasters of:

a doctrine that springs up in times of misery and despair. [. . .] I know the communists. [. . .] I was the first to infect these people, when I introduced into Italian socialism a little Bergson and mixed in quite a lot of Blanqui. There is a philosopher in the ministers' bench, and he certainly taught me that neo-spiritualistic philosophies, with their continuous swaying between metaphysics and lyricism, are extremely pernicious for small brains. They are like oysters: very tasty . . . but difficult to digest. (Rauti and Sermonti p. 455)

He used the same approach with the other parties. He attacked them, but he never shut them out completely, he always left a sliver of space for them to join him at any time. Threat and seduction; the carrot and the stick. Those who initially opposed him had to have the feeling that deciding to support him was an exercise of their own free will. This ambiguity was his winning strategy and it lasted for the entire *Ventennio*.

The number of Trump's followers has already been discussed. But web hits are one thing, what happens within a voting booth is quite different. How many of those followers would become his voters? Statistical research showed that the 70 percent of those interviewed declared they were drawn to Trump, and 90 percent were actually willing to vote for him. Given the very high rate of abstention in U.S. elections, such statistics can have a huge impact on an election. On *YouTube* Trump had an average of 30,000 viewers per streaming; Clinton only had 500. On *Instagram*: Trump had 2.5 million followers, Clinton only 2.1 million. On *Facebook*: Trump 10,772,000 fans, Clinton 6,171,000. Trump had 75 million conversations on *Twitter* over the course of his campaign, add to this figure all his posts on *Facebook* and other media. It is on this swarm of buzzes, grumbles, and hilarity that Trump's victory became more and more likely. On *Facebook*, Trump's posts were the most shared and grew exponentially. Those of Hillary Clinton dropped especially toward the end of the race. We all know who went to Washington.

In the meantime, Trump continued moving to the right. His speeches became increasingly inflammatory. The overriding theme was *us vs. them*. He exacerbated the racial, class, and gender divides. He even exacerbated cultural differences. Rather than trying to mend the country's torn social fabric he fueled the flames of dissention. Addressing his supporters after his victory at the Nevada caucus on February 23, 2016, his third victory in a month before the Super Tuesday challenge in March, he thanked them as follows:

We won with young. We won with old. We won with highly educated. We won with poorly educated. I love the poorly educated. We're the smartest people, we're the most loyal people, and you know what I'm happy about? Because I've been saying it for a long time. 46% were the Hispanics—46%, N.1 . . . with Hispanics [. . .] we're going in the wrong direction. We're going to keep—as you know—Gitmo, we're keeping that open, and we're going to load it up with bad dudes. We're going to load it up with a lot of bad dudes out there. We're going to have our borders nice and strong. We're going to build the wall, you know that. We're going to build the wall. And I have a lot of respect from Mexico, and you just heard we won Hispanics. But let me tell you Mexico is going to pay for the wall, right? It's going to happen. It's going to happen. . . . We have a trade deficit with Mexico. They'll pay for the wall. They'll be very happy about it. Believe me. I'll talk to them. They're going to be very, very thrilled. They're going to be thrilled to be paying for the wall. [. . .] So tonight folks, this was a great evening. I love this place. I love this state. I love Las Vegas. I have spent and invested so much money over here. Trump International Hotel . . . I was so proud. Remember: Make America great again. We're going to do it, and it's going to happen fast. Thank you very much everybody. Thank you.

There was something fundamentally different about the 2016 election from previous elections. As already observed, people were voting primarily against someone, rather than for someone. Trump used a rhetoric, as Jason Stanley affirmed in *How Fascism Works: The Politics of Us and Them*, that served to inflame his base and erode the country's democratic roots. Trump's approach was to evoke a nostalgia for a mythical past that was intentionally considered mythical and had to remain mythical. It only existed to charm voters. What made it dangerous was that it was only a tactic to acquire and maintain power. The culpability for this tactic is to be equally divided between the Republican Party and Trump, as for both of them respect for the law and institutions was no longer of any importance.

It was important for the Republican Party to have a candidate that could win the election and for Trump to win for himself and his companies.

The swarm of Fascists entering the Italian Parliament made quite an impression. For some it was as if barbarians had entered civil society. One imagined Chamber desks destroyed with shouts and blows levied against political opponents. This occurred to some extent, such as in the case of the Socialist deputy Francesco Misiano who was badly beaten. No one expected that violence would shortly break out among the Fascist deputies themselves.

The violence occurred between the two factions that represented Fascism: the rural and the urban. Once in the Chamber they were forced to face each other in taking political decisions. In the summer of 1921, Giolitti was succeeded by Ivanoe Bonomi as Prime Minister. Bonomi set off the dispute between the Fascists. He put forth the somewhat bizarre idea that the two opposites, Fascists and Socialists, join forces. The President of the Chamber of Deputies, Enrico De Nicola, who would be the first President of the Italian Republic after the war, was also persuaded that the idea was valid. Mussolini even agreed with the idea to the extent that he made it his own by announcing a Pacification Pact on July 23, 1921. The Fascist deputies who were veterans of the assaults on the Red Leagues, on the Socialist clubs, and on the Catholic Popular Party were dumfounded by the announcement. He excluded the liberals. He wanted an alliance only among the three mass parties: Fascist, Socialist, and the Popular Parties, so that policy could be enacted with the support of the consent of the vast majority of Italians. In order to be taken seriously, he wanted to resolutely tackle the problem of violence, by imposing a Pacification Pact to finally end the guerrilla warfare between the Fascists and the Socialists. Above all he wanted the cooperation of the Italian labor Union, the *Confederazione Generale del Lavoro* (CGL) whose leaders Mussolini defined as being "quite reasonable."

CGL executive Gino Baldesi appreciated the compliment. Turati showed his appreciation for the project in the pages of *Avanti!* The Popular Party and the Republican Party refused to participate, as did the Communists. Among the Fascists, however, pandemonium ensued. The Pacification Pact was seen as a gratuitous truce that Mussolini was gifting to the Socialists so they could reorganize. The gulf that divided the rural *squadristi* from Mussolini suddenly became very wide.

All that the rural *squadristi* had in common with the Fascist vision of Mussolini was anti-Bolshevism, nationalism, and solidarity with former combatants. The rural Fascism of the *squadristi* was bourgeois in the narrowest sense of the word, devoid of any ideal other than that of intransigence which could not see beyond its own class interests.

Mussolini and the old Fascists were different, at times even contradictory. This was not so much for demagoguery, but in order to keep alive events that had become mythical, such as World War I and the rebellion against the *Biennio Rosso*. The differences between the two factions of Fascism were remarkable. For the very young *squadrista*, the Milanese leaders, the group to which Mussolini belonged, were "old men" with an old concept of revolution. The divisions were such that the communist leader Antonio Gramsci wrongly assumed that the rift would lead to a split. In fact, many of Mussolini's followers would have liked a sort of "socialist Fascism."

Not so long ago no one would have ever thought that a man such as Trump could be elected President. However, the myth that he was elected only by the ignorant poorer classes must be dismissed. Many of his voters came from areas that for years had been Democratic strongholds. This included the Midwestern "rust belt," which encompassed the states of Michigan, Illinois, Indiana, Iowa, Wisconsin, and other states such as West Virginia, Ohio, and Pennsylvania where the highly unionized working class had always voted Democrat. These voters completely changed their support in the 2016 election. In fact, it was evident that Trump gained more support than Romney among those Americans with annual incomes of less than $30,000, while Clinton gained support among those with annual incomes over $100,000. It was also clear that after the Great Recession of 2008[6] the composition of the social classes had changed. The number of people excluded from the productive processes increased as did their anger, and the number of those who felt neglected by political forces grew exponentially. Trump also gained the votes of the more religious citizens and, in particular, among Catholics (52%

versus Clinton's 45%) and White evangelicals (81% versus Clinton's 16%). A vote for Trump was an anti-establishment vote as was the *Brexit* vote in the United Kingdom. But were those who voted for Trump really just racists, homophobes, xenophobes, and Islamophobes? Or is this simply terminology that has become established among elites since the Civil Rights struggles of the 1960s? Could it have been instead the cry of all those who had been subjected to a kind of "reverse discrimination" put in place in the name of *political correctness*?

It seems that Trump and Brexit are only the first expressions of a widespread, common distress toward immigration policies perceived as senseless, invasive, and threatening to livelihoods. These policies appear to weaken and denigrate traditions, the culture and the religious roots of the West. It is as if citizens should feel a pervasive sense of guilt for being what they are (Cfr. *Huffington Post* February 10, 2017).

After Brexit, any political prediction became hazardous. Exit polls at the time of the 2016 U.S. election showed that the candidates were very close. There were only a few points of difference between them. James Comey, head of the FBI, during the campaign had investigated Hillary Clinton for using her personal email for government business during her tenure as Secretary of State and interestingly had even re-opened the investigation just before election day. However, not long after the election, in a public letter, he acquitted her of legal wrongdoing. In the meantime, Clinton's image had been damaged just before the election, which she ultimately lost.

The discourse of the candidates was not a programmatic one based on a worldview, or a *Weltanschauung*.[7] This was a huge departure from previous campaigns. It emphasized the fact that both candidates were the product of calculated choices of their Parties, rather than the expression of popular sentiment and of a real political program that, even in its diversity, had the common good at its core. Trump's saving grace though was that he appeared to not be associated with the political establishment. Moreover, the mechanisms of choosing a candidate within the parties were guided by anything, but democratic procedures that respected the will of the people. Trump was able to stretch to such proportions this lack of respect for the people that he was able to question the validity of the electoral system asserting that the process was rigged. That gave rise to the idea that the results could be contested. Something never seen before in American politics. It is a system in which the loser accepts the election results regardless of how questionable those results may be. As can be seen in recent history with the 2000 election in which Al Gore lost to George W. Bush by a handful of votes. This is the true meaning of American democracy.

Dan Rather wrote in his blog, which was then reported on CNN and MSNBC shortly before the 2016 election, that what made the difference was the tone and level of the political discourse. Rather identified the "never mind" attitude as the danger of the country's future and against which citizens should rebel. After stating that he was an optimist by nature and a skeptic, but not a cynic, by profession, Rather lashed out at the tenets of this philosophy which he traced back mainly to the Republicans whom he accused of electing Trump out of pure political cynicism and not in the interest of the country. He also laid blame on the press for indifferently allowing Trump to broadcast his lies providing a sort of false equivalence between the two candidates, on those who encouraged xenophobia and misogyny to heat up the electorate and finally on those who fanned the fire of lies against the truth. Against these groups Rather urged people to pay attention to the current situation without forgetting what happened in the past. The future of the country depended on this focus, which, after November 8, should try to demand more from its politicians, its press, and its citizens.

However, there are other factors to take into account in the 2016 election: the transformation of the political landscape, the crisis of the two-party system, and the appearance of populism with its assertion of avoiding ideology, particularly that of political correctness. In a book written by John B. Judis with the significant title *The Populist Explosion: How the Great Recession Transformed American and European Politics* the author pondered the question of why there was such love for Donald Trump's populism. Judis makes a distinction between populism of the right and populism of the left. To the latter category belong Sanders in the United States and Podemos in Spain (anti-elite movements that take the side of the people against the richest 1 percent), while to the right are the followers of Trump and many parties in European countries, including Italy. Both are destabilizing elements. The right-wing populists, however, in addition to lashing out at progressives whom they accuse of being Communists, also accuse the power elites of being responsible for current-day disasters. In fact, they champion the people against a political elite that is accused of favoring immigrants, African Americans, and terrorists. According to Judis it is exactly this mindset that characterizes right-wing populism, especially in Europe.

Rather than noting similarities between the right wing of Trumpian populism and Fascism, a theory Judis discarded, because Trumpian populism lacked territorial ambitions, Judis only saw a similarity between Trump and Berlusconi, as they were businessmen with media backgrounds. A point these two have in common is they removed certain ideological principles that had previously acted as a barrier to making certain statements or taking certain positions. It should also be noted that Berlusconi also had much in common with Mussolini, both with respect to their backgrounds as media entrepreneurs and their media expertise, as well as the absence, at least initially, of a true rigid ideological grid which allowed them to capture unexplored political terrain.

Further the territorial element is no longer the most important component of Fascism. The Trumpian rhetoric that praised a mythical past to be restored, in some cases even praising violence and the techniques he used for the conquest of power, is nevertheless part of the Fascist *outillage.* Ideological principles have also been used by Trump in an unscrupulous way. They are stretched and pulled from one end to the other depending on convenience and circumstances. He claims he is not ideological, but when opponents are accused of being communists, he is judging them within the parameters of ideology, at the heart of which lies that political correctness, which stems from positions of the political left, and the thinking that formed the Civil Rights battles. Those struggles were fought not only by the left. The Civil Rights Act of 1964, which was part of President Lyndon Johnson's Great Society agenda, was supported by many conservatives and was voted for by many Republicans. Ideology has never really been part of American politics in the way it made its back door appearance in the 2016 election. This was thanks to Trump. It was based on individual prejudices of the voters linked more to the personality of Trump than to a precise political program. Apparently, Trump's prejudices were due to the influence of his father who had been a sympathizer of the Ku Klux Klan, and was arrested in a Klan protest in the streets of New York in the 1920s. His father's real estate empire had mainly been built on low-income housing rented for the most part to African Americans against whom, it has been said, he used discriminatory criteria. Trump's expression of his prejudices clearly encouraged unprecedented popular animosity and incited violence. Further Trump has never claimed to have programmatic or ideological coherence, he does not even follow a political ethic. A bit like Frank Underwood in the *House of Cards* series, without, Frank's strategic and long-term ability and without his tragic nature. With time we learned that the behavior of the protagonist in the television series was only a pale copy of what Trump has put into place.

If physical violence was the prime feature that distinguished Fascism from any other party, what kept it at the helm was another, more subtle, intangible, almost harmless element that would diabolically rip apart peoples' consciences, completely distorting them. It is no coincidence that Gaetano Salvemini,[8] one of the many forced into exile by persecution during the Fascist period, defined Fascism as the creation of a propaganda genius, of a manipulator so skillful as to deceive his own people, making them believe that words had more power than reality and indeed could modify it.

Moreover, it was this same ability to persuade and backlight through cinema, radio, newspapers, songs, and architecture that created worlds in the heads of individuals; that type of propaganda infected graphic designers, painters, philosophers, soldiers, poets, bankers, futurist artists all moved by a motion so strong that they did not hesitate to fight in the name of those ideas. It provided an iconographic scheme for choreographies, parades, marching bands, advertisements, and symbols that praised the bright future of the nation. It molded the minds of the people, it made them feel young and, therefore entitled to conquer other countries and receive their obeisance. Mussolini's propaganda was dominating; it was based on charisma, violence, tampering with the collective memory, and it always ambiguously pressed the most seductive buttons: war and fear.

It was a propaganda that annihilated the need for peace, democracy, freedom, and autonomy of thought. The people identified with the Leader who first emptied their minds and then filled them to the brim with slogans, diktats, and his own policies without leaving any room for the individual's own thoughts. Every citizen's brain was like a hard disk that had to be rewired.

The ease with which people's minds can be penetrated can be seen from the success of Mussolini's March on Rome. It was the clever sale by the newspapers of that rough mobilization that convinced the King, and the political forces, to open the doors of the Government to Fascism.

Meanwhile, Mussolini's plan to enter into the Pacification Pact with the socialists continued igniting the rebellion of the reactionary Fascists financed by the rural landowners. In order to boycott the agreement, they caused unspeakable episodes of civil war violence to spread throughout Central and Northern Italy. These included the reckless failed attack of 600 black shirts on the prisons of Sarzana and the atrocities carried out in the cities of Bologna, Padua, and Carrara. The price was dozens of deaths. Mussolini intervened, resentfully declaring, "This circle of hatred must be broken. We have built our fortunes on biers. The squares have become Sunday slaughterhouses. The country needs peace" (Pini, and Susmel p. 127).

He persisted with the Pact. He was not intimidated; he not only negotiated with the CGL and the socialists, but also with the Popular Party. On August 13, 1921, in Rome he signed the Pact in the study of the President of the Chamber of Deputies, Enrico De Nicola. Consistent with his position, on August 18, he also resigned from the Fascist party Directorate.

Arpinati, Grandi, Balbo, and Farinacci, the leaders of the opposition to the Pacification Pact, did not have the political stature to assume control of the entire Fascist movement and to continue on without Mussolini. The only man who could have done so was D'Annunzio, but after being contacted by one of their emissaries, refused.

The conservative rural wing meanwhile cut off Mussolini's supply of financial oxygen, by financing only the *Fasci di Combattimento* and their local newspapers and not *Il Popolo d'Italia*. The industrialists made it clear to Mussolini as well that the current state of affairs could not continue. The number of supporters and the sales of his newspaper plummeted and he risked bankruptcy. Moreover, there was complete complicity between the *squadristi* and the forces of law and order who felt that they were almost allies; even the judiciary favored the Fascists. In the first half of 1921, the Fascist to socialist arrest ratio was 396 to 1421. The same solidarity existed in the army; some soldiers became Fascists while enrolled in the army.

A large part of Italy was an accomplice to the rural Fascism that Mussolini detested. However, he had no choice. Either he abandoned politics or played the only political card available to him. He had to betray the commitment he undertook with the Socialists. If he found this ethically reprehensible, it was not because of ideology. In fact, his Fascism had no doctrine. This was unlike the socialists who could never deny Marx, or the Popular Party which would never deny its Catholic roots. His political stance was so ambiguous that any choice in any direction was open to him, without inhibitions of any kind.

Years later Mussolini would write in the *Enciclopedia italiana* entry on Fascism that his doctrine, from the beginning, had always been a doctrine of action. This meant that the deep ideological body of his movement first, then of the Fascist Party itself, was non-existent. Only later would clarifications be made by intellectuals and philosophers such as Giovanni Gentile. It was this indefiniteness that would allow Mussolini to be a republican and then a monarchist, a reactionary and a progressive, a socialist and a pro-capitalist, oligarchic and populist, anti-Germany and then pro-Germany. It made him able to develop the bizarre form capitalism known as *corporativismo*, or corporatism, in which the economy was collectively managed by employers, workers, and state officials through formal mechanisms at the national level. Mussolini chose compromise, he had to recover his balance, and he toned down the revolutionary rhetoric to regain the trust of his newspaper's advertisers. Although he had to backtrack, he did not want to appear as if he had lost. Fortunately, for Mussolini, luck was with him.

Disappointed by D'Annunzio's refusal, his internal opponents proposed that Mussolini be rehabilitated, provided that he renounce the Pacification Pact. Mussolini agreed and was even able to impose a condition. Fascism could no longer be a movement without rules where anyone could take initiatives; it needed to be transformed into a real political party. It needed a secretary, by-laws, and a governing body. In this way those who did not respect the rules could be expelled.

Mussolini was able to successfully rehabilitate himself and Fascism in the eyes of bourgeois public opinion, regaining his position as its leader.

How much was the media coverage received by Trump from early 2015 to March 2016 worth? Rumor has it that its value was about $2 billion. How true are the rumors of his financial difficulties? Trump has never made his tax returns public. He is said to have spent only ten million, with all of this expenditure being for online services. The point was to get the media to talk about him; like when Justin Bieber, the teenage idol "liked" a Trump post. Trump was quick to invite Bieber to sing at one of his rallies, offering him the unthinkable sum of five million dollars. Bieber's manager forbade him from appearing. Memory of the concert faded, but the news of it would bounce on all the newspapers and TVs worldwide. Trump not only saved five million dollars, but his image gained so much more.

Frank Luntz the Republican political consultant for many TV programs and columnist for such dailies as the *Los Angeles Times*, the *New York Times*, the *Financial Times*, the *Wall Street Journal*, and the *Washington Post* explained that the web won over television two to one. When choosing a candidate for whom to vote an individual will spend two hours on the web, but only one hour watching television. Anyone running for office anywhere must keep this in mind. Trump's staff certainly did. Trump was consistently the underdog in all the polls; he came from behind only by using the Internet. The key is to continuously monitor hot topics that capture the attention of the reader or the audience in the press and in television, respectively. These topics are then loaded onto the web, updated, and revised according to the candidate's opinion, strengthened and specifically tailored. Old news must be revised and even falsified. People on social networks must be provoked, and those who may be indifferent forced to take a position. Blogs must be activated in order to create murky reactionary pools that prompt people to make choices contrary to forecasts. Speed is a must. In order to achieve a result topicality is essential. Posts and tweets must be launched at the speed of a missile attack with disposable contents that may have relevance for only a short period of time. These make one feel like they are on the crest of a media wave. All this must be done while affirming that one is contrary to ideology.

Trump and Mussolini are not ideologues, but have used ideologies as props bending them to their purposes. They both came from a *liberal* past, but moved quickly to the conservative side of the political spectrum. They created new dangerous ideologies that are rigid in approach and contents, and exclude compromise and any type of dissent. They need an enemy, an *other* to blame, socialists and communists for Mussolini, Antifa and liberals for Trump. They both progressively endanger the roots of Democracy by impoverishing the political discourse.

NOTES

1. *Trasformismo* in Italian politics refers to the method of making a flexible centrist coalition of government thereby isolating the extremes on the left and the right in Italian politics. The policy was first embraced by the Count of Cavour

Figure 5.1 Mussolini and Trump Address the Crowds. By the authors.

Camillo Benso and the Historical Right when Italy was unified during the Risorgimento (the social movement that resulted in the political unification of the country under the Kingdom of Savoy in 1861). One of the most successful *trasformismo* politicians was Giovanni Giolitti, who was Prime Minister on five occasions over twenty years. Under his influence the liberals did not develop as a structured party, they were a series of informal personal groupings with no formal links to political constituencies.

2. The Treaty of Rapallo (1920), signed in Rapallo, a town in the region of Liguria, established relations between Italy and the Kingdom of Serbs, Croatians, and Slovenes (later Yugoslavia). Italy obtained the Istrian peninsula while Dalmatia went to Yugoslavia. Fiume (Rijeka) was to be a free city.

3. Villa Cargnacco had belonged to the German art historian of the Italian Renaissance Henry Thode from whom it was confiscated by the Italian state. It is also referred to as the *Vittoriale degli italiani* ("*The shrine of Italian victories*"). It is a hillside estate in the town of Gardone Riviera overlooking Lake Garda in the province of Brescia in the Lombardy region. The Italian writer Gabriele D'Annunzio lived there from 1921 until his death in 1938. The estate consists of D'Annunzio's residence called the *Prioria* (priory), an amphitheater, the cruiser *Puglia* set into a hillside, a boathouse containing the MAS vessel used by D'Annunzio in 1918 when he participated in the Bakar Raid, and a circular mausoleum.

D'Annunzio began renting the estate in 1921. Because of his continuing popularity and his disagreement with the Fascist government on several issues, such as the alliance with Nazi Germany, the Fascists did what they could to keep D'Annunzio happy and away from politics. Part of the strategy was to make large sums available to him to expand the property, to construct and alter buildings, and to create an impressive art and literature collection.

4. A region in Northern Italy, bordering with Austria, which had (and still has) a large German-speaking minority. The region changed hands in its history from Italy

to Austria and back to Italy. Since 1946 it has been part of Italy and has special status as an autonomous region.

5. The *Ventennio*, or twenty years, refers to the period that runs from Mussolini's ascension to power, officially October 31, 1922, to the end of his regime, which occurred formally on July 25, 1943.

6. This was another trauma that, together with September 11, irreversibly changed the face of America and which is beyond the scope of this work: cfr. Anna Camaiti Hostert *Trump non è Una Fiction* [Trump is not a fiction].

7. German term which means a comprehensive conception or apprehension of the world especially from a specific standpoint.

8. Gaetano Salvemini (September 8, 1873–September 6, 1957) was an Italian anti-Fascist politician, historian, and writer. He was well respected as a historian both in Italy and abroad, particularly in the United States, where he lived after being forced into exile by the Fascist regime. His transatlantic exile experience endowed him with new insights and a fresh perspective to explain the rise of Fascism and shaped the memory of the war and political life in Italy after 1945.

Chapter 6

Achieving Internal Consensus

The founding convention of the National Fascist Party was held at the *Teatro Augusteo* in Rome from November 7 to November 9, 1921. Until that time Fascism had been a movement. The convention was supposed to be a peaceful meeting in the Eternal City, and its citizens appeared quite uninterested in the event. However, as Fascists arrived in ever greater numbers, indifference turned to concern. There were skirmishes between Fascists and the police leaving 6 dead, and 180 wounded. The parties on the left called for a general strike in Rome. The convention attendees were unanimously in favor of Mussolini. He won across the board. None of the *squadristi ras* became part of the leadership. Mussolini was acclaimed *Duce dei Fascisti*, its undisputed leader. Once the new party was formed, Mussolini returned to Milan to attend to certain urgent matters at *Il Popolo d'Italia*. The newspaper was ready to be relaunched, and it would now finally also come out on Mondays. Seven years from its inception, Mussolini now had financing to purchase more modern printing presses and a new headquarters. He also created the cultural magazine *Gerarchia* (*Hierarchy*) to reach political intellectuals.

With the founding of the Fascist Party Mussolini was able to rein in the most troublesome elements in the party. Further with the exception of being forced to renounce the Pacification Pact he paid no political price in Parliament. He was free to create political ties with Giolitti, Salandra, Facta, Bonomi, Orlando, and other party leaders or members of Parliament. He was free to act based on his intuition, without having to answer to anyone. He could use the Fascist Party as a cloak or a club and, depending on the situation. There were still some grumblings from the more difficult *ras* such as Roberto Farinacci. However, Mussolini was able to conveniently isolate him (and those like him), summoning him when he was once again needed.

The Fascist Party was a pyramid, as well as a network. At the top of the pyramid was Benito Mussolini. Beneath him was a Directorate led by the Secretary General, Michele Bianchi, beneath the Directorate was the Administrative Secretary, Giovanni Marinelli. These two positions were flanked by a National Council consisting of the heads of all the bodies of the associations related to the party such as trade unions or businesses. The next body in the pyramid was the National Inspectorate with a host of inspectors that had oversight over the provincial federations which were headed by a federal secretary, and had a federal inspector, and a political secretary of the *Fascio di Combattimento*. Beneath that body were the municipal bodies, which were organized like the provincial ones, and under the municipal bodies were local neighborhood groups, each having a head of that neighborhood group. Charged with expelling wayward members, at any level in the pyramid was a Disciplinary Committee. The party was organized as a grid forming a cage encapsulating each element of it. Each member was called a *gerarca* and, contemptuously, given a diminutive of that title: *gerarchetto* if he had an inferior role. The *squadre d'azione*, which continued to exist, were under the jurisdiction of the local directorate of the Fascist Party and the squad's commander.

Mussolini's mistrust for the party was constant throughout the *Ventennio*; he was careful not to involve the party apparatus in government appointments. In fact, in an ungenerous manner he removed the two most valuable party secretaries, Arturo Turati and Giovanni Giuriati, to appoint the puppet Achille Starace,[1] who was a perfect obedient sycophant.

Looking back to the period of 1921–1922, before the March on Rome and the Fascist Party, was there something in the fascists' thinking that kept them united beyond their past as fighters on the Isonzo, as Fiume Legionnaires, or as *squadristi*? Was there a collective vision of the future for which to fight? Did the violence have a focus?

Norberto Bobbio in *"L'ideologia del fascismo"* ("Fascist Ideology") *in Quaderni della F.I.A.P* took up these issues and found that the ideological ties of the diverse currents of early Fascism only had in common a negative or destructive culture. They were against democracy; they exalted war, courage, daring, and fearlessness. For these men their leadership examples were charismatic authoritarian leaders, conquistadors, and statesmen with a violent streak. "When society is dominated by businessmen, by bankers, by industrialists, by speculators . . . [the Fascists] believed that it had entered a declining phase: plutocracy"(Bobbio p. 12). Bobbio confirmed that in order to coalesce this uneducated mass "a supporting solidarity between classes (*interclassismo*) was needed in society. This concept usually took the form of a national or nationalistic (and therefore super-classist) theory of economic interests" (Ibid.).

Trump's campaign speeches became more and more fiery and his independence from the Republican Party became more and more marked. He began
to criticize the most important figures of the Party. He attacked Senator
John McCain accusing him of not being a national hero. Trump claimed that
McCain had only become a hero because he had been captured. He stated
that he preferred heroes that had not been captured, because they were winners. McCain later denied his vote when it was needed by Trump to repeal
Obama's healthcare reform. When he died in August 2018, he left written
wishes that he did not want President Trump at his funeral. However, it was
attended by all the living past presidents, Democrats and Republicans alike.
Trump is not part of the Republican Party elite, which includes the Bush
family, Mitt Romney, and John McCain, all of whom have levied heavy
criticism at him. John McCain who embodied the conservative Eurocentric
values still infused with certain ethical principles was particularly critical of
Trump. McCain appeared as the opposite of the unscrupulous Trump.

In reality, as Jeet Heer pointed out in the article *How the Southern Strategy
Made Donald Trump Possible* published in *The New Republic* on February
18, 2016, two weeks before the Super Tuesday that gave Trump the South,
the contrast between the old Republican establishment and the new populism
Trump represented was a "false dichotomy." Trump simply shifted the bar
further to the right and exposed the Party's true hidden soul. To understand
this, the scholar suggested, looking back to 1964, when the Civil Rights Act
was passed, the GOP won all the Southern states in the country. The voters
of those states felt abandoned by the Democrats who, thanks to President
Johnson, had pushed the law through. In that article Heer wrote:

> The Southern Strategy was the original sin that made Donald Trump possible.
> If Republican voters were anywhere near as diverse as the Democrats', a candi-
> date like Trump would have been marginalized quickly. Conservative elites can
> denounce Trump all they want as a "cancer" or an impostor. In truth, he is their
> true heir, the beneficiary of the policies the party has pursued for more than half
> a century. Trump does represent an innovation, or perhaps a return to form, in
> one way. The Southern Strategy has long relied on coded appeals to racism—an
> emphasis on "law and order," denunciations of racial quotas, and so on—that
> enticed the bigoted base while still giving the Republican Party plausible deni-
> ability. This sort of winking racism no longer works, in part because the base
> feels the party hasn't delivered. Trump's signature trait is that he doesn't hide
> his bigotry, so he excites voters who feel that here, at last, they have the real
> thing. (Heer 2016)

Heer concluded, "If Trump is victorious in South Carolina and the six
upcoming Southern contests on Super Tuesday, he'll owe much of his success

to the racial politics crafted by the conservative movement that reshaped the Republican Party. There's no denying that" (Ibid.).

Moreover, in recent years the Republican Party has fought against intellectuals, has shown that it does not believe the science regarding the dangers of climate change or the coronavirus, and has begun to flirt with religious movements of dubious credibility. It has not sufficiently fought corruption and has encouraged unscrupulous individuals. Otherwise, how could it be possible that someone like Roger Stone, nicknamed Dirty Trickster, arrested for collusion during *Russiagate* (convicted in November 2019, evidence at trial showed collusion with Wikileaks and Putin's men) could have collaborated with presidents Nixon and Reagan and with Bob Dole and then become an advisor to Trump? How could it be that a man like Paul Manafort, chairman of the Trump campaign, sentenced to jail until 2024,[2] who had also met with Reagan and Dole, have such a successful career and become so influential? With such examples it is not difficult to prove that since the days of Newt Gingrich, the Republican Party has fed on bigotry, prejudice, and lack of ethics.

One need only scroll through the pages of the 1995 Contract with America, which later inspired Silvio Berlusconi, in order to understand that cuts in education, the lauding greater legality promoted by the forces of law and order, the withdrawal of American troops from the UN, and the revision of all trade treaties were not a Trump brainchild. What was missing with Trump was political mediation and negotiations. There was only an unfettered and politically unfiltered release of opinions by the President, often only via Twitter. These opinions fueled a desire for revenge against immigrants, against Muslims, and against America's enemies in general; but also, against his personal

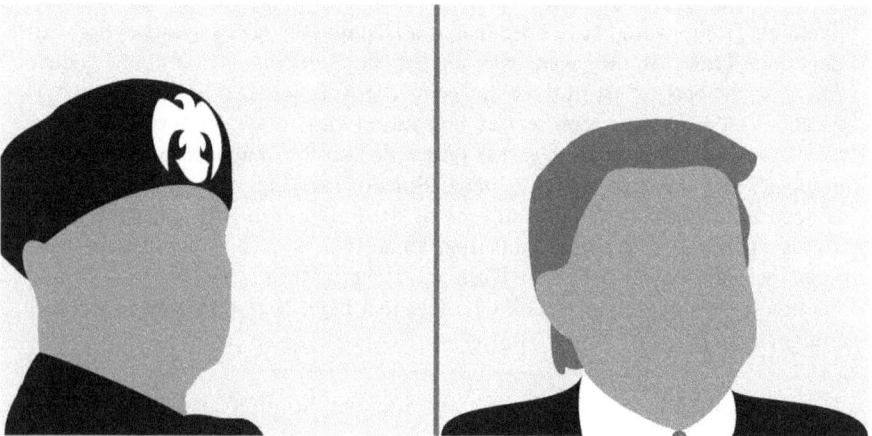

Figure 6.1   Mussolini and Trump Exhibit Similar Profiles. By the authors.

enemies and political opponents in particular. This is the primordial sludge which generated Trump and from which he began his climb in the Party that culminated in his obtaining the support of the entire Republican establishment. Unfortunately, this is a confirmation of a general crisis in Western democracies and their institutions, which have been incapable of recognizing that they actually caused it.

Let's return to the Fascist convention in Rome, and its closing event at the *Altare della Patria*,[3] which was attended by about 30,000 Fascists. At this point, a little-known fact that occurred during the founding convention of the PNF should be mentioned as it underscores the emotional and strategic position that Mussolini had assumed in the general Fascist image repertoire. In a climate overheated by massive violence many participants proposed strategic actions for Mussolini to take immediately: attempt a coup d'état seizing key points in the city, arresting Prime Minister, Ivanoe Bonomi, and informing the representatives of local government (Prefects) that the Fascists had taken power. All the above would transform their presence in Rome into an *ante litteram* March on Rome. This had been the dream of Gabriele D'Annunzio and his Legionnaires. Since there were many former Fiume Legionnaires among the Fascists it is not surprising that this idea had gained momentum. Mussolini stated peremptorily that it was not the right time.

Indeed, Mussolini never shared the Party's enthusiasm for the March as he was not convinced it would actually be effective. For Mussolini, the real "March" would be to be called by the King officially to Rome to form a new government. His goal was to become Prime Minister with the consent of the political system. How was this goal to be achieved? At this point, the PNF set the wheels in motion as it was convinced that a great demonstration of Fascists through all of Italy with a focus on Rome was unavoidable and took action so that it could take place without bloodshed. This could only happen if the King was involved.

The key to contacting the King was through the Queen Mother, Margaret of Savoy, who at the time was vacationing in Bordighera in the region of Liguria. Her support for Fascism was well known and she was a regular reader of *Il Popolo d'Italia*. On October 16, several high-ranking *gerarchi*, many of them aristocrats, met with her. The group included the Count of Val Cismon, Cesare Maria De Vecchi; the Count of Cortellazzo, Costanzo Ciano; General Emilio De Bono; Deputy secretary of the party Attilio Teruzzi; and Italo Balbo. However, only De Vecchi and De Bono, the two most ardent monarchists, attended her private audience as the others had republican leanings. They immediately informed her of what was happening within the PNF, certain that she, in turn, would have informed Vittorio Emanuele III. A broad understanding on the part of the monarchy would be the only way to avoid a violent clash with the army and ensure that the crisis, now inevitable, remained limited and political in nature. The Queen Mother, after expressing words of praise for their discipline and their organization of the Militia, which she had read in Mussolini's newspaper, promised that she would personally intervene with her son. In the meantime, knowledge of the March began to spread, and many started setting the stage in Parliament.

And who helped Trump? How did he come to win a majority in the Republican Party, which initially saw in him only a kind of "crazy horse"?

There were certainly some television channels, such as Fox News, that favored him unequivocally from the start. The Trump and Clinton debates were watched by more than 100 million people. Election predictions continued to favor Clinton. According to CNN she received a 62 percent approval rating from the debates. Another fact to be considered was that in the last year of the campaign Americans spent 110 million hours viewing news coverage and campaign spots. Although he began from an unfavorable and unaligned position, Trump was able to convince the Republican Party to follow him and by the end of the campaign had basically conquered the party. Looking back at the Republican Presidential primaries there were seventeen Republicans vying for the nomination, including Jeb Bush and John Kasich both with political experience as governors of Florida and Ohio, respectively and yet the party chose Donald Trump. Why? Perhaps because of those internal divisions that had torn the Party apart in previous years. And Trump knew this very well.

"Does it have to be unified? I'm very different than everybody else, perhaps, that's ever run for office. I actually don't think so" asserted Trump, rightly, in an interview with George Stephanopoulos broadcast on ABCS News *This Week* on May 8, 2016, a few months before the election, almost amused by the party's difficulty in making a decision regarding his candidacy. After this assertion a series of meetings between Trump and congressional leaders in Washington concluded with assuring him the nomination. The then speaker of the House, Paul Ryan, who previously was "just not ready to back Trump" one week after that shifted to "totally committed to working together." What happened? It was a complete turnaround in the Party's position. The missing unity had been found. According to *The Guardian* article by Tom McCarthy *How Donald Trump Convinced the Republican Party to Revolve Around Him* of May 14, 2016, "45 of 54 Republican senators either support Trump wholeheartedly or have pledged to support the nominee. Only three senators have said they will not back Trump." A few of them, such as Senator Susan Collins of Maine took a wait-and-see position and reserved their decision for the Republican convention in July 2016. But eventually one by one they gave in, believing that the other candidates for various reasons, ranging from the social policies of Governor Kasich to the feeble and permissive policies of Jeb Bush, would not guarantee a victory against Hillary Clinton. It should be clarified that internally the Republican Party was still divided, although it had generally continued its move to the right, especially during the Obama presidency, when its chief weapon became ideological obstructionism.

These internal divisions predated Trump's candidacy. The Republican establishment had bitterly fought several internal battles against conservative populists on different goals including that of immigration. During the Obama presidency there had been internal tactical battles over the government shutdown arising from failing to approve the budget, or to decide how many and which compromises (very few) to make with the Democrats. Small factions within the party, such as libertarians, fought bitterly to move their political agenda to the top of the Party's priorities. Added to this was Donald Trump, who unlike the other candidates went against everything the loyalists thought they knew about the GOP and its voters. The Republican Party would have had to go through an unprecedented second founding if it wanted to avoid Trump whose agenda violated the party's orthodox positions on trade, reform, economic aid, and national security. He never pledged allegiance to the party. Rather, he gave voice and brought out a huge portion of the base that disagreed with leaders on key measures, or who were not interested in the old, hypocritical, stale formulas. In a sense, the candidate-celebrity challenged the idea that policy proposals or a political agenda mattered. He mocked the need for any long-term strategy or subtlety in the political game. And he did so with his body language and a simplified, direct narrative. Trump's dynamic professional and personal history, along with his crude and sometimes vulgar bombast, were thrown in the face of the religious, conservative, and cowardly image that the party had come to assume, due to the cumbersome and reactionary presence of the Tea Party movement that had held it hostage in recent years. Trump's appeal to certain forms of bigotry forced some Republicans to confront the left's portrayal of the GOP as well as how the party of White resentment was far more present among its voters than the Party leaders had ever imagined. Faced with a reality that forced it to take note of the transformation of its voter base, the Party succumbed to Donald Trump's anti-establishment position. When the conservative candidate, Ted Cruz, Trump's fiercest rival, dropped out, Trump's victory in the party was complete, although there were still strong dissents and many rejections. Katie Packer, a Republican consultant, and strategist as well as the former deputy campaign manager for Mitt Romney expressed her misgivings about Trump's nomination by stating in the NBC news report entitled *Beyond Trump. Where Will the Republican Party go after 2016?* by Lee Ann Caldwell and Benny Sarlin of August 25, 2016, "Donald Trump's success has made me question some days whether I have a home in this party anymore. His long pattern of disrespect for women, his mocking of the disabled and prisoners of war, his openly racist comments make me wonder who the people are who believe he is a leader fit to fill the shoes of George Washington, Abraham Lincoln, Dwight D. Eisenhower, Ronald Reagan and both George Bushes."

Those who believed that the founding of the Fascist Party would put an end to the violence would be disappointed. On May 29, 1922, the *Prefettura di Bologna* was occupied for four days. In Milan, Palazzo Marino (Milan's city hall) was occupied.

In Parma, the anti-Fascist population, attacked by Italo Balbo's *squadre*, reacted with weapons from behind barricades built with market carts and stones removed from the streets. The city resisted for three days. The violence continued.

By now it had become clear to even the most hesitant parts of the historical right that it could not govern without, or against, Fascism. Consensus for Fascists had skyrocketed. Membership in the Fascist union had gone from 450,000 members in June 1922 to 700,000 members in September. The readership of *Il Popolo d'Italia* had grown exponentially. In fact, it is a historical paradox, that precisely this growth, particularly among workers, placed Mussolini before his most serious threat.

As fate would have it, the Fascist Party faced several threats. The most dangerous was the fact that Fascist union members felt they had been abandoned by the Party and there was a possibility of a clash with the rural Fascists.

Power had to be seized quickly to avoid a new war between the opposing Fascist factions and to avoid the bankruptcy of the Party.

In October 1922 Italian Fascism faced a chasm. It seemed to have no future. But it was precisely the absence of a future that brought Fascism back from this abyss. Mussolini realized that a legal path to power would take too long. He had to take power through a show of force: a quick *March on Rome*, but the PNF lacked a well-trained militia. The best path forward, according to Mussolini, was the parliamentary route, which also had to be taken quickly. Mussolini shrewdly allowed himself to be courted by all the liberal and conservative leaders who wanted to create a stable government with his support. He made everyone believe that he agreed with them, that he had no pretentions; he even promised to take on the task, frightening to others, of firing on the Fascists if needed. He played on the rivalries, ambitions, and ambiguities of the various leaders, with no holds barred. He cleverly took advantage of their hypocrisies. He simply conned them. Meanwhile, the first government of Luigi Facta, which had replaced the Bonomi government in the Spring, was succeeded in August by a second Facta government.

Mussolini was able to bring events to a head only by negotiating with everyone. In the meantime, Italo Balbo was appointed to train a militia and, he immediately pointed out that the men entrusted to him were a rabble impossible to educate and discipline. Mussolini's intuition once again came to the fore: he decided to use them as a psychological weapon, an instrument of pressure on the political establishment, in order to bend it to his will.

With this haste and these premises, extra funding had to be sought that went beyond limited spontaneous donations. Italo Balbo was also involved in the search for financing. On the eve of the March, he had managed to obtain five million *Liras* from the Masons.

Another twenty million would come from the banking association in view of future favors, six million from agrarians, and a couple of million from Milanese industrialists who would visit Mussolini at his famous *Covo* (Lair), at his *Il Popolo d'Italia* office and would conveniently "forget" cash on Mussolini's desk. Meanwhile Mussolini tested the waters by leaking the idea of the March on Rome in the newspapers. Strangely enough, there was no particular reaction. No political leader protested. No one was indignant.

Mussolini cleverly played Prime Minister Facta. He convinced him that should his government fall, he would be able to form another one with Fascist support. By making Facta believe that it would be possible to form an alliance with a member of Giolitti's party, Mussolini was able to neutralize Giolitti himself. In order to make the government of the Giolittian Facta fall, Mussolini sought Salandra's help and, on October 17, 1922, Salandra convinced his only minister in the government, Vincenzo Riccio, to resign. The crisis had begun.

The Fascists had to act quickly. On October 21, 1922, the Fascist party leadership ceded power to the *quadrumviri* Balbo, De Bono, De Vecchi, and Bianchi. When the order was given, Fascists from the various Italian regions converged on their respective capitals or on the most important nearby towns to assume control of the most crucial cities.

Mussolini clearly stated that the March was to be a formality. A show of strength. This behavior based on a bluff is symptomatic of his character.

NOTES

1. Achille Starace (August 18, 1889–April 29, 1945) joined the Fascist movement in Trento in 1920 and shortly thereafter became the local political secretary. In October 1921, Starace became vice-secretary of the National Fascist Party March on Rome. His career reached its peak when he was made Party Secretary of the National Fascist Party. He was appointed to the position primarily for his unquestioning loyalty to Mussolini. As secretary, Starace staged huge parades and marches, and proposed anti-Semitic racial segregation measures. He was dismissed as Party Secretary in 1939. In 1943, after the collapse of the regime he was arrested even though his real power had ended two years earlier. He was subsequently released. He attempted unsuccessfully to regain Mussolini's favor in the *Repubblica Sociale* and was arrested once again, but this time by his former colleagues on charges that he had weakened

the party during his tenure as Party Secretary and sent to a concentration camp in Verona. He was once again released and settled in Milan, where on April 29, 1945, he was recognized by partisans, subsequently executed, and strung up next to Mussolini in Piazzale Loreto.

2. Roger Stone and Paul Manafort were both pardoned by Donald Trump shortly before he left office in December 2020.

3. The Victor Emmanuel II National Monument also referred to as the *Altare della Patria* (Altar of the Fatherland) as it holds the guarded eternal flame at the tomb of an unknown Italian soldier from WWI. The monument was built in honor of Victor Emmanuel II, the first king of unified Italy, and is located in *Piazza Venezia* in the center of Rome. The monument itself is often regarded as pompous and too large. Foreigners often call it "the wedding cake"; Romans commonly call it "the typewriter."

Chapter 7

Geopolitics

In this chapter we have kept in mind, without specifically delving into it, the underlying conflict between President Trump and what he has contemptuously referred to as the "deep state": The Pentagon, the State Department, the CIA, the FBI are all parts of that "hidden" government according to him. Trump came to power with the specific strategy of toppling "the American empire" and transforming the United States into a nationalist and even protectionist nation state. This strategy was contrary to the vision of the role that those agencies of the federal government thought the United States should have in the world.

The U.S. federal government employs several million people. Approximately three million of those employees work for the U.S. Department of Defense, making it the world's largest employer. To place this in perspective, the world's second largest employer is the Chinese People's Army, the third is Walmart, and the seventh is McDonald's. In issue 8/18 of the September 2018 *Limes* magazine entitled *Stati profondi gli abissi del potere* (*Deep States the abyss of power*), the journalist Dario Fabbri theorized in his article *Negli abbissi della superpotenza* (*In the abyss of the superpower*) that it is thanks to the "deep state" that "the American empire" endures. The large number of federal employees probably horrifies many Americans, hostile to a large central government, and may have even been horrifying to America's founding fathers. The founding fathers created the United States with the idea that the power of a president would be limited by checks and balances, and they probably never envisioned such an exponential growth of the federal bureaucracy. We share Fabbri's view that even though Trump as an atypical president sought to diminish their influence and therefore the U.S. influence in the world, there is no doubt that America's "superpower status has maintained intact the structural characteristics that made it the dominant world power," as Fabbri wrote in *L'Espresso* (one of Italy's most important weeklies) in a January 18, 2017 article with the significant title *Donald Trump è un incapace: ma nonostante lui gli Stati Uniti restano padroni del mondo* (Donald Trump is incompetent: but despite this the United States remains master of the world). These federal agencies are connected with Congress, which sets their budget, and they are beyond a president's control. In that *L'Espresso* article Fabbri states "[h]egemony always weighs on the nation that created the empire. Every superpower [Fabbri continues, in a less convincing statement] needs to import goods in large quantities in order to make its currency global, and to welcome people to keep its population young and violent, as they are often called upon to go to war." He then compares the United States with Ancient Rome at the end of the third Punic war which had made Rome a universal superpower with the consequence that many Romans became convinced that their enemies and rivals were jealous. The Gracchi[1] proposed a revival of Latin ethnicity and a respective isolation of Roman power.

As we noted above the structural characteristics that made the United States a dominant power remain intact. It controls the seas, has an enormous capacity to absorb goods, and continues to enjoy a strong currency. It still holds an invincible supremacy that has prevented Trump from turning it into a conventional nation.

Traditionally when we speak about the relationship between the United States and the Soviet Union first and now Russia, as far as anyone can remember, it has never been good. Even when they were allies during World War II their respective ideologies kept them apart and made them rivals: the most important capitalist country pitted against the leader of Socialism. The Cold War certainly did not simplify matters and when in 1991 the Soviet Union dissolved, the long-awaited transition to democracy underwent alternating phases culminating in a new more or less veiled form of a regime under Putin's leadership. The relationship with Russia beginning with George W. Bush, who had numerous disagreements with Putin, despite their cordial personal relationship, to Obama, with whom there was bad blood even on a private level, even before the Ukrainian crisis (Snowden *docet*), has always been tense. This completely changed with Donald Trump. Apart from accusing each other from time to time, when it was convenient, of interfering in the other's domestic politics, the two countries began not only to collaborate, but to use their respective spheres of influence to assist one another in the world arena.

Trump's fondness for authoritarian regimes is well-known. However, his relationship with Russia seemed to go beyond fondness. It is worth noting that in Putin's Russia, the Soviet regime, reappears in many forms as Putin, a former KGB agent, uses many of its same methods. In an article published in *The Guardian* on July 10, 2019, Irina Scherbakova, historian, writer and well-known civil rights activist in Russia, in reference to Stalinist crimes and the Gulags, wrote, "Every day our freedom seems to shrink as quickly as it expanded 30 years ago." According to Scherbakova, Vladimir Putin came to power accompanied by a new form of patriotism based on the heroic and glorious Soviet past in which Stalin was seen as a strong leader who led the Soviet Union to victory in World War II. In this way his image resurfaces as positive and

[t]he millions who perished in waves of political repression were pushed to the margins of collective consciousness. Today, the 1989 liberation of eastern Europe, the fall of the Berlin Wall and the end of the Cold War are understood by many Russians in terms of defeat, disaster even. No wonder, given that Putin has called the fall of the Soviet Union "the greatest geopolitical catastrophe of the 20th century." Today Stalin's face watches you ubiquitously from billboards, subway train walls, and bookstore windows. Dozens of monuments to him have sprouted around Russia. It is difficult today to recall 1989 without a deep feeling of lost opportunity and shattered hope. In the early Putin years, a silent majority traded the possibility of freedom for promises of "stability," and later for the national pride of "great Russia," a power that draws borders around itself and feels like a besieged fortress. (Sherbakova 2019)

After this miserable picture of the country, Scherbakova refers to her own non-governmental organization as strongly opposed by the Putin government for the work it does in bringing to light the tragic events of the Stalin era and the many victims whose names and stories have been forgotten. What seems most interesting is that among the accusations that Putin has levied against this organization, and many of the same type, is that of being in the service of a "foreign agent" intent on destabilizing the Russian government.

This accusation is an old trick used by bureaucrats of the Soviet Union to demonize internal dissent when the dissenters tried to introduce elements of democracy into the regime. It was the denunciation Stalin used to begin his Great Purge, which, according to his paranoia, was justified not only against ordinary citizens, but also against certain members of the Communist Party of the Soviet Union (CPSU) whom he accused of having collaborated with the Nazis. However, when the Soviet army intervened in the domestic affairs of developing countries later on, (mostly in Africa, Asia, and South America), their bureaucrats used it as an excuse to encourage freedom from colonialism and establish socialism instead of calling these invasions the action of a foreign power. As it is evident, this is a double standard, or we could say speaking with a forked tongue.

Putin's strategy for restoring Russia to its glorious past—to its *grandeur*—to recreate the dream of *the Great Mother Russia*, is complex, long-range, but relatively clear-cut and executed by a politician of great ability who knows what he wants and who can implement a Machiavellian approach to achieve his goals. Thus, it is not only the concept of Democracy that is in danger, but all Western culture and Europe in particular, as the cradle of Western culture. In this sense Trump's, who only has short-range objectives tied more to his personal gain than to a far-sighted policy, and Putin's goals are aligned. Making America great again and restoring Russia to its past glory are both based on a weakening of Europe. Putin is banking on an old dream, espoused by Ivan Ilyin, a reactionary Russian philosopher with Fascist sympathies who died in 1954, and who is increasingly cited by Putin. Ilyin envisaged the isolation of the West and Russian expansion in Asia, culminating with the formation of an entity called Eurasia, with Russia as the center of power. Europe is currently in a precarious state. It is dealing with the growth of populist movements that have often been funded by Russia and the tariffs imposed by Trump make it fertile ground for Putin's plan. To describe the Russia Putin would like, the words of Russian journalist Viktor Vladimirovic Erofeev come to mind. In an article in *La Repubblica,* (one the most popular daily newspapers in Italy) on October 30, 2009, he wrote, "[w]hat is Russia? Perhaps to understand it she should accept her feminine nature. She calls herself Holy Mother Russia, yet for much of her history she has aspired to be a man. She wants a sex change. She wears a skirt, but she wants pants."

A transformation that Trump liked very much as he called for Russia's help during his election campaign. In July 2016 when Donald Trump asked Putin's Russia to hack Hillary Clinton's emails: "Russia: If you're listening, I hope you're able to find the 30,000 emails that are missing," referring to emails that had been deleted from Hillary Clinton's private email server when she was Secretary of State. The events that followed that request are well known as the email scandal played a significant role in the election of Donald Trump as President of the United States.

Italy 1922. Mussolini was quite clear about what Italy's relationship with the Soviet Union should have been. On January 14, 2018, Giorgio Fabre wrote in *Il Manifesto*, a daily leftist newspaper, referring to a book by Emilio Gentile (*Mussolini contro Lenin*, [*Mussolini versus Lenin*] that in his articles in *Il Popolo d'Italia*:

Mussolini was violently anti-Leninist, because Lenin took the Russian Army out of World War I leaving its Western Allies in great difficulty. [Mussolini's] articles referred to a Jewish plot in which Ulyanov (Lenin) was also a participant. A leitmotif repeated from '17 to '19. As Fascism [Fabre added] settled in and the movement became a party, and as the Bolshevik leadership took root in Russia, Mussolini, always a realist, changed his mind. First (July 1920, and then again in June 1921) he called Lenin "an artist who molded men; he had failed, but he was still an artist." And the description of the Soviet state led by the "red tsar" was tinged with envy, because it had overcome the political chaos of the West: "the red state is the state par excellence." . . . Then when Lenin twisted the Bolshevik policy with the NEP [New Economic Policy], by introducing elements of small-scale capitalism, Mussolini crowed victory, claiming that, as he had predicted, Russia was bowing to the West and the Revolution had been defeated. (Fabre 2018)

Mussolini quoted Lenin in two articles in June 1920 and July 1921 and the Soviet leader actually mentioned him in his writings, circa 1915. As the historian Emilio Gentile wrote in *Il Sole 24 Ore* on May 4, 2017, the two would even have crossed paths in Switzerland during Mussolini's wanderings.

In 1903 Lenin moved [from Munich] to Geneva. There [in the Brasserie Handwerk], on March 18, 1904, he participated in a large rally to commemorate the Paris Commune. A young Mussolini, who had immigrated to Switzerland two years before, where he earned his living as a propagandist and journalist among Italian workers, also spoke at the rally. Participation in the commemoration of the Paris Commune would have been the only occasion for them to have encountered one another, but there is no evidence to show that they actually did meet.

Further according to Emilio Gentile in July 1912, when with the Congress of Reggio Emilia, the revolutionary left wing of the Italian Socialist Party led by Mussolini removed control of the Party from the reformists and he took over the direction of *Avanti!*, "Lenin without mentioning Mussolini commented on the event in *Pravda*, stating that in Italy the Socialist party 'was on the right path.' But it does not appear that Mussolini had ever heard of Lenin, and he knew nothing about the Bolshevik party, which Lenin conceived as an organization of professional revolutionaries."

Aside from the controversies in the pages of *Il Popolo d'Italia*, Mussolini was aware that Italy was in dire need of raw materials: coal, oil, and iron. The Soviet Union had unlimited resources and above all could sell these at a good price. Why not tap into these resources by establishing normal diplomatic relations? In fact, right after the March on Rome, he had a cordial meeting with the Soviet representative in Rome, Vaclav Vaclavovič Vorovskij, to whom he explained that he intended to recognize the Soviet government; no European power had ever done this before. In his inaugural speech to the Chamber and Senate on November 16, 1922, Mussolini mentioned his intention creating a great deal of alarm among the parliamentarians who were concerned that his position on communism had changed. He reassured them stating that the diversity of the two countries would not be an obstacle provided that neither country interfered in the domestic affairs of the other.

On November 30, 1923, he officially informed the Chamber of Deputies that he would proceed with diplomatic recognition of the USSR with an exchange of ambassadors. Moreover, in a friendly gesture to his ally, England, Mussolini agreed with its government that both countries would proceed with this recognition on the same day. However, due to a misunderstanding this did not occur.

On January 12, 1924, the Soviet delegates arrived in Rome for the preliminaries. At the last minute certain diplomatic points emerged that were not in line with the foundations of the Soviet State. In the meantime, the day of Anglo-Italian recognition of the Soviet Union was set for February 3, 1924. In the confusion, however, Ramsay MacDonald's new Labour government which took office on January 23, 1924, signed the exchange of ambassadors on February 2, 1924, bringing recognition forward by one day. Mussolini was disappointed that, rather than being the first country to recognize the USSR, Italy would now only be the second. Mussolini was so sincerely disappointed that the Bolsheviks at a later date would show their fondness by supporting his regime in a moment of crisis.

The first ambassador of the USSR to the Kingdom of Italy was Konstantin Jurenev. He arrived on March 12, 1924, and took lodgings in Via Gaeta No. 5, the former seat of the Tsarist embassy. The Consulate General of the USSR was opened in Milan. Career diplomat and nobleman Gaetano Manzoni was appointed Ambassador to the USSR in Moscow. Italian consulates were opened in Odessa, Kiev, Leningrad, and Tiflis. The new president of the Council of People's Commissars, Aleksej Rykov, soon came to Rome and he then visited Sorrento where he had a historic meeting with Gorky, the exiled famous Russian poet, and then traveled to Naples and Venice. Upon his return to Moscow, he was so enthusiastic that he wrote with the assistance of Ambassador Manzoni a warm thank you to Mussolini for the hospitality received and praise for the policy of order and rapid development of the country under his leadership. Moreover, he extended an invitation to Italian industrialists to exploit the Black Sea mineral resources.

The moment for the Bolsheviks to exhibit their fondness for Mussolini occurred not long after, as in June 1924 the Matteotti murder occurred. As we have noted the political fallout that followed was overwhelming. Apart from the Soviet Union the entire world focused on Mussolini's expected fall. At the beginning of July 1924, Ambassador Jurenev invited Mussolini to lunch in Via Gaeta on the orders of the Bolshevik government to the great dismay of the Italian Communist Party.

Antonio Gramsci, the founder of the Italian Communist Party, wrote irritated that due to that courtesy Mussolini had regained his authority and accused the ambassador of having undermined Soviet prestige among Italian workers. In response to the contentious article in *L'Unità*, Jurenev never even blinked; it seems that the idea for the lunch came directly from Stalin who had him extend another invitation on November 7, 1924, on the occasion of the anniversary of the Soviet revolution. The entire anti-Fascist left was devastated. During the *Ventennio* the relationship between Stalin and Mussolini fluctuated, but in substance it was very positive to the point that in the spring of 1941 a trip to Moscow had been planned for Mussolini to sign important trade and friendship agreements, as shown by Carlo Lozzi's *Mussolini-Stalin: storia delle relazioni italo-sovietiche prima e durante il fascismo (Mussolini and Stalin: A History of Italian-Soviet relations Before and During the Fascist Regime)*.

On October 28, 2016,[2] just a few days before the election, James Comey, then Director of the FBI, announced that he would reopen the case on Hillary Clinton's emails wreaking havoc in Clinton's campaign and most likely causing a cascade of votes to be cast for Donald Trump, giving him that last push to victory. In July of that year, Comey had also launched an investigation into Russia's interference in the elections, scrutinizing the ties of then candidate Trump's staff with Russia. He had investigated General Michael Flynn, who was Trump's national security adviser for the first few months of Trump's term and had contacts with Russian diplomatic staff and who had received payments for working with Russian lobbyists. In March 2017, Attorney General Jeff Sessions, one of Trump's first supporters, came under scrutiny for his meetings with Russia's then ambassador to America, Sergei Kislyak, during the 2016 election campaign. When James Comey was working under DOJ oversight, Sessions recused himself from the Russia investigation. Later he refused to halt the Flynn investigation, and subsequently, in April, he refused to stop his own department's prosecution of the General. He refused to change his position even under pressure from Trump's lawyers. This infuriated the President, who on several occasions publicly complained about him, until November 7, 2018, when Sessions submitted his specifically requested resignation. Matthew George Whitaker replaced Sessions as Acting Attorney General from November 2018 to February 2019 until William Pelham Barr was appointed Attorney General.

In May 2017, Trump fired Comey. Deputy Attorney General Rod Rosenstein appointed Robert Mueller as special prosecutor for the investigation that became known as *Russiagate* and was focused on the specific contacts of Trump and his staff with Russia, which was accused of intervening, upon request, in the 2016 election.

The *Russiagate* investigation dragged on for months without producing conclusive evidence to indict President Trump for collusion with Russia. When Mueller finally concluded his investigation, the Democratic speaker of the House of Representatives, Nancy Pelosi, requested that the entire Mueller Report of roughly 400 pages be made public. However, Attorney General Barr in March 2019 only released to Congress the "Barr Report," a four-page summary of Mueller's Report (claiming the remainder of the Mueller Report could not be fully released for national security reasons), asserting that the investigation did not establish that members of the Trump Campaign conspired or coordinated with the Russian government in its election interference activities and that the special counsel had not concluded one way or the other as to whether the examined conduct constituted obstruction.

Russia, as reflected in several statements made by Putin, was obviously relieved by the report's findings. Fareed Zakaria commented on CNN and in the *Washington Post* that what was worth noting in the investigation was the President's heavy-handed interference in the judiciary. A conflict between the different branches of government that fail to maintain separation and independence undermines the heart of democracy. The Democratic Chair of the Intelligence Committee of the House of Representatives, Adam Schiff, pointed out that beyond the conclusion that there was a lack of evidence to tie Trump to collusion, there were other alarming elements. On March 28, 2019, shortly after the Mueller Report was delivered, Schiff gave a speech with a rundown of what might be okay for Republicans and Trump, such as accepting the numerous meetings of the President's family and friends with Russian officials and then lying about it, asking a foreign power to publicly smear Hillary Clinton during the 2016 election, falsifying polls, having a relationship with Wikileaks, and finally exploiting his position of power to conclude advantageous business deals. Schiff stated that for him all this *was not okay*. He asked his colleagues, especially Republicans, to come to their senses, because even if this was not criminal behavior he stated, "I think it's immoral. I think it's unethical. And I think it is unpatriotic. And yes, I think it is corrupt. And evidence of collusion. . . . The day that America accepts all this it will have lost itself forever."

Later "Ukrainegate" for which Trump was impeached by the Democratic-controlled House, but not convicted by the Republican-held Senate, only confirmed Trump's ties to Putin, as House Speaker Nancy Pelosi said, "This has been going on for 2 1/2 years. This isn't about Ukraine. It's about Russia. Who benefited by our withholding of that military assistance? Russia. . . . Well, our adversary in this is Russia. All roads lead to Putin. Understand that" (Mascaro and Jalonick 2019).

Mussolini had a perception of the USSR based on his school days. This is shown by historian Emilio Gentile in *Il Sole 24 Ore* of May 4, 2017, in which he printed excerpts of essays eighteen-year-old Benito Mussolini had written for the literary supplement of the magazine *I Diritti della Scuola*, (*School Rights*) in its December 1901 issue. The article deals with the Russian novel, defined by Mussolini as

a novel that transcends the boundaries of the land in which it was written and identifies with the universal [. . .]. The Russian novel takes a corrupted side of society and vivisects its gangrene [. . .]. The Russian writer is a man who lives humanely, he is a man and contemporaneously an apostle [. . .] among the people, who are undergoing very distressing times. The Tsar's absolutism weighs upon them—a huge leaden cloak—on their minds. The Cossack spies on them insidiously from the barracks and censorship attempts to monopolize their thoughts; but the forces of youth hasten the hour of redemption with their work and their blood.

The young socialist Mussolini identified with that.

Sixteen years before the October Revolution and months after writing that essay he began his controversial wanderings in Switzerland among the Italian and French blue-collar workers in factories and in construction. Literature was the lens with which he viewed Russia. Through literature he almost foresaw and feared the two revolutions: the first failed attempt in 1905, the second, successful one, in 1917. It was the redemption he hoped for. It may be what spurred him, as head of government, to want to exchange ambassadors so quickly. However, he never fully grasped the strategic advantage of a friendship with that titanic country that had all the raw materials needed for the development of new technologies, and, as Napoleon learned, was impenetrable to armies.

The commercial agreement signed in 1924 became even more profitable due to the friendship that developed between the two countries Ministers for Foreign Affairs, Maxim Maximovich Litvinov and Dino Grandi.[3]

On November 24, 1925, the two Foreign Ministers met again in Milan. During lunch the police commissioner approached Grandi whispering that he had dispersed a group of communists in the square who wanted to applaud on Litvinov's exit. "Oh, how I wish, on your visit to Moscow, I could do the same with a group of Fascists upon your exit from the Kremlin!" was Litvinov's smiling retort.

Shortly after that lunch, the Russians ordered 150 engines from Isotta Fraschini S.P.A.[4] and 75 hydroplanes from SIAI Marchetti.[5] The most important cooperation, however, was in a contract signed on April 28, 1931, which provided Stalin with a team of engineers to oversee industrial production, as he had shot all company directors who had received degrees under the Tsar, especially directors of electric power plants. Mussolini even sent the engineer who had been responsible for the dam on the Tirso river in Sardinia, Angelo Omodeo to make the dams on the Dnjepr River safe.

More commercial interaction took place when a delegation formed by the managers of Montecatini, Isotta Fraschini, Pirelli, and Breda Locomotive, headed by Giovanni Agnelli accompanied by Professor Felice Guarneri, finance expert and Mussolini's Minister for Trade and Currency from 1937 to 1939, traveled to Moscow.

During this period there was also a very close collaboration between Fiat and the USSR. Fiat not only agreed to sell vehicles, trucks, and autos built in Italy, but it also set up a ball bearing factory in the USSR in the immediate vicinity of Moscow. Fiat built a second plant to produce light alloy metal castings. This explains the close relationship between the Agnelli family and the CPSU in the post-war period when in 1969 Fiat began manufacturing autos in the Togliattigrad plant.

Italy's leading shipbuilder, Ansaldo of Genoa, was awarded the contract for the design of merchant and military vessels. The enthusiasm for trade between the two countries was such that in 1931 as an exporter to the USSR, Italy went from sixteenth to eighth place. Imports, from the USSR in particular those of oil, went from ninth to sixth place, placing it just behind Germany, the United States, England, France, and Argentina. Fuel storage facilities were built in Savona, in the Italian region of Liguria, for the storage over 50,000 tons of fuel. At a certain point Italy had so much fuel that Agip[6] began to sell it in the domestic market for a lower price than it was sold in the United States.

Despite the success of the commercial relationship with the USSR, Mussolini toyed with it. He was haughty and condescending; he did not understand the enormous internal strength of the country and the power it could wield in the future. He also failed to take into consideration that the USSR was a loyal, outspoken ally, unlike Hitler, and that the country's physical distance prevented any real political friction.

Mussolini should have involved the USSR at least in two key historical moments. The first was at the Stresa[7] conference in April 1935, where he looked only to France and England to create a common policy against the invasiveness and rearmament of the Reich. The USSR was actually the only European power that had a tangible interest in containing Germany because it rightly perceived it as a threat.

Stalin was also excluded from the Munich Pact of September 1938.[8] Once again Stalin would have been a stalwart opponent to Hitler's expansionist greed. This arm's length treatment by Italy created bitterness, but not enough to spoil relations between the two countries.

Even the opposition of the USSR to the Italian invasion of Ethiopia with which it had friendly relations since the time of Peter the Great had no real impact. The friendship between USSR and Abyssinia was a long-standing relationship. In fact in the first Italian Ethiopian War (1895–1896) during the Francesco Crispi government, the Tsar sent a group of advisors to Africa to train the Abyssinians.

Between August and September 1939, during the two Molotov-Ribbentrop meetings to negotiate the Treaty of Non-Aggression between Germany and the Soviet Union (Molotov-Ribbentrop Pact),[9] Stalin let Mussolini know that he would have no objection to Italy's expansion into the Balkans. Mussolini, however, was indifferent to the offer as it was not without strings attached.

Stalin wanted Italy to agree to the USSR's claim of control over the Bosporus and the Dardanelles Straits, removing them from Turkey's control. The sovereignty over these Straits would eliminate the claustrophobic conditions of the Black Sea and provide an outlet to the Mediterranean.

Stalin's first real involvement in Europe occurred late, in the fall of 1940, when Germany and Italy proposed the USSR's entry as a fourth member of the Axis. They were betting on the collapse of the British Empire, now at war with the Axis. Molotov was sent to Germany to negotiate, but the negotiations failed as the Germans refused the USSR's demand to control the Straits. Enmity arose between Italy and the USSR in December, after the outbreak of the first Soviet-Finnish war, when the Fascist press clearly took the side of Finland. Italy sent fifty Fiat G50 fighter planes to assist Finland. It was only the diplomatic pressure of the Nazis that forced Stalin to stop the aggression. Thereafter trade between Italy and the USSR resumed and there was talk of a new trade agreement to provide Italy with a quantity of goods adequate for its war needs. Mussolini was to travel to Moscow to sign it; instead, he remained in Italy and the troops of the Royal Army invaded the USSR alongside the Germans. Mussolini clearly did not understand anything about the *universality* of Russia. The Russian novel had not opened up his mind and he had clearly failed to understand anything about the political relevance of the USSR.

From the beginning of his campaign Trump had an ambivalent attitude toward Europe. He asserted that the NATO countries did not sufficiently contribute their share to the budget as compared to the United States. In a speech in Racine, Wisconsin, on April 2, 2016, he stated, "[t]hat means we are protecting them, giving them military protection and other things, and they're ripping off the United States. And you know what we do? Nothing. Either they have to pay up for past deficiencies or they have to get out."

He concluded that speech with: "[a]nd if it breaks up NATO, it breaks up NATO." He also accused NATO of being obsolete, of being more suitable to the Cold War period, than to the current time of terrorism. He later modified his position. It is well known that Putin does not like NATO and would like to see it weakened so that Russia could represent a third player having the same importance, placed between Europe and the United States. A withdrawal of the United States from NATO, or a split within the Atlantic alliance, would destabilize Western Europe, and would have achieved one of Putin's top priorities without Russia moving a finger. Although any move by a U.S. president with respect to NATO must necessarily go through Congress, U.S. policy toward Russia is an area where even Republicans have clamored for the levy of new sanctions. They also criticized Trump after the Helsinki conference in July 2018 where Trump warmly greeted Putin and stated that Russia had not interfered in the 2016 elections because Putin told him that it had not. Trump's criticism of NATO, however, failed to grasp a fundamental fact that the United States has always proclaimed that it was a superpower, a leader of the Western world, the very leadership of which the so-called "deep state" is the custodian. Trump's assertion that he would not defend the Baltic States if they did not pay their dues goes precisely in the direction Putin would like, because it created a rift and a difference in treatment among the NATO alliance.

As a whole the European Union was taken aback by Trump's election, with his flirtation with European populism and its far-right parties with which he shares a hostility to globalization and international trade, as well as certain authoritarian and discriminatory leanings toward immigration. If the international trade system splinters due to a war caused by Trump between the United States and China, Mexico or Japan the economic effects reverberate throughout Europe. Brexit set a precedent for the disintegration of European unity. The identity crisis of the West is now at an advanced stage, and the problems of external immigration are used to instill fear and anger in people. These sentiments help the extreme positions of populist parties that are cropping up throughout Europe, which often have Russian backing. For more than seventy years, the stability of U.S. democracy has generally been a beacon and a cornerstone for Western world order. When democracy was threatened in Europe, the United States was the shield against the rising tide of authoritarian regimes. It is no coincidence that when Angela Merkel (with whom Trump was particularly annoyed over Germany's small NATO contribution) congratulated him on his election in November 2016, she recalled the two countries' shared values of democracy, freedom, respect for the law, as well as the dignity of human beings regardless of their origin, skin color, religion,

Figure 7.1   Mussolini and Trump with Adolf Hitler and Vladimir Putin, Their Favorite Leaders. By the authors.

gender, sexual, or political orientation. "On the basis of these values," Merkel concluded, "I offer the future president of the United States, Donald Trump, close cooperation."

On the eve of coming to power, Mussolini had very clear ideas concerning Italy's relationships with other European countries and the world. In fact, he assumed control of the Foreign Ministry. His goal was to avoid ill-conceived adventures undertaken for the taste of controversy, he set aside his demagoguery.

He was genuinely angered by the snubbing of Italy's territorial claims at Versailles.[10] He had to content himself with the annexation of the territories of Istria, Dalmatia, Alto Adige, and Trento and Trieste for which he had officially fought. Italy's requests for a portion of the German colonies in Africa and Asia, or the Middle East regions of the Ottoman Empire were ignored. Instead France and England were the countries that took the spoils.

Mussolini had close ties to France. In *La Repubblica* of December 14, 2008, the journalist Massimo Novelli, in his review of the book written by the historian Roberto Gremmo *Mussolini e il soldo infame* (*Mussolini and the Infamous Money*), pointed out that a few days after the March on Rome, two *Sureté Nationale* informers notified their superiors of information, gathered in the political circles of Paris, regarding Mussolini's relationship with exponents of the French government in 1914, immediately after the outbreak of the World War I. In particular, these informers referred to the large sums of money, roughly ten million francs, that the future *Duce* had allegedly received from the deputy Charles Dumas, chief of staff of Minister Jules Guesdes, to encourage Mussolini to champion in *Il Popolo d'Italia* Italy's entry into the war on the side of the Allied powers. In another confidential note Mussolini was even referred to as "an agent of the French Ministry in Rome" (Novelli 2008).

Therefore, it was natural that in 1935 the French Prime Minister Pierre Laval did not hide his esteem and affection for the *Duce*. At the end of his January visit to Italy, Laval enthusiastically stated, "I do not want to leave Rome without expressing to the Italian press my admiration for Mr. Mussolini. We have developed a camaraderie that I will be able to use in the service of the French-Italian friendship" (*Corriere della Sera*, January 8, 1935).

This made Mussolini's about-face on Italian–French relations all the more incredible when on March 26, 1939, in his *Discorso Ventennale dei fasci* (Twentieth anniversary of Fascism speech) he stated, "[w]e wish that there would be no more talk of brotherhood, sisterhood, cousinhood or any other bastard kinships, relationships between countries are relationships based on force and these interactions of force are the determining features of their policy" (Mussolini 1939).

Italy's relationship with England did not fare any better, despite the fact that the relationship was also based on personal friendships established during World War I. Mussolini befriended several important British officers with whom he created lasting ties when he was stationed on the Isonzo front. One of these was Samuel Hoare, who in 1935 became Foreign Secretary and skillfully supported Italian aggression against Ethiopia. It has been proven that beginning in 1917 *Il Popolo d'Italia* received "[a] contribution of one hundred pounds a week (about six thousand euros today) as an offering to the former socialist leader by the British Intelligence agent Samuel Hoare" (Messina, *Corriere della Sera*, Aug 1, 2013).

The honeymoon with England was such that when, on April 7, 1925, a deranged Englishwoman, Violet Gibson, daughter of the powerful Lord Ashbourne, shot Mussolini, slightly injuring him, without any enmity Mussolini allowed her to be deported to England. The *Times* published a long article with the eloquent title, *Mussolini Trionfante* ("Mussolini Triumphs"—the title of the article was in Italian), in which the paper praised the very clever Fascist propaganda which had transformed the crazy gesture of a British citizen . . . into a sign of generous magnanimity with a resounding success to its image" (Saunders note 10, p. 334).

Winston Churchill, who was then Chancellor of the Exchequer in the Conservative government, met Mussolini in mid-January 1927, and formed a flattering impression of him. The English continued in their love affair with Mussolini so much that on January 17, 1933, Lloyd George did not hesitate to affirm to the *Manchester Guardian* that the Fascist corporative state was the greatest social reform of the modern era, and sometime later, addressing Dino Grandi, he confided that either the world decided to follow Mussolini, or it was lost. In England, public opinion was fascinated with Mussolini, but also baffled by his ways. As Mussolini celebrated victory over Ethiopia in 1936, the thirty-five-year-old anti-Fascist journalist John Gunther on May 10 in the *Daily News* wrote "[he] is the most formidable combination of turncoat, rascal and man of genius in modern history."

Overall, Mussolini's mood toward England and France was mixed. On the one hand, he resented Italy's *mutilated victory* and the embarrassment inflicted by France and England on Italy at Versailles. On the other hand, he was grateful for their financing. When he came to power, as a statesman, the situation became more ambiguous. Relations were good enough for him to exploit their conflicts to gain greater geopolitical influence in the Balkans, the Middle East, and Africa. "Italy," Mussolini told a group of journalists on November 3, 1922, "wants to be treated by the great nations of the world as a sister, not as a maid" (Susmel and Susmel, Vol. XIX, p. 3).

Turning to Germany, Hitler was not initially interested in Italy. Like the Weimar Republic after Germany's defeat in World War I, the Third Reich was seeking a way out of Germany's political and military isolation. As the historian Hans Woller, wrote:

> After World War I, the German Reich was powerless and isolated: if it could expect any support from outside, it was certainly not from Paris or Moscow, not even from London for the time being, but from Rome, whose feverish expectations of war gains after 1918 had remained unheard. Like Germany, Italy too had to shake up the Versailles peace order sooner or later if it did not want to completely neglect its own national interests. (Woller p. 493)
>
> In line with this goal and so as not to irritate Italy the young Adolf Hitler, decided that it would be good to "leave the South Tyrolean question unresolved, despite the fact that this exposed him to violent hostility at the national level and even within his own party." (Ibid.)

Hitler expressed his satisfaction after the March on Rome in his *Zweites Buch*, the unpublished continuation of *Mein Kampf*, when in a pleased tone he wrote, "[w]ith the victory of Fascism, the feeble Italian government, subject to international influence, was removed from power and in its place was put a power that had made its maxim the exclusive representation of Italian interests" (Hitler p. 187).

In 1932 Giuseppe Renzetti, Mussolini's trusted man in Germany, advised him that the Führer's admiration for him was unconditional. Hitler considered Mussolini a brilliant statesman and referred to him "as the last of the Romans." Moreover, "he is dying to meet the *Duce*" wrote Giuseppe Renzetti to the Private Secretariat of the head of government on June 21, 1932.[11] Despite Italy and Germany's common antipathy for the outcome of Versailles, it did not generate a friendly relationship between the two countries. On the contrary, it remained cold and unfriendly for a long period of time. The subsequent failure of Stresa in 1935 left Italy alone to oppose the Third Reich. The antipathy for the Reich was also caused by the total contempt that the Führer had for Italians. He considered them "Mediterranean negroids, with the exception of the *Duce*, his teacher in the art of conquering power" (Cicchino 2010).

The United States has traditionally supported Israel from the time it was created, even during conflicts with the Palestinians when the United States should have shown greater respect for the human rights of the Palestinians. A change takes place with the Obama administration. The relationship between that American President and Netanyahu was so strained that Netanyahu claimed that Obama did not have a "special feeling" for Israel. Netanyahu also believed that Obama's attempt to balance power between Saudi Arabia and Iran was naive and had underestimated the persistence of Iran's bad intentions in the Middle East. The truth is that Obama was not anti-Israel.

Quite the contrary. This is evidenced by the strong military and intelligence support he provided to Israel. He also protected Israel in 2011 when the United States vetoed the UN Security Council resolution condemning new Israeli settlements. Obama later also blocked Palestinian efforts to join the International Criminal Court after Netanyahu emphasized the Palestinian danger in crude and vulgar terms by talking about "a nuclear warhead aimed at my crotch." During Obama's term the relationship between the two leaders continued to deteriorate. The Israeli Prime Minister tried throughout Obama's term in office to persuade the administration to take a military stance against Iran. Nevertheless, Obama had not been naive with respect to Iran: he had succeeded in curbing its power with the nuclear agreement. However, he was very puzzled over entering into an agreement with Saudi Arabia, which certainly was not a champion of democracy and human rights within its own borders. In addition, an agreement with Saudi Arabia would have dragged the United States further into the Middle East conflicts.

The climate from the time of the 1993 Oslo Accords has changed. The hope that Palestinians had of having their own state that would include Gaza, the West Bank, and East Jerusalem as its capital has slowly dissipated, despite the fact that half of the Israeli population also supports a two-state solution, even though at this point neither side believes that it will ever happen.

With Trump's election and Obama out of the picture, Netanyahu was able to focus on a strategy of transforming the direction of Middle East policy. His main objectives were to diminish the Palestinian cause in the eyes of the world and to form an anti-Iranian coalition between Saudi Arabia and the Arab Emirates as Iran, a longtime supporter of Hezbollah in Lebanon and Hamas in Gaza, had benefited from the American folly in Iraq and the war in Syria.

The election of Trump completely unbalanced the situation to the disadvantage of the Palestinians. In an excellent recently released book by Rashid Khalidi, *The Hundred Years' War on Palestine: A History of Settler Colonialism and Resistance, 1917–2017*, the author reviews the troubled Israeli–Palestinian relationship and explains how Trump's policies have reversed ongoing negotiations and created the likelihood of further conflict. President Trump for years has had a privileged relationship with Israel partially due to the ties that bind Jared Kushner's family to Israel. Netanyahu has a longstanding friendship with Jared Kushner's father, Charles. The Kushner family, which made its fortune in the real estate market, shares Netanyahu's conservative policy ideas. They donated large sums of money to the Israeli cause and have invested hundreds of thousands of dollars in West Bank settlements. When Netanyahu visits the United States, he often stops by the Kushner family residence. As early as September 2016 before he was even elected, Trump met with Ron Dermer, the Israeli ambassador to the United

States who by that time believed that Israel had found in Trump someone who would espouse their views. In reality, Trump who had presented himself as non-interventionist with the slogan "America First" had no interest in meddling in Middle Eastern affairs. As far as he was concerned:

[A]ll of this was an annoyance. . . . The Sunnis, the Shias, the Jews, the Palestinians have been doing this for thousands of years, and I, Donald Trump, am not going to continue to add to the already outrageous investment of trillions of dollars in a region that breeds and funds terrorists against America while we starve our infrastructure investments at home! (Entous 2018)[12]

During his term Trump has put Netanyahu's policies into practice, doing nothing to prevent the expansion of Israeli settlements, moving the U.S. Embassy from Tel Aviv to Jerusalem and finally abandoning the two-state policy. Trump also made anti-Iranian deals with Saudi Arabia, abandoned the Kurds, who had helped the United States defeat Isis, to Turkish violence, and killed Iran's beloved General Qasem Soleimani all with the approval and exultation of Russia that has very strong interests and alliances in the region starting with Saudi Arabia and Turkey. Only China and India which have conflicting economic interests with the United States may be able to intervene to modify the dangerous unstable status quo created.

A part of the conflict between Italy and England was due to the Middle East. Open wounds for Italy were the oil wells in Iraq, which the British Empire had acquired with the Peace of Versailles. The boundaries of Iraq, as Churchill boasted in his Memoirs, were created during a night in March 1921 in a large hotel in Cairo along with the man who would become King of Iraq, Faisal I bin Al-Hussein bin Ali Al-Hashemi. The creation of Iraq was a stroke of genius for British interests. Churchill managed to bring under British control a vast territory rich in oil resources. Using the United States as a lever, Mussolini demanded that the more than 600,000 dead on the Karst deserved at least a portion of the oil. Mussolini had to wait ten years, but in May 1932, the BOD (British Oil Development), an oil company, formed by the companies of various European nations was incorporated. Italy participated in the venture through Agip, which had been incorporated in 1926. King Faisal granted BOD a concession to extract oil along the right bank of the Tigris River. An increasing annual concession fee was paid to Iraq. It went from 100,000 pounds in 1933 to 200,000 pounds in 1937, when the contract was to terminate. This project was so important to Mussolini that by the beginning of 1935 Italy had a controlling 53 percent share of BOD. A few months later in a sudden turn of events Mussolini summoned the then president of Agip, Umberto Puppini, and ordered him to sell Agip's entire interest to the British. The Ethiopian War had begun, and the League of Nations had placed an embargo on Fascist Italy. Italy was in a state of absolute emergency, or it seemed to be. The restrictions were actually only on consumer goods not on raw materials needed to wage a war, such as oil; the Iraqi oil, however, would not be enough to fuel the conflict. Mussolini had sought assistance from the United States as it was not a member of the League of Nations and was isolationist. American companies happily provided Italy with the needed oil. England did not hinder the Abyssinian enterprise; it allowed Italian ships to pass through the British-controlled Suez Canal carrying their troops, materials, means, and supplies without batting an eye. Some form of compensation was necessary. This is when Mussolini decided to sell Agip's controlling share in BOD to the British.

Mussolini's relationship with certain revisionist Zionists led by Zeev Jabotinsky was quite surprising. These relationships were established in July 1922 before Mussolini took power. Jabotinsky had written a letter to Mussolini in which he set forth the vulnerability of the dismemberment of the former Ottoman Arab territories after World War I, with the possibility of a return of part of the Jewish people to these areas. He proposed working together for this purpose with the *quid pro quo* of using the Italian language among the Jews of the Mediterranean, which Jabotinsky spoke because he had studied in Italy.

In the proceedings of the *Conference Italy-Israel: The Last One Hundred and Fifty Years* held in Jerusalem on May 16–17, 2011, Simonetta Della Seta wrote,

> [b]efore Mussolini decided to impose the race policy on the Italians, Italy was one of the most liberal European countries towards its Jewish population, and the leaders of the world Zionist movement had additional hopes that Mussolini would succeed in moderating Hitler's fierce anti-Jewish policy. In September 1926, Chaim Weizmann, then head of the World Zionist Federation, met with Mussolini. (Della Seta 2011)

Weizmann pointed out the difficulties imposed by the British on Jews who wanted to immigrate to Palestine and asked for a pass through the Italian ports. Mussolini was willing to do that. All he wanted in exchange was that the construction of the port of Haifa be given to Italian companies. The following year he granted an audience to the new president of the World Zionist Federation Nahum Sokolov. He did not alter his stance even when in 1929 friction between Arabs and Jews in Palestine escalated and he signed the Lateran Pacts[13] which regulated the relationship between the Holy See and Italy and made Catholicism the state religion in the country. In 1933 Jabotinsky was able to participate in the eighteenth Zionist World Congress as a representative of Italy.

Mussolini's presenting himself as a friend to the Jewish people allowed him to clearly differentiate himself from the Nazis, to be a credible arbiter of European politics, and to gain the sympathy of the Israeli lobby in the world.

At Mussolini's next meeting with Weizmann at Palazzo Venezia on April 26, 1933, Weizmann asked him to intervene with the Führer to save 50,000 German Jews, allowing them to transit through Italy. Although the Italian ambassador in Berlin insisted, Germany refused.

In the meantime, Mussolini's political flair led him to develop a parallel pro-Arab policy, trying to act as a mediator between these two groups. The harmony with Weizmann and Nahum Goldmann was such that they converged on the far-sighted project of the birth of two states in Palestine, one Jewish and one Arab, with the result of undermining British hegemony. In a conversation of February 17, 1934, Weizmann again asked for Mussolini's support for Jewish immigration to Palestine; Italian help was given by intervening along with the French and the English to persuade the Nazis to let 7,000 Jews leave the Saarland (an Anglo-French protectorate since 1920 under the Treaty of Versailles) without any loss of property, after the Saarland, through a plebiscite, had asked for its reintegration into Germany.

However, Mussolini was unsuccessful in convincing Hitler to curb his racial policy and failed to persuade the Arabs to accept the idea of a Jewish state.

Della Seta adds an even more interesting detail.

During those years, the Fascist regime had allowed the Zionist Revisionists to open their own naval school in Civitavecchia (active since 1934) where, until its closure in 1938, the dozens of men trained there would form the first nucleus of the Israeli navy. The importance for Mussolini was obvious: it was essential to form a group of young people who could become propagandists of Italy and Fascism in the world and especially in Palestine, where the revisionist Zionists had proven to be the ardently opposed to the English. (Della Seta 2011)

The relations between Jabotinsky's agents and the Italian government, through the Consulate in Jerusalem, were stable for most of the 1930s to the extent that they provoked several complaints from England.

This harmony slowly crumbled. Mussolini's dormant paranoia of internationalism, first socialist, now Jewish, regained strength. The abomination of the racial laws of 1938, which stripped Italian Jewish citizens of their rights subjecting them to discrimination and in many cases sending them to concentration camps, operated also as a blunt weapon to push them to flee the country. This caused a great damage to Italy and the consequent brain drain of intellectuals and scientists, including great physicists such as Enrico Fermi of the famous "boys from *Via Panisperna*."[14]

Two days before the Super Tuesday of 2016 in which Donald Trump solidified his position as the Republican candidate, with the intent to create a media event and attract attention, he quoted Mussolini: "better to live one day as a lion than one hundred years as a sheep." On Sunday, February 28, 2016, shortly after re-tweeting with this phrase to the @ilduce2016 account, Trump was interviewed by Chuck Todd on NBC's *Meet the Press*. When asked if he wanted to be compared to the Italian dictator, Trump replied:

> Chuck, Sure, it's okay to know it's Mussolini. Look, Mussolini was Mussolini. It's okay to—it's a very good quote, it's a very interesting quote, and I know it. I saw it. I saw what—and I know who said it. But what difference does it make whether it's Mussolini or somebody else? It's certainly a very interesting quote . . . I want to be associated with interesting quotes. And people, you know, I have almost 14 million people between Instagram and Facebook and Twitter and all of that. And we do interesting things. And I sent it out. And certainly, hey, it got your attention, didn't it?

Madeleine Albright, Secretary of State during the Clinton administration and the first woman to hold that post, who escaped European Fascism, reflected on this comparison. She wrote the book *Fascism: A Warning* with Bill Woodward. Among her many observations was that undemocratic leaders today win through democratic elections, as happened with Putin. She also noted the bond that links the past with the present and that affirms the gradualness of those moments that can empty the soul of democracy. Albright compares it to plucking a chicken's feathers little by little to muffle its moans in order to make as little noise as possible. The comparison with Trump is obvious: her advice is to pay attention to even the most inconsequential signals that come from his presidency. Albright referred to him the first undemocratic President in modern U.S. history.

Trump's victory represented for Italy a strengthening of the right of Italy's political spectrum: from Matteo Salvini's *Lega* to Giorgia Meloni's *Fratelli D'Italia* to Silvio Berlusconi's *Forza Italia*. With Berlusconi he not only has in common immense wealth but, they made entering politics possible to anyone without the requiring competence in the field. The fundamental requirement is to be a good communicator. This has changed not only the way of doing politics in Italy but it has set a precedent for Western democracy in general. When a state of uncertainty exists over the ability of institutions to solve their problems, voters turn to people who are perceived as outsiders to the system despite the fact that these individuals may not really be outsiders, as in the case of Berlusconi or Trump. When Trump was elected, Salvini gloated and thanked Americans for having voted for the American tycoon. Trump's xenophobia is at the heart of Salvini's political project.

When Matteo Salvini became Minister of the Interior, the Italy-U.S. relationship became even closer. In June 2019, he visited Washington and met with Secretary of State Mike Pompeo and Vice President Mike Pence. He declared that Italy was America's closest European partner as the two countries shared "a common vision" not only in the economic and trade fields, but also with respect to the values of work, family, and civil rights. Salvini also pointed out that the results of these policies seem to prove Trump right. Moreover, the slogan "America First" goes perfectly with Salvini's *Prima gli Italiani* (Italians First). In those June meetings, the discussions covered European security against Russian and Iranian threats, China's predatory investment in infrastructure in Italy and Europe, and the need to strengthen defense cooperation between Italy and the United States. The trip took place during the crisis with Europe over Italy's national debt and the disagreement between Salvini's party the *Lega* (League) and its coalition partner the *Cinque Stelle* (Five Stars Movement).[15] The *Lega* had received 34 percent of the vote in the European parliamentary elections and had become the largest party in Italy. Salvini nourished the hope that if he broke with his government ally, he would become Prime Minister. That did not happen, and Giuseppe Conte remained Prime Minister after the *Cinque Stelle* formed a government with the *Partito Democratico* (PD, Italian Democratic Party). Salvini had banked on the fact that Conte had angered Trump over the Belt and Road agreement with China and his refusal to recognize Venezuelan opposition leader Juan Guaidò as President. However, he had not factored in the possibility that other party alliances could be formed. Shortly before the formation of Conte *bis* (the second Conte government), Trump changed his mind and declared in a tweet that he was in favor of the confirmation of the premier as he considered Giuseppe Conte (to the great amusement of Italians, Trump famously misspelled his first name as *Giuseppi*) a man who "Loves his Country greatly & works well with the USA. A very talented man who will hopefully remain Prime Minister!" What united Trump and Conte as Trump previously stated in 2018 at their first official meeting in Washington was the fact that they were both "political outsiders."

We will not address the merits of Italy's traditional historical relationship with the United States. To understand the Trumpian transformation of the relationship it is important to keep in mind that beginning with the immediate post-war period Italy has been a country of primary strategic importance for the United States. It guaranteed access to the Mediterranean and represented a physical wedge in the Balkan Soviet zone of influence during the Cold War. For these reasons, the United States has always kept Italy and its governments under control, being careful to systematically keep the Italian Communist Party, the largest European party in the West and too close to the Soviet Union, out of power. Things changed after the fall of the Berlin Wall. With Trump things changed even more. Italy is still strategic, but it also became, in Trump's mind, vital because of the election of the first European populist government.[16]

The attitude toward the United States during Mussolini's time can be seen on the pages of his many articles in *Il Popolo d'Italia* full of admiration for President Woodrow Wilson. On October 1, 1918, in fact, he wrote:

> In Wilson's speeches you hear something new. The President lifts you [the European allies] up higher. To the peaks. It seems to take you by the hand and says to you: men, lift your eyes for a moment from the battle that inflames and exalts you. Take comfort in the vision of a better tomorrow that has been made fruitful from your infinite torment. It is for this tomorrow—the tomorrow not of just one people, but of all humanity—for which millions of men suffered and died. . . . The president is ahead of the leaders of our country, he precedes them.

On January 19 he added, "All of Europe lies prostrate before this man, who comes from across the ocean and is not an emperor, captain or prophet, but is all that, in a harmonious synthesis that draws people together."

Despite Mussolini's complaints of the rigidness of the United States toward Fiume, the mutual appreciation between the two countries remained intact. At the beginning of the *Ventennio*, even Ernest Hemingway expressed admiration for Mussolini when in June 1922, while a correspondent for the *Toronto Star*, the writer met Mussolini during a press conference in the headquarters of *Il Popolo d'Italia.*

Hemingway described him as "a great man. And with a dark complexion, a high forehead, a slow smile and big hands." He then specified, "He is not the monster as he has been painted, he is not a socialist renegade. He had many good reasons for leaving the [Socialist] party" (Canali, pp. 90–91).

Articles by and about Mussolini began to appear in the most well-known foreign newspapers. He was also interviewed by some of the most important journalists of the time such as Edgar A. Mowrer, Hiram K. Mode Well, Carroll Binder, and William H. Stoneman of the *Chicago Daily News*; George Selders, John Clayton, and David Darrah of the *Chicago Tribune*; and Ralf Barnes for the *New York Herald Tribune* and Arnaldo Cortesi for the *New York Times* who were correspondents in Italy. There were also important women journalists in this group, such as Anne O'Hare McCormick, who visited Rome shortly before the seizure of power, and defined Mussolini as a "new man" and Fascism as a revolt of youth, "made up of vital energies tired of the wisdom of the old, of the tinkering of parliaments, of the prudent formulas of the reason of state" (Canali, p. 88).

This hype was so convincing that the naturalized U.S. citizen Generoso Pope bought and developed in support of Fascism a substantial network of U.S. newspapers. In 1928, he took over one of the most prestigious Italian language newspapers, *Il Progresso Italo-Americano*. It had an average circulation of 95,000 copies. In 1929 he bought *Bollettino della sera* and in 1931 *Il Corriere d'America*, becoming the leader among Italian American newspapers in New York. In 1932, he added to his papers *l'Opinione*, in Philadelphia. With these tools, Pope took on the role of Mussolini's trusted man in the United States, wisely directing public opinion in favor of Fascist Italy. He created an incisive, strong, and ambitious image of Italy as a modern nation that had become a military power. With the birth of the cinematographic information exchange agencies, the black shirt parades directly entered not only the homes of New Yorkers, but of the entire country. Families overseas become familiar with Fascist symbols.

Admiration for Fascism was so strong that at the beginning of the Ethiopian War the public opinion of the Italian Americans convinced President Franklin Delano Roosevelt to abandon several proposals for an embargo against Italy. This love spilled over into the film industry as well. In 1933, Columbia Pictures, at the behest of the German-born Jewish producer Harry Cohn, produced the documentary *Mussolini Speaks* written by the famous journalist Lowell Thomas. The film distributed in theaters grossed a record one million dollars, which today corresponds to about ten million euros.

During the early 1930s, President Roosevelt's faith in Italy was so strong that he declared "Mussolini must go down in history as a builder of a better form of coexistence among peoples" (De Felice, p. 911).

Mussolini also did not skimp on his praise for President Roosevelt. At the beginning of the 1930s their relationship was so close that on April 24, 1933, Mussolini wrote to Roosevelt:

My dear President, in response to your request for an exchange of ideas on the economic and political problems which are of mutual interest to the United States and Italy, I have asked the Minister of Finance, Hon. Guido Jung, to come to Washington as my representative. He will tell you with how much interest I follow the work of the United States government, in its efforts to resolve the world's current difficulties, which can only be solved through mutual collaboration and the good will of nations. (Villari p. 53)

And he accompanied the letter with a precious gift.

It is with great pleasure that I have entrusted to Mr. Jung the reproduction of the codices of Virgil and Horace which are preserved in the Laurentian Library in Florence. . . . I have chosen these two authors not only because their poetic works are the greatest literary legacy of Rome, but also because they are examples of that nobility of spirit and human understanding which I believe to be the two fundamental qualities of the American character. (Ibid.)

In harmony with this climax, in 1934 Roosevelt sent Rexford Tugwell, a member of Roosevelt's "Brain Trust," to Italy to meet with Mussolini to study the achievements of Fascism, land reclamation, and its new cities. Everyone knew that only Italy and the United States were looking for a third way out of the Great Depression, which was beyond capitalism and communism: on the one hand, the Fascist Corporative State, and on the other, Roosevelt's New Deal.

Roosevelt really believed that an agreement could be reached between Italy and the United States. In fact, in 1937 when Mussolini's son, Vittorio, came to the United States to try his luck in Hollywood, Roosevelt summoned him to Washington for a private meeting (Mussolini and Giannini p. 105). Roosevelt expressed his desire to invite Mussolini to the United States; he confided that they could find an understanding and would find a solution for Italy in relation to current world events. Mussolini, however, ignored the request and pretended that the meeting never occurred.

With highs and lows, this correspondence between the two leaders continued until shortly before the beginning of World War II, in April–May 1940; in one of the last, perhaps most important letter, Roosevelt guaranteed that Italy would be able to sit at the peace negotiating table at the end of the conflict with the same rights as a belligerent state if it remained neutral. But once again Mussolini turned a deaf ear.

Trump's relationship with China has had numerous vicissitudes even before he was elected to office. During his campaign Trump expressed his isolationist ideology which consisted of three fundamental elements: 1) opposition to alliances pursued up to then by the United States; 2) opposition to free trade; 3) support for authoritarian regimes. He maintained this ideology once in office, and it meant that Europe and NATO took second place to a privileged relationship with Russia, then with China, becoming the real enemy to confront. There is an interesting essay on the subject titled *The China U.S. Trade War and Future Economic Relations* published by the Chinese University of Hong Kong, Hong Kong, in 2019. In it, the author, Lawrence J. Lan, a Stanford professor of economics for forty years and president of the Chinese University of Hong Kong, explained how given the relations between the two great countries, it was desirable to escape the certainty of the "Thucydides' trap," which is based on the conviction that when an emerging power threatens to displace an existing great one from regional or international predominance, war will break out. Instead, Lau argued, a collaboration between them could be achieved at an economic level, not only because it would create their interdependence, maximizing unused resources in both countries, but also because it would lead to a "new normal" preferable by far to a devastating conflict.

Trump's fluctuating relationship with China has gone from tariff wars to stalemates on both economic and geopolitical fronts. But Trump has always remained guarded. Some have even spoken of a return to the Cold War, although, as Fareed Zakaria says in his opinion piece "Why Trump Caved on China" in the *Washington Post* of January 16, 2020, it would be wrong to see the relationship between the two giants in these terms.

China, according to Zakaria seeks to achieve stature as a world superpower precisely within the order forged in the West since 1945. China is in fact not a rogue nation seeking to interfere in the internal affairs of nations as Russia does. While with Obama U.S. policy had moved in the direction of a recovery of the relationship with China, the second largest economy in the world, with Trump things would change. Obama was the first American president to visit China since Nixon who opened up to Mao's China to the West in 1972. Xi Jinping at the time of Obama's visit spoke of a new type of power relationship between the two countries, established by "eight years of an impressive degree of constructive cooperation." Trump sparked the tariff war by slowing down the world economy. In January 2020, Trump executed with the vice premier of the People's Republic of China "phase one" of a trade agreement to end the tensions that had lasted for more than eighteen months. In that agreement China committed to purchase goods for 200 million dollars, while the United States agreed to not impose new tariffs although those already in force would remain until "phase two" which would take place a year later.

This policy has been criticized by Democrats who accused the President of being vague and of being fooled in view of a hypothetical "phase two" based only on ambiguous promises. Even the agricultural sector will benefit little from these new economic agreements that have already cost enough. Robert Reich, Secretary of Labor during the Clinton administration, explained it well in a January 15, 2020 tweet: "China agrees to buy $50B of ag products this year. That's a gain of $29B from before Trump tariffs. Trump tariffs have cost U.S. farmers $11B. U.S. taxpayers have spent $28B on emergency payouts to farmers. So loss to U.S. is $39B. You do the math."

This is why Zakaria hopes that competition between the United States and China will take place within a framework of alliances and negotiations within the international system. In fact, if contentiousness and contrasts should prevail, this could not only destroy the open global economy, but it would march dangerously toward non-peaceful solutions, which are much more dangerous. "With China," Zakaria states, "the challenge is not how tough you can be, but how smart you can be."

Portions of this book were written before the Coronavirus pandemic exploded around the world and has forced many into house arrest. As we all know the virus originally manifested in China, which allowed Trump to immediately label it, with his usual contempt, "the Chinese virus," and later with a derogatory racial epithet, "Kung flu," names that he almost immediately backed away from following protests and counter accusations by China. This, however, gives the measure of how the American administration sees the Asian power not as a competitor with whom to make agreements and negotiate, but as an enemy to defeat.

When Mussolini took power, he did not neglect China. Italy had established economic relations with China in 1866, and China was very attentive to what was happening in Italy, since it had granted Italy the territory of Tianjin.[17] It had become the remotest colonial strip of Italian possessions. The Society of the Blue Shirts, a secret organization created within the Kuomintang, was inspired by Fascism, as was General Chang Kai-Shek, who had the idea of reproducing parts of the Italian model in China (Pini p. 41). Chinese State officials came to Rome to study Fascist welfare programs, the new strategies for agricultural production, urban settlement, the new cities, and land reclamation, and especially the administration of the state and the balanced budget. In 1936 Mussolini sent as a consultant to China, the Minister of Finance and Treasury, Alberto De Stefani. Legal scholars and professors from Italian academies went to the universities of Peking (now Beijing) and Shanghai to bring the Asian country up to date with the European systems; naval and aviation officers were also requested to train sailors and pilots. A consortium of Italian aeronautical companies was even created to build aircraft in China for China. But then Mussolini switched sides and allied himself with China's mortal enemy: Japan. At the end of 1937, the Italians had to return home.

NOTES

1. The Gracchi brothers, Tiberius and Gaius, were Romans who both served as tribunes of the plebs between 133 and 121 BCE.

2. It is interesting to note that this is exactly ninety-four years after the Fascist October 28, 1922, March on Rome.

3. On August 2, 1930, with the approval of Mussolini the two signed a broader exchange agreement that lasted through the 1930s.

4. Isotta Fraschini S.p.a. was an Italian luxury car manufacturer that also produced trucks and engines for marine and aviation use. Incorporated in Milan in 1900 by Cesare Isotta and the brothers Vincenzo, Antonio, and Oreste Fraschini, in 1955 it was merged with engine manufacturer Breda Motori and renamed F.A. Isotta Fraschini e Motori Breda. The company went bankrupt in 1999.

5. SIAI-Marchetti was an Italian aircraft manufacturer originally founded in 1915 as SIAI. It was re-named SIAI-Marchetti in 1943. The company's manufacturing facilities were a particularly high-priority target for enemy bombers, and the facilities were virtually destroyed toward the end of World War II. By the end of the War the company was basically insolvent and attempts to diversify production did not bring it back to solvency. It declared bankruptcy in 1951. In 1953 it emerged from the bankruptcy process and began to focus its development efforts on the emerging helicopter market. In 1983 SIAI-Marchetti was acquired by the Italian helicopter specialist company Agusta.

6. AGIP—*Azienda Generale Italiana Petroli*, (General Italian Oil Company)—is an Italian automotive gasoline, diesel, LPG, lubricants, fuel oil, and bitumen retailer established in 1926.

7. The Stresa Pact was made in Stresa, a town on the banks of Lake Maggiore located in the Piedmont region. It was an agreement between Britain, France, and

Italy formalizing opposition to German rearmament. It committed Britain, France, and Italy to work together against Germany. The Pact was negotiated around the time of the Abyssinian crisis, but no mention was made of it. Mussolini took the silence as acquiescence for Italy to proceed with the invasion.

8. The pact was concluded in Munich on September 30, 1938, among Germany, England, France, and Italy. It provided for ceding to Germany the Sudeten German territory of the then Czechoslovakia despite the existence of a 1924 alliance agreement and 1925 military pact between France and the Czechoslovak Republic.

9. The Treaty of Non-Aggression between Germany and the Soviet Union was concluded on August 23, 1939 between the Soviet Union and Nazi Germany. The Treaty provided a written guarantee of peace between the two parties and a commitment that neither government would ally itself with or aid an enemy of the other. It also had a secret protocol which defined the borders of Soviet and German spheres of influence across Poland, Lithuania, Latvia, Estonia, and Finland. On September 1, 1939, shortly after the Treaty was signed, Germany invaded Poland, which signaled the beginning of World War II in Europe.

10. Signed on June 28, 1919, in the Palace of Versailles in France, the Treaty of Versailles was the most important of the peace treaties ending World War I as it provided for the end of the state of war between Germany and the Allied Powers.

11. See *I documenti diplomatici italiani* (Italian Diplomatic Documents), seventh series, 1922–1935, edited by the Ministry of Foreign Affairs.

12. Comment told by a Trump confidant to Adam Entous, Staff reporter for the *New Yorker*, and published in Entous's article with the headline "The Enemy of My Enemy," in the print edition of the *New Yorker* on June 18, 2018.

13. The Lateran Pacts of 1929 were agreements between the Kingdom of Italy and the Holy See to settle the long-standing "Roman Question." These were signed on February 11, 1929, and the Italian Parliament ratified them on June 7, 1929. The Vatican City was recognized as an independent state under the sovereignty of the Holy See. Among other things, the Italian government also agreed to give the Roman Catholic Church financial compensation for the loss of the Papal States and Catholicism was made the state religion of Italy.

14. The boys from *Via Panisperna* (*I ragazzi di Via Panisperna*) were young scientists led by Enrico Fermi who in 1934 in Rome made the famous discovery of slow neutrons which later made the nuclear reactor possible, and then first atomic bomb. The nickname of the group comes from the address of the Physics Institute of the University of Rome La Sapienza located at Via Panisperna, a street in the city center where they met.

15. The Movimento Cinque Stelle (Five Stars Movement) began as a political movement (it is now a political party), founded on October 4, 2009 by Beppe Grillo, a comedian and blogger, and Gianroberto Casaleggio, a web strategist. The *Movimento* has been variously considered populist, anti-establishment, environmentalist, anti-immigration, anti-globalist, and Eurosceptic. It has also been described as "right wing" because of its anti-immigration stance, even though it has promoted policies usually advocated by the Italian left such as "citizen's income" (*reddito di cittadinanza*) and green-inspired environmental policies. Its members stress that

the *Movimento* is not a party but a "movement," and it is not to be included in the traditional left–right paradigm. The "five stars" are a reference to the five key issues that are key to the movement: public water, sustainable transportation, sustainable development, the right to Internet access, and environmentalism.

16. See two recently published volumes Timothy Snyder, *The Road to Unfreedom: Russia, Europe, America*, The Duggan Books, New York, *2018* e Andrew S. Weiss, *With Friends Like These: The Kremlin's Far Right and Populist Connections in Italy and Austria,* Carnegie Endowment for International Peace, Washington D.C. 2020.

17. Tianjin (formerly Romanized as "Tientsin") was a small strip of territory in central Tianjin, a large city in Northern China on the coast of the Bohai Sea. As part of the aftermath of the Boxer Rebellion, China ceded it to the Kingdom of Italy on September 7, 1901. The territory granted in concession totaled 46 hectares. Control by the Italians was formally taken on June 7, 1902 and was placed under the administration of an Italian consul. The territory was officially ceded back to China in 1947.

Chapter 8

The Women

Both Trump and Mussolini are often called "serial predators." Despite their differences in personal history and time periods, they have a relationship with women based on the use and consumption of their bodies. Women are disposable trophies to display in the living room of their personal egos. It is true that women during Mussolini's regime did not yet have the right to vote, which they would only fully acquire in Italy in 1945; although, in 1924 Mussolini had granted them the right to vote only in municipal elections. This, however, was abolished by the *Leggi Fascistissime* (*Very Fascist Laws*) of 1925–1926. It should also be acknowledged that Trump has promoted women to positions of responsibility in his companies, believing, as he has often said, in their professionalism and work ethic.

It is also true that the position of women in the Fascist era is not comparable to the position of women today, where after years of struggle and social and political battles they are no longer invisible, have won many rights (although worldwide they have not yet fully won the right to equal pay for comparable work), and feminist movements have a voice and a physical presence almost everywhere in the world. It is nevertheless true that the two men share a compulsive use of a predatory sexuality that, despite their differences, constitutes a characteristic of their individual personalities. Not all powerful men had and have it in these terms. Rather for these two men it is a fundamental and constitutive element of their approach to power.

Benito Mussolini was an unscrupulous man both in politics and in his personal life. He knew how to manage power to obtain money and how to use money to obtain power—and keep it. His predatory instinct gave him a simple approach. He would see a woman, be interested, make a move, and usually the woman would accept. This behavior created complications as the numerous lovers, escapades, and illegitimate children were scandals that had to be covered up. His sexual diversions were hit-and-runs. His encounters would often take place on a marble seat, covered by a quilted cushion, in the compartment of one of the large windows of the Map Room (*Sala Mappamondo*) in Palazzo Venezia.

Since he considered women only a momentary instrument of pleasure, he often did not even invite them to sit down; they were also forbidden to put their handbags or anything else on his huge desk. When he was finished, he paid them with money inserted in the pages of a book that he gave to them as a gift. He used them and then threw them away. He would never see them again.

His crudeness was in line with the Fascist mentality that exalted only prolific mothers, generators of heroes and war widows. His joke to the Assembly of the Milanese *Fascio* in 1921 to justify the alliance with the liberals is still famous:

> We do not belong to that crowd of insignificant spinster virgins, always afraid of losing their virginity (privilege) and—deep down—would love to! We do not belong to those who are constantly terrified of contaminating themselves, of diminishing themselves, of tarnishing, even with a veil, their splendid and onanistic isolation. Effects of a physiological weakness. Those who are strong do not have such fears. (Pini and Susmel, p. 113)

Giovanni Papini, one of Italy's most illustrious poets, and a misogynist, expressed the worst possible vision of women in the following manner: "the female body is only the happy musical flute for young male virility, prize of the winning male." He contemptuously offended women by defining them as "meat urinals." The famous medical anthropologist Mario Francesco Canella, Chair of Biology of Races at the University of Bologna in the 1930s, added to this description with:

> By morphology, structure and physiology men and women can be considered two different racial types, this is not only the opinion of scientists, but is a belief and a widespread feeling. Remember that the female creative power in art and science, in technology and philosophy has always been nonexistent. Women lack, because of an important biological necessity, the intellectual and spiritual gifts that allow the male genius to reach lofty heights. (Canella 1940, p. 222)

The machismo of the black shirts was explained by Maria Antonietta Macciocchi as follows:

> From its inception, Fascism aimed for an acceptance that I have defined as masochistic by women: an acceptance of every "torture" and of an "impulse toward death" (Freud) celebrated as the eternal ritual of the dead in battle and of widows who exalt the sacrifice of their chastity. From this renunciation of

life, women achieved a self-negating joy: it is a "joy" of denial between power and women: renunciation, subordination, domestic slavery, in exchange for an abstract, verbose, demagogic love of their leader, the *Duce*, the great and virile Fascist clown. (Macciocchi, p. 38)

Antonio Scurati's book *M. Il figlio del Secolo* (*M. The Son of the Century*) illustrated that Mussolini's success was due to his personality and to his lust as a conqueror. His sexual voracity allowed him to dominate Italy, exploiting the masses for his use and consumption, exactly as he did with women; to then state with contempt that they gave him the same sense of inner loneliness of a desert. As Mussolini learned from Gustave Le Bon, the crowd is female and it was up to him, the male, to dominate *her*. He expressed the same disappointed detachment toward the entire nation: "governing the Italians is not difficult, it is useless."

Even the conquest of an Empire was like the conquest of a woman. In 1936 the totality of the land in the Italian Empire was about ten times the size of Italy. Mussolini should have been satisfied. Nevertheless, he still coveted Sudan, the Anglo-French colonies of East Africa, and the Near East. Insatiable, as with women. The fact that for Mussolini politics was identical to sex is not a new idea. It was amply illustrated in the Memoirs of his personal valet Quinto Navarra, in those of his chauffeur Ercole Boratto, but above all in the diary of Claretta Petacci which was published in 2009 with the title *Mussolini Segreto. Diari 1932–1938*, (*Secret Mussolini. Diaries 1932–1938*).

Politics and sex. But also, a rapacity that had a death wish: Mussolini was crazy about dueling and subjugating his opponents. He fought dozens of duels from 1915 to 1922. Some of his more famous duels were with the anarchist Libero Merlino, the socialist leader Claudio Treves, the journalist Mario Missiroli, and the socialist deputy Francesco Ciccotti Scozzese. Antonio Scurati writes of this last duel in his *M. Il figlio del secolo* to illustrate Mussolini's merciless and violent personality. Scurati revealed aspects of Mussolini's life that were less glamorous and less boisterous. His novel used several interesting aspects of Mussolini's personality using elements everyone already knew. In an interview with the journalist Guido Caldiron in *Il Manifesto* published on April 23 2019, Scurati said:

Giving voice to Mussolini means getting rid of him. Above all it means facing the removal from the roots of our collective conscience of Fascism as one of our national identity template, and I am doing this through an inclusive and popular form of narrative: the novel. What gave me the impetus to do this was the conviction that after the collapse of the anti-Fascist attitude a novel on Mussolini would be beneficial to rekindle the reasons for anti-Fascism.

Lifting the curtain on well-known facts allowed Scurati to tell us that despite the admiration of democratic nations and politicians all over the world, Mussolini was a disgrace for both Italians and for the world, and was the essence of Fascist violence in its purest form.

There have been numerous works on Mussolini, ranging from books to television programs to films. For example, there is the monumental multi-volume work by Renzo De Felice: *Mussolini.* Italian public television broadcasted Sergio Zavoli's masterpiece: *Nascita di una dittatura (Birth of a Dictatorship).* Broadcast in 1972 it was a five-episode program in which Zavoli interviewed all the still living men of the *Ventennio*, as well as Mussolini's wife, Rachele, who, for the first time, told the story of her life with the *Duce* on television.

Another important work was Carlo Lizzani's 1974 movie *Mussolini Ultimo Atto (Last Days of Mussolini)* with Rod Steiger as Mussolini, which at the time caused some perplexity, because it made Mussolini a credibly human figure and portrayed Claretta Petacci (played by the actress Lisa Gastoni) as a victim who sacrificed her life to remain at his side, though she could have been saved.

Mussolini's sexuality was, as we have said, insatiable and destined to unhappy endings and it even raises the idea of a strongly repressed latent homosexuality. There are some suggestive elements of this that can be seen from footage in the *Istituto Luce*'s archives. One such example is the documentary *Il Viaggio del Duce in Piemonte*[1] *(The Duce's Trip to Piedmont)* filmed in May 1939 by the *Istituto Luce*. The visit takes place about a month and a half after his threatening speech against France's colonial selfishness toward Italy. The words he had used against France printed in the typical Fascist cubital form are plastered everywhere as is his image. His posture is striking: erect in his black uniform, alive in his puffed baggy pants, a dazzling smile. He is infused by a certain sensuality aimed at his male followers. The camera roves around taking in the mantras, diktats, and solemn phrases of his speech. His body language is carefully planned for the cameras (he would have been a great movie director). He seemed to wink at the men but carefully intends to seduce the women who respond with cries of approval. These scenes are expertly recorded by the sound engineers of the *Istituto Luce* who had carefully placed microphones in strategic places. The camera operators were masters at capturing in a single shot a close-up of the *Duce* speaking and then panning out to the 100,000 strong crowd. Everything was aimed at the *Duce* being the Nation itself. This footage brings to mind the phrase with which the legionnaires defined Caesar: "husband of all wives, wife of all husbands."

An example of eroticism is illustrated in the image below in the Junoesque posture of the Fascist woman (Fig. 8.1). She is wearing a Fascist uniform and is speaking to him with her head slightly down and has an expression of adoration making it appear that she intends to kiss him. Mussolini's gaze cannot be completely seen in the drawing, but the image still seems to convey his cool indifference as if he is toying with her. Mussolini carefully screened all the material shot by *Istituto Luce* and decided which images would appear on screen, so we can surmise that he was pleased to convey the subliminal image of sexuality.

What was incredible is that he also applied the power sex paradigm to international relations. He had unconsummated flirtations with both Stalin's Russia and Roosevelt's America. However, he seemed to have three favorite lovers: Germany, France, and England. He would use France and England to make Hitler jealous, who would spitefully cause the others to argue, as occurred with the Hoare-Laval Pact between Italy, France, and England. The Pact was intended to make the independent nation of Abyssinia into an Italian colony to partially satisfy Mussolini's colonial aspirations without dragging Italy into a war. Hitler leaked the details of the Pact to the English press causing a huge public outcry, forcing Foreign Minister Samuel Hoare to resign. The failure of the Pact was among the factors that would bring about the birth of the Rome-Berlin axis the following year.

However, Mussolini had awkward relationships with women who had more power than he did. One such woman was Maria José, the daughter of the King of Belgium and the wife of Crown Prince Umberto. Once Mussolini came to power, King Vittorio Emanuele III of Savoy granted him the use of a portion of the royal estate at *Castel Porziano*. Mussolini would often visit the estate alone or more often with one of his mistresses. One afternoon he met with Maria Josè, and she indicated that she would be a willing partner.

Figure 8.1 **Mussolini and Trump with Women**. By the authors.

Mussolini was apparently quite taken aback and was unable to perform—her noble lineage seemed to have caused him embarrassment. Mussolini's driver, Ercole Boratto, confirmed this anecdote in his memoirs, *A spasso col Duce*, (*Going Out with the Duce*) published in 2014. Maria Josè's temperament created such a fear in him that he confided to Claretta Petacci that he found her body "repulsive" (Petacci and Suttora p. 507).

Mussolini's relationship with his only legitimate daughter Edda was also enigmatic. Her ambiguous relationship with her father was revealed in a long interview given in the 1970s in the then dilapidated Villa Torlonia[2] to Nicola Caracciolo.[3] During her story, Edda Ciano slipped up and referred to her father as "my husband."

There was definitely ambivalence in the relationship, at least on Mussolini's part. In the interview Edda recounted that on the evening of her marriage, on April 24, 1930, the couple was driving on the Appian Way to Naples to then embark a boat for Capri; at a certain point, they noticed the headlights of a car following them. She recognized that it was her father's car. It seemed that he did not want to leave her, or at least for her not to leave unaccompanied. He continued following them for so long that about halfway to Naples she had to get out of the car to implore him to return home.

Mussolini was submissive with men, who were more aggressive, such as Roberto Farinacci. His relationship with Hitler also seems to have been one of subjugation. In certain photos of the two, Mussolini is clearly both complicit and dominated (Cicchino 2010).

Gossip has attributed about sixty "verified" relationships to Mussolini. Among the first was the socialist activist Angelica Balabanoff. She was from a wealthy Ukrainian Jewish family and met Mussolini in Lausanne, Switzerland. She referred to him at the time as "wretched human being," but then became a faithful colleague in the direction of *Avanti!* They conveniently lived on the same street in Milan: Angelica lived on Via Castelmorrone, number 9; Mussolini, with his wife Rachele and young daughter Edda, at number 18. Margherita Sarfatti followed Angelica Balabanoff. She was a well-educated journalist and a writer. She too was Jewish. In 1925 she published in England the famous biography *Dux*, which was translated into twenty languages and was a monumental success, creating the myth of Mussolini worldwide. She was an art historian and became the editor of *Gerarchia*, the official political magazine of Fascism founded by Mussolini in 1922. She was later forced to leave Italy with the advent of the racial laws.

Neither Balabanoff nor Sarfatti had children with Mussolini. However, he did have numerous children: five with his wife Rachele, and at least another ten, perhaps eleven, illegitimate children that created serious problems for him due to paternity suits brought by their mothers. This situation was even more problematic after the signing of the Lateran Pacts, because of the potential indignant reaction of the Catholic Church. These children were therefore a weapon of blackmail. To avoid this Mussolini restricted their freedom and placed them under the control of OVRA agents.

His first verified relationship from which a child resulted was in 1907 when he was a teacher in Carnia, in the Italian region of Friuli. The relationship was with a young blue-collar worker who gave birth to his first son, Candido. In 1909 Mussolini's second son was born; he died at the age of two, nothing more is known of these two children. His daughter Edda born in 1910 was his third child; her mother was Rachele Guidi, who at the time was not yet married to Mussolini.

Although it has never been proven, there were rumors that the Fascists Pino Romualdi, and Asvero Gravelli were also Mussolini's offspring. He was very close to both men. Gravelli was an intransigent Fascist. In the 1930s he became the director of the magazine *Antieuropa*. Many people claimed that this appointment was due to his extraordinary resemblance to Mussolini. Romualdi and Gravelli were among the Fascists with Mussolini in 1944 when he formed the *Repubblica Sociale* (Italian Social Republic).[4] In 1944, Romualdi was for a few months vice-secretary of the *Republichino Fascist Party* of the *Italian Social Republic*. After the war, he was one of the founders of the *Movimento Sociale Italiano*[5] (*MSI* Italian Social Movement) and was elected to Parliament.

Particularly interesting is the story of Mussolini's seventh child. Benito Albino was born in Milan in 1915 to Ida Dalser, who was utterly devoted to Mussolini. Mussolini abandoned her and she died in the criminal asylum of San Clemente in Venice in July 1937, at fifty-seven years of age. Benito Albino did not have a fortunate life either. Mussolini even prevented him from creating his own life. He forced Benito Albino to leave Italy, made him enlist in the Navy, and sent him to the Far East from where he returned only in 1938 to be interned in a mental hospital. He died in the psychiatric institute of Mombello di Limbiate in the Lombardy region in 1942.

His wife, Rachele, gave birth to Vittorio in 1917: Mussolini's ninth child. He became a movie screenwriter and co-founded the magazine *Cinema*. In 1918 Rachele gave birth to his son Bruno who became an aviator. He died in Pisa in 1941 while piloting the first modern four-engine aircraft of the Italian Air Force.

In 1923 a twelfth purported child was born: a girl named Elena. Her mother was a fashion designer named Angela Curti Cucciati. Elena followed Mussolini to Salò and was active in the *Repubblica Sociale Italiana*; she was also with him when he was brought to Dongo, where he was executed. According to the letters exchanged between Claretta Petacci and Mussolini during that time, he denied paternity of Elena. In 1927 Rachele gave birth to Mussolini's thirteenth child—Romano, a future jazz pianist. In 1929, she gave birth to his fourteenth child, Anna Maria.

At the time of Edda's marriage Mussolini was involved with the very famous pianist Magda Brard, a former child prodigy and the daughter of a radical socialist French senator. It is rumored that her second child, Vanna, who was born in 1932, was Mussolini's daughter. Brard opened a music academy in Turin. However, she came into conflict with the Prefect who refused to renew her membership in the National Fascist Party. Moreover, out of fear that she may have been an agent of the French secret service, her home was searched and every element, document, or photograph that could refer to Benito Mussolini was confiscated. She withdrew to live in the villa Roccabruna Blevio on Lake Como. In the years 1943 to 1945 she used her past with Mussolini to save many leaders of the *Comitato di Liberazione Nazionale* (CLN National Liberation Committee)[6] including Enrico Mattei.[7]

It is generally assumed that Mussolini had many other illegitimate children. For years he received a woman every day for a fleeting mid-morning meeting. They were all chosen, after careful investigation, by his private secretary. The daily procession did not stop even in 1936, when he took his last lover the very young Claretta, daughter of Francesco Saverio Petacci, a physician at the Vatican. Her family was quite ambitious and was determined to profit from her relationship with Mussolini. In fact, thanks to Mussolini her sister Miriam had a movie career. Edda and Galeazzo, who were opposed to the relationship, attempted to smear Claretta and her family. These actions just made the couple more determined. It was apparently an intense, manic, passionate love. "Jealousy makes me crazy: for it I would be capable of any act"—said Mussolini (Guspini, p. 143). The relationship also had numerous betrayals and even some grotesque occurrences. The historian Mauro Canali discovered in the Central State Archives a rather colorful *velina* of a police informant, with the code name *Francis*, who reported a memorable jealous tirade by Mussolini over a certain Luciano Antonetti. The quarrel ended with Claretta bursting ". . . into a broken cry, invoking forgiveness. The *Duce* was moved and you could see it. The argument . . . ended by resting Clara's head on his chest" (Canali 2020).

There was also some type of relationship with Margherita Sarfatti's then eighteen-year-old daughter Fiammetta. Ercole Boratto, in his memoirs, *A Spasso col Duce*, wrote that one day the three of them took a trip in a motorboat. According to Boratto the girl was clearly in love with Mussolini and she could not wait to be alone with him. Boratto also claimed that Mussolini had passionate feelings for her (Boratto p. 80).

The Fascist regime took great care to maintain absolute secrecy on all of his extramarital affairs and was extremely rigorous in keeping the names and faces of his mistresses secret. Maniacal precautions were taken to guarantee secrecy for his trysts with Claretta Petacci. She was forced to come to Palazzo Venezia sitting in a sidecar dressed as a policeman and completely hooded.

The same discretion was also demanded by his occasional lovers who were accompanied to his private apartment directly by the security services.

When, due to carelessness, it was Mussolini himself who made a mistake, both photographers and the *Istituto Luce* were forced to remedy the situation, erasing all traces of it, as happened in 1932 in Naples, when during his speech one of his lovers inadvertently stood next to him. Since it was impossible to cancel the cinematographic testimony, he gave orders to obscure the part of the frame where the woman appeared.

Although Mussolini was an unfaithful husband, his image for Italians had to be that of a father, an uncle, a grandfather, or parent who worked hard and provided for his family in both good and bad times. The regime took on the commitment to censor all images discordant with Mussolini's image in photographs, film footage, and newspapers, and to only disseminate those that Mussolini approved. Thus, in newsreels to shore up this image, he would be shown as the happy father, as on the occasion of the wedding of his daughter Edda to Galeazzo Ciano, or accompanying the brides of his sons and his grandchildren to the altar. The newsreels also showed his terrible moments of grief such as his desperation over the loss of his brother Arnaldo, and alongside Rachele, suffering over the loss of their son Bruno.

Because of Mussolini's sexual proclivities he was convinced that men revealed their most important secrets in pillow talk as he did. Once he was in power it is not surprising that among the tools he would use to exert control over his *gerarchi* would be sex. The political police kept brothels under strict surveillance as they were inexhaustible sources of information. The favorite haunt of the *squadristi* in Milan was brothel in Via San Carpòforo. It was owned by the Knight Cesare Albino Bianchi, an enthusiastic Fascist and sex industry entrepreneur who had twelve lucrative brothels.

The legislation in force at the time provided that a woman could begin her career as a sex worker at twenty-one, or even eighteen, as long as she was *emancipated*, which meant in those days that she was married.

If a woman was fortunate enough to work in a luxury brothel, it meant she would have a smaller number of patrons to service in an evening and more income. Clothing in such brothels had to be impeccable. In a Milan brothel located on Via Chiaravalle, the clothes worn by the young ladies were made by a famous designer of the time, Biki.[8]

The brothel was an intimate place, where male camaraderie was strengthened. "Of course we are friends, we go to the brothel together!" became a figure of speech. Between one joke and another, the sexual habits of the habitué of these brothels were recorded and were available to the regime for use as needed.

One of Mussolini's most valuable sources of information was the madame Fedora Sandelli. She owned several brothels and had one in a villa in Rome on the Appian Way, which had ten girls destined for a very small circle of VIPs. At the opening of that brothel the women were dressed in a sexy version of the latest fashions. The rates ranged from 500 *liras* for a simple performance to 2,000 *liras* for an entire night. At that time a switchboard operator in Italy made barely 500 *liras* per month (about $975 today).

The regime made wide-ranging strategic use of *Pensione Sandelli*. High-ranking Nazi officials were even brought there, including Sepp Dietrich, the SS commander of the *Leibstandarte*, who was brought to *Pensione Sandelli* to obtain information on secret German projects concerning Italy. In her memoirs Sandelli wrote that in 1938, during Hitler's visit to Rome, a senior Nazi officer impregnated one of her girls. The SS induced her to go to Germany promising an abortion, but she was poisoned instead (Pagani p. 164). Three of her other sex workers impregnated by Fascist *gerarchi* also died. One committed suicide, two others died of exsanguination caused by clandestine abortions. Among the illustrious guests were Mussolini's son-in-law, Galeazzo Ciano, Alessandro Pavolini, Roberto Farinacci, and even the elderly General Emilio De Bono.

The proudest of his brothel visits was the multi-decorated aviator and Fascist politician Ettore Muti[9] who was happy to provide his comrades with the secrets to his virility: "[d]rink a glass of honey with a dozen almonds every night. Or eat two roasted hyena eyes accompanied by licorice root!" (Padiglione p. 30).

The fact that Trump is a serial predator is well known. His relationships with women have always been controversial and animated by a deep misogyny.

An image from the 1964 school yearbook of the New York Military Academy shows Trump pictured with a young woman with the caption "Ladies Man." Rather than being voted as one of his classmates "Most Likely to Succeed" he was voted "Ladies Man." The young woman in the photo was not his girlfriend, but simply a school employee, as Barry Levine and Monique El-Faizy reveal in a book about Donald Trump's behavior toward women, titled *All The President's Women: Donald Trump and the Making of a Predator*. It is one of the few books on the subject, and it is also revealing of Trump's attitude toward power as well. The authors wrote "[t]he woman in the picture is 19-year-old Fran D'Agati Dunn, a secretary who worked at the school at the time and was asked to step in for the photo. Nothing more than a prop (Levine and El-Faizy p. 9)."

In an interview with the *Huffington Post* on October 24, 2019, Monique El-Faizy, one of the authors, when asked by journalist Emma Gray if considering women objects started early in Trump's life, replied:

Absolutely. That's why I chartered the book the way I did. In his graduation photo from the military academy, the woman standing next to him is an accessory. To me, that said it all. And I think that that comes from his father, too. His father would bring these young, pretty girls up to the academy. From what his classmates say, these were not women that Donald Trump knew or had any kind of relationship with. They were just girls that his dad would bring up for him, presumably for the image of it. So I think that he didn't develop that attitude in a vacuum.

This image is one that the authors find emblematic of Trump's attitude toward women. In the introduction to the book they wrote:

Our investigation, found at least sixty-seven instances of inappropriate behavior, including twenty-six instances of unwanted sexual contact. On the basis of that evidence, this book will show that Trump repeatedly and systematically engaged in aggressive sexual pursuit of women over many decades. It will show that this behavior was neither random nor occasional nor casual. Our investigation found Trump's sexual misconduct, particularly during the 1980s and 1990s, was far more frequent than has been previously reported . . . and followed patterns. It will show that he was not just sexist, misogynistic or even a harasser. The behavior he has admitted to—grabbing women by the "pussy"—and many of the credible accusations that he denies, were they to be proven in a court of law would qualify as crimes, some of them serious. . . . After considering all the evidence, one cannot but conclude that Donald Trump is and has for some time been a full-blown predator. So what does this mean for our nation? Multiple allegations of sexual assault against any man must be taken seriously; all the more so when that man holds a position of power. (Levine and El-Faizy pp. 2–3)

In one of the notes at the beginning of the book the authors also wrote:

When the man with the largest bully pulpit in the world espouses the idea that women are objects, that they can be grabbed or kissed or insulted at whim, he is sending a signal to men everywhere that such attitudes and behaviors are acceptable. And when we as citizens stop being shocked, we normalize it, not just for Trump, but for all men. . . . We cannot let even the slightest idea of sexism or misogyny go unchallenged if we have any hope of creating a world that values women and men equally. Since we cannot confront what we cannot see, revealing and carefully considering these alleged incidents of sexual misconduct is essential. All too often women who come forward with stories about harassment, assault and verbal, emotional and physical abuse are shunted aside, brushed off, dismissed or disbelieved. As a result, women keep their experiences to themselves far more frequently than they make them public. And when they do report them, the repercussions are often so unpleasant that they regret having done so. Victims get re-victimized. It is essential that those who came forward with allegations against Trump are given the fair hearing, they are so often denied—especially given the efforts of Trump and other powerful people to discredit them. Having carefully considered all the evidence we found, we believe the stories of the women whom we have included in this book. (Levine and El-Faizy p. XX)

In the same interview with Gray the *Huffington Post* in October 2019, Monique El-Faizy then commented that they wanted to examine not only the things he had done, "but why and what it meant. How he came to be formed as the predator he became." The authors' interest in the project apparently began when porn star Stormy Daniels admitted in early 2018 that she was paid under the table in 2016 along with twenty other women who had accused Trump of inappropriate sexual conduct not to reveal the details of their encounters. This would have hurt the then U.S. presidential candidate's campaign. With more than a 100 interviews under their belt, the two authors reveal that they discovered a pattern to his behavior.

> [Trump] clearly has a thing for younger women. He started talking about Ivanka being sexy when she was around the same age as these models that he was kind of staring at backstage and pursuing at parties. So that's one of the patterns. He likes porn stars, as we've seen. . . . And he has these habits. He'll push somebody against the wall and try and kiss them. He'll grab a breast or a buttock. When he's in a property that he owns . . . he feels that he has the right to walk in on a woman in her room. . . . What's interesting is that there were very few one-offs. We only put things in . . . that fit the pattern, because he has such well-established patterns over the years. What was powerful [is that] when we would interview the women, almost all of them in some way blamed themselves: "What kind of vibe was I putting off? What was I wearing?" And when you look at them in the context of these patterns, you realize it has almost nothing to do with that woman. If it wasn't that woman, it would've been another woman wearing something else and putting off a totally different vibe. (Grey 2019)

Trump's attitude toward women, as already noted, developed early. Shortly after giving birth to her fifth child, his mother experienced hemorrhaging, and had to undergo several operations, including a hysterectomy. Therefore, she had neither the time nor the physical strength to devote attention to her children, including Donald. Some have pointed out that Trump, who was only two and a half years old, experienced a trauma that had a decisive influence on the development of his personality, because it occurred in the midst of the formation of his character, and affected his sense of security and self-confidence, leading to consequences in the formation of his identity. In Steven Buser and Leonard Cruz's book *A Clear and Present Danger: Narcissism in the Era of President Trump*, the authors stated that what is perceived as an abandonment of the mother figure can generate progressively bombastic and excessive behavior. The child becomes exaggeratedly needy of attention and can develop character disorders that make him easily irritable, sometimes irritating, always in spasmodic search for approval and attention. The authors point out that this seems to be precisely the case with Donald Trump. When he was still a teenager, both parents together, as Michael Kruse wrote in a November 15, 2017 article in *Politico*, titled *The Mystery of Mary Trump*, decided to send "their fourth and most incorrigible child, who as a boy threw cake at kids at parties and erasers at his teachers at his private elementary school, first to Sunday morning Bible classes, like his siblings—and then, unlike his siblings, to a stringent military academy an hour and a half upstate shortly after he turned 13."

The military school was to straighten out their rebellious and unruly son. His father tried first to curb Donald's behavior through the discipline imposed by the military institution and then with his own discipline. Trump's father often went to visit on weekends and would take him out to dinner; his mother very rarely visited. Sandy McIntosh, a schoolmate of Trump, said that he excelled in sports (baseball, basketball, soccer, and football) and, along with one of Trump's leaders and mentors, Theodore Dobias, recalled that his father was "inflexible" with the young Donald, constantly telling him: "be a killer and be a king." Both asserted, however, that young Donald spoke little about his mother, that he "didn't say anything about her. Not a word." A distant unaffectionate mother, who was very fond of the splendor of the English Crown she idolized and found the time to follow on TV; a domineering father, who considered his eldest son, who had shunned his father's career to be an airplane pilot, a failure, and never failed to remind him of it in public and in private. These parents served as the backdrop for the formation of Trump.

Fred Trump Sr. had begun his career building military barracks for naval personnel and had then expanded his business to create a real estate empire constructing homes for the middle class, especially war veterans, and then with rental housing for low-income families. His empire was also built on allegations of having twice defrauded the U.S. government. The U.S. Senate Committee on Banking Housing and Urban Affairs, which carried out the investigation, defined him as "a shrewd character with a particular talent for obtaining every ounce of profit from public housing." He was never indicted, but since that time, procedures for obtaining funds for the public sector became more restrictive to minimize the risk of entrepreneurs obtaining windfall profits. Trump Sr. was accused by some of his tenants of being a racist and excluding African Americans as tenants in his apartments. It has been rumored that he was sympathetic to the Ku Klux Klan. This stemmed from his 1927 arrest arising from his participation in a Ku Klux Klan march which was protesting against the New York Catholic police[10] for assaulting native-born protestant Americans. He was released in June 1927 and the charges were dropped.

Among his five siblings, Donald became Fred Sr.'s favorite son, and was chosen to carry on the family business. Freddy Jr., the oldest son, would grow up to be an alcoholic and die of a heart attack at the age of forty-three. It is said that Trump has never touched a drop of alcohol precisely because of this sad family legacy. Trump has also rarely spoken of his two sisters, who are still living, and his recently deceased younger brother. However, Trump's most difficult familial relationship to understand remains the one with his mother. Trump has a portrait of his father, of whom he had been "in awe" since he was a boy, hanging on the twenty-sixth floor of his Trump Tower office in New York. When he took office in January 2017, Fred Sr.'s portrait could immediately be seen behind the Resolute Desk in the Oval Office. His mother's portrait only appeared in the spring as witnessed by the then White House communications director Hope Hicks.

Trump, on the rare occasions that he has spoken of his mother, has described her as "fantastic," "formidable," "a wonderful person," "one who always encouraged me to believe in God and in myself." He has said that he learned from her his "sense of entertainment" as he explains in his book *Art of the Deal* written in collaboration with Tony Schwartz. However, the absence of a true close relationship with her was a constant feature of his life. It has been repeated several times, even by Trump himself in 2005 to his biographer Tim O'Brien that, while with his father he was directly in touch, because there was more harmony, "my mother was a wife who really was a great home-maker." Although when he was a child, household chores would have been performed by domestics and when he played with other children, she was never present. In his *Think Big and Kick Ass in Business and in Life*, written in collaboration with Bill Zanker, he stated that the one who really understood him the most, because he absolutely wanted him to succeed, was his father.

Fred Sr. died at the age of 93 after a decade of suffering Alzheimer's disease. In June 1999 there were more than 650 people at his funeral, including many of New York's VIPs. When Donald Trump gave the eulogy, he spoke only of himself. He began by saying that he had learned of his father's death immediately after reading on the front page of the *New York Times* the positive opinion surrounding his new project to build the Trump World Tower in Manhattan and said that his father would have been proud of what he had accomplished. He concluded by saying that his father was always aware of whatever he had in mind and was confident that he would be able to pull it off. Fred Trump's funeral became an opportunity for Donald to show off. His pronouns were almost all in the first person—I, me, mine—and far surpassed those in the third person, referring to his father. He was not even able to let the life of his father be the center of attention at his funeral. Trump is utterly incapable of affection and emotion. He has said when his parents died—his mother died a year after his father in 2000—it was the closest he ever came to shedding tears. Journalist Gwenda Blair in an article in *Politico* on September 1, 2018, reported that Trump confessed this to his biographer Tim O'Brien in

2005, saying: "[Crying] It's just not my thing. I have nothing against it when someone cries, but when I see a man cry I view it as a weakness. I don't like seeing men cry. I'll give you an example. I never met John Gotti, I know nothing about John Gotti, but he went through years of trials. He sat with a stone face. He said, 'Fuck you.'"

Donald Trump was not the only Trump family member to never speak of Mary Trump; his other three siblings never have, nor have his children (Donald Junior or daughter Ivanka), nor his first wife Ivana who knew her. Only Eric, the youngest of the sons, told reporter Michael Kruse of *Politico* in the November 17, 2017 article *The Mystery of Mary Trump* that his grandmother was amazing and "was strong, smart, charismatic and incredibly loving. She had an amazing smile and an incredible sense of humor. Looking down, there is no doubt that she would be unbelievably proud of my father and all that he has accomplished."

Donald Trump has five children from his three marriages: Ivanka and his two oldest sons Donald Jr. born in 1977 and Eric born in 1984 from his first marriage to Ivana Zelnickova. Trump's other two children are from his second and third marriages. Tiffany was born in 1993 from his second marriage to model Marla Maples for whom he divorced Ivana in 1991. Barron born in 2006 is the only offspring of Trump and Melania Knauss.

Trump may not have had a great relationship with his mother, but things are different with his daughter Ivanka. Ivanka's relationship with her father is so privileged that she was given a special position in the White House as "Advisor to the President" without having any previous government experience whatsoever. She is not only Trump's favorite child, but at times their relationship even seems peculiar and ambiguous. It is nothing like he has with his other children or even his second daughter, Tiffany. In February 2013 father and daughter, as guests on the *Wendy Williams Show*, were asked by the host what they have in common. While Ivanka answered "either real estate or golf," Trump answered "I was going to say sex but I can't relate that to her." And even before that, in 2006, he was invited along with Ivanka to the ABC talk show, *The View*, to promote his show *The Apprentice*. When asked how he would react if he saw a nude photo of his daughter Ivanka on the cover of *Playboy*, he first replied that he would be disappointed, then added in a whisper "not really" and then added "I don't think Ivanka would do it, although she does have a very nice figure. I've always said that if Ivanka wasn't my daughter perhaps I'd be dating her," adding, "Is that terrible?" And when Joy Behar, said, "Who are you, Woody Allen?" Trump complimented her with a "that's good!" And again when in 2004 Howard Stern, the controversial and provocative radio and television personality, invited Trump on his program and called then twenty-three-year-old Ivanka "a piece of ass, [asking] can I say it?" Trump did not blink an eye and authorized the expression.

In a later Stern interview in 2006 Trump reiterated that Ivanka had "actually always been very voluptuous." He also added, "You know who's one of the great beauties of the world, according to everybody? And I helped create her: Ivanka. My daughter, Ivanka. She's 6 feet tall, she's got the best body. She made a lot money as a model—a tremendous amount."

In 2016 Adam Withnall writing for *The Independent* published the article, *Donald Trump's unsettling record of comments about his daughter Ivanka*. Among the various comments he chronicled was a comment made in a September 9, 2015, piece in the *Rolling Stone* written by Paul Solotaroff. In the interview Solotaroff had commented that he had met Ivanka and praised her. Trump then commented: "Yeah, she's really something, and what a beauty, that one. If I weren't happily married and, ya know, her father. . . ."

On May 18, 2016, Ivanka gave a long interview to "CBS This Morning" co-host Norah O'Donnell after the article in the *New York Times* by Michael Barbaro and Megan Twohey titled *Crossing the Line: How Donald Trump Behaved With Women in Private* of May 14, 2016 had been published. The O'Donnell interview addressed in detail her father's relationships with women. Among other things it was stated that her father asked people if they thought his daughter was "hot." Ivanka responded that she had read the article and found it "disturbing." "I was bothered by it, but its largely been discredited since," she said in the interview. "He's not a groper. I've known my father obviously my whole life, he has total respect for women, . . . because he believes ultimately in merit." But that does not seem to be the case if one thinks back to the video that a few months prior accompanied the October 7, 2016 *Washington Post* article just before the election. In it Donald Trump in the company of Billy Bush from NBC Universal's *Access Hollywood* was talking about women. While they were in the bus that would take them to the location where the taping of the broadcast would take place Trump recounted his attempts to seduce married women and said he would begin to kiss the woman they would meet shortly for the broadcast, adding "I don't even have to wait. When you're a star, they let you do whatever you want. You can do anything . . . grab them by the pussy. You can do anything."

In that *New York Times* May 14 article by Michael Barbaro and Megan Twohey, *Crossing the Line: How Donald Trump Behaved With Women in Private* the two journalists disclosed quite a bit about Trump's attitudes toward women. Starting with the fact that he described Rosie O'Donnell, television host and lesbian activist in the LGBTQ movement, has having a "fat ugly face."

What emerges from the interviews is a complex, at times contradictory portrait of a wealthy, well known and provocative man and the women around him, one that defies simple categorization. Some women found him gracious and encouraging. He promoted several to the loftiest heights of his company, a daring move for a major estate developer at the time. He simultaneously nurtured women's career and mocked their physical appearance. . . . He could be lewd one moment and gentlemanly the next. (Barbaro and Twohey 2016)

Trump has always affirmed that hiring women is something that has made him and still makes him proud, "I have always treated women with great respect. And women will tell you" (Ibid.). He said they have an unparalleled work and professional ethic: "It would just seem that there was something they want to really prove" (Ibid.). The fact is that he has always had an advantage over them that in most cases they did not have as the two journalists wrote: "In many cases there was an unmistakable dynamic at play: Mr. Trump had the power and the women did not. He had celebrity. He had wealth. He had connections. Even after he had behaved crudely toward them, some of the women sought his assistance with their careers or remained on his side" (Ibid.).

With the purchase of the Miss Universe organization, however, he entered a realm populated by beautiful young women who were hungry for advice, approval, and success. It has been said that Trump likes his women very young. At the time he bought the pageant he was married to his second wife Marla Maples, a former model with whom—he previously said publicly—"he had the best sex of his life." His involvement in the event was immediately very intense. Many of the participants have testified to his misbehavior and his invasion of their privacy, his obsessive comments on their appearance, and his constant inspections as if they were a platoon of soldiers. He made comments on their bodies out loud and in front of everyone.

Barbara Res, whom Trump hired in the 1980s in his construction company, was also interviewed for the Barbaro and Twohey article, *Crossing the Line: How Donald Trump Behaved With Women in Private*, and she recalled a comment Trump made about a project he was to develop in Los Angeles. Out of nowhere he made a comment about the appearance of Marina del Rey's California women: "They take care of their asses. 'The architect and I did not know where he was coming from,' Mrs. Res said. Years later after she had gained a significant amount of weight, Mrs. Res endured a stinging work place observation about her own body from Mr. Trump. 'You like your candy,' she recalled him telling her. 'It was him reminding me that I was overweight.'"

But it is politically that Trump has hurt women. He has disempowered them. He has promoted hundreds of anti-abortion judges, most of whom are White men, including two to the Supreme Court. He has encouraged through his behavior a toxic masculinity among his supporters. Nina Burlington, who in 2011 published the essay *Golden Handcuffs: The Secret History of Trump's Women*, wrote in *The New Republic* on April 13, 2020:

> If Trump can be said to "empower" women at all, it is in the same way that he empowers the women closest to him, promoting them as commodities; as deal enhancers. Trump's wife, daughters, and daughters-in-law must resemble in style and stature the thousands of women this *impresario* of female flesh has lined up beside himself for years in his beauty pageants and reality television escapades. Branding women has been his avocation. He opened his "T Model" agency at a time when model industry practices were just a few legalities removed from human trafficking. Jeffrey Epstein is not the only one of Trump's running buddies to be credibly accused of pedophilia. Trump not only attended parties for aspiring models, many of them underage girls; he hosted them on his yacht and in halls at his hotel in New York. The goal of all the New York "modelizers" was to interact sexually with as many nubile out-of-towners as physically possible. Ambitious, disoriented young girls would submit to, if they were lucky, just a thorough ogling or manhandling; and if unlucky, rape.

NOTES

1. *Piemonte* (Piedmont) is a region in northwest Italy. It is bordered by the Italian region of Liguria to the south, the Lombardy and Emilia-Romagna regions to the east, the Aosta Valley region to the northwest, and borders Switzerland to the northeast and France to the west.

2. Villa Torlonia is located on the Via Nomentana in Rome and formerly belonged to the Torlonia family. It was the Mussolini family residence from 1922 to 1943. It was completely abandoned after 1945 and allowed to decay in the ensuing decades. Recent restoration work has allowed it to be opened to the public as a museum owned and operated by the municipality of Rome.

3. This interview was re-broadcast on Rai 3 for the Program Mixer/Format PII in November 1997.

4. The Italian Social Republic is more commonly known as the "Republic of Salò" (*Repubblica di Salò*) as it was located in the town of Salò in the Northern Italian region of Lombardy on the banks of Lake Garda. The Republic of Salò was a German puppet state with limited recognition created during the latter part of World War II. It existed from the beginning of the German occupation of Italy in September 1943 until the surrender of German troops in Italy in May 1945. During the civil war, which split Italy in two, it fought against the Italian Resistance. The Italian Social Republic was the second and last incarnation of the Italian Fascist state and was led by Mussolini and his reformed anti-monarchist Republican Fascist Party.

5. The *Movimento Sociale Italiano* (*MSI* talian Social Movement), renamed in 1972 as *Movimento Sociale Italiano—Destra Nazionale* (Italian Social Movement—National Right), was a neo-Fascist, nationalist, and national-conservative political

party in Italy. It was created in 1946 by supporters of Mussolini, most of whom took part in the Italian Social Republic and the Republican Fascist Party. By the early 1960s the MSI had become the fourth largest party in Italy.

6. The *Comitato di Liberazione Nazionale* (National Liberation Committee, CNL) was a political umbrella organization and the main representative of the Italian resistance movement fighting against Nazi Germany's forces during the German occupation of Italy and Italian Fascists during the Italian Civil War. It was a multi-party entity whose members were united by their anti-Fascism. It coordinated and directed the Italian resistance and was subdivided into the Central Committee for National Liberation (CCLN) based in Rome and the later National Liberation Committee for Northern Italy (CLNAI) based in Milan.

7. Enrico Mattei (April 9, 1906–October 27, 1962) was an Italian public administrator. He was initially a Fascist party member, albeit an inactive one. In 1943 he was introduced into anti-Fascist circles in Milan. After July 25, 1943, when Mussolini was forced to resign, Mattei joined a partisan group of the Italian resistance movement supplying them with weapons. He was able to join the resistance, despite suspicion over his former membership in the Fascist Party. After World War II he was given the task of dismantling the Italian Petroleum Agency Agip. Instead, Mattei enlarged and reorganized it into the National Fuel Trust, *Ente Nazionale Idrocarburi* (ENI).

8. Biki was the professional name of the designer Elvira Leonardi Bouyeure (June 1, 1906–February 24, 1999) and was based in Milan.

9. Ettore Muti (May 2, 1902–August 24, 1943) was an aviator and Fascist politician. He replaced Achille Starace as PNF Party Secretary in October 1939 and held the office until shortly after the entry of Italy into World War II on June 10, 1940.

10. During that period of time many American police officers in those years were of Irish origin and Catholic. The Ku Klux Klan as a hate group targets not only Blacks but basically anyone who is not a WASP (White Anglo-Saxon Protestant). During the early part of the twentieth century many Americans of the time viewed the Irish as a subordinate ethnic group to be isolated because they were Catholic despite being English-speaking Whites. Noel Ignatiev, a great scholar of racism in the United States, in his beautiful book *How the Irish Became White* explains in fact how an initial discrimination against them because they were Catholics was later transformed into an Irish oppression of Blacks that allowed them to become effectively "white," in the sense of escaping the discrimination and oppression of which African Americans continue to be victims.

Interview with U.S. Ambassador
Robert J. Callahan

Q. It has been said that, more than the 1930s, the decade of the 1920s, as Mussolini was coming into power is similar to the time preceding Trump's election. What similarities do you see between the two historical periods and what do you think these similarities are driven by?

A. I don't see a lot of political or socio-economic similarities between the 1920s and the ten years that preceded Trump's election. The '20s followed the unspeakable horrors of the Great War closely and then the Spanish flu pandemic. In the United States, people wanted a release from their sacrifices and embarked on a spree that became the Roaring '20s. But there was political stability, a "return to normalcy," and the economy boomed.

In Europe, to the contrary, there was political chaos and, in many places, economic uncertainty. The great imperial dynasties of Germany, Austria, and Russia had collapsed.

Many countries, most notably Germany, endured hyperinflation. Communism made political gains, and this frightened the establishment. The far-right also began to emerge, and the more moderate political parties saw them as a counterweight to the communists and largely ignored their threat. There were violent battles on the streets of Paris, Berlin, and Rome. In this maelstrom, Lenin, Stalin, Mussolini, Hitler, and Franco took power. Democracy faltered and disappeared in Italy, Germany, and Spain, and it had never taken hold in Russia. It became the age of the totalitarians.

In the decade before Trump's election in 2016, the United States did suffer a severe recession, the worst since the Great Depression of the 1930s. Still, the economy had recovered and was well on the way to full employment and record highs in the stock markets. There was political stability, although partisanship had reached an emotional pitch not seen since the pre-Civil War era.

There was, however, a demographic factor at play that may have helped Trump win the election. To be sure, many Trump supporters embraced his promise to expand the economy and get better trade deals. Ohers liked his blunt speech and pledge to save American industry. Still others resented Hillary Clinton for asserting that they were among the "deplorables." But others no doubt reacted favorably to his condemnation of illegal immigration and his thinly veiled racism. Whites in America were destined to become a minority within a generation or two. Some of them, especially those with modest educations, feared that they were losing their way of life and their ability to secure well-paying employment. They wanted Trump to save their jobs and keep the immigrants out. They wanted to preserve a world that was changing rapidly and forever.

So, in the sense that Trump demonized immigrants and blamed foreigners for America's problems, he resembled the dictators of the 20s, who played on their people's fears and prejudices—Lenin the capitalists, Mussolini the communists, Hitler the Jews. But in fairness, his demagoguery is neither as venomous nor as dangerous as the others. It is just nasty.

Q. Do you see any similarities between Mussolini's personality and Trump's?

A. Both are egomaniacal and narcissistic. Both are messianic and think that they alone can save their countries and people. Both seek short-term success and act impulsively. Both are vain about their appearance. Both resent criticism and deflect blame. Both are dishonest. Both demand total loyalty from subordinates but are reluctant to reciprocate it. Both are showmen and love the stage. Both are salesmen and think they can persuade anyone of anything.

But Mussolini was better read and more thoughtful than Trump. He was also multilingual, a successful journalist, and devoted to healthy habits in his diet and exercise routine. Trump is none of these things. He doesn't read even short briefing papers, much less books on philosophy and history, as Mussolini did, has little idea of correct punctuation and spelling in his native and only language, believes that physical exercise is deleterious, and enjoys junk food.

Q. Both Mussolini and Trump, with great foresight with respect to their times understood the power of new technologies, utilizing the not yet widespread new mass media as tools for creating political consensus: cinema, newsreels, radio for Mussolini; social networks, television, Fox News channel for Trump. Do these means really influence voters and if so how? And what has been the effect of fake news, that Trump has so shrewdly made popular?

A. Yes, Mussolini and Trump know how to use modern communication media for their political benefit. Mussolini seized on newsreels and the radio to enhance his coordinated propaganda efforts and to good effect. Trump was among the first and most successful in using Twitter and other social media for political ends.

Mussolini quickly eliminated the free press and used radio and film to enhance his image and reinforce his propaganda. Trump, of course, confronts daily an open and skeptical press. He has used Twitter to bypass the established media and speak directly to his constituents with his version of the truth. He has also had the advantage of a compelling, sympathetic, and largely sycophantic news outlet—Fox—and they have created a symbiotic relationship. Fox scores high viewer ratings, and Trump gets unconditionally favorable coverage.

But both Trump and Mussolini use perhaps the most traditional political technique to their advantage—the mass rally—and both seem to thrive when in front of a large crowd.

Q. Both Mussolini and Trump have been called serial predators with women. Do you think this characteristic influences their relationship with power? And why is power, dominance, and winning, so important to them?

A. It is well documented that Trump and Mussolini have used their positions of wealth and/or power to exploit and abuse women. In Trump's case, it's on tape. And Mussolini was notorious not only for his mistresses but also for his brief and almost feral encounters with women, often in his office.

But it should be noted that their behavior is not unusual in the annals of powerful men. In the United States, for example, Franklin Roosevelt, John Kennedy, and Lyndon Johnson all carried on numerous affairs, some lasting not more than a single session. And in a celebrated case that needs no comment, Bill Clinton seduced a young intern in the Oval Office.

It is unfortunate, but hardly surprising, that powerful men use the allure of their office or wealth to seduce women, often young and impressionable women. We need only read Suetonius' "Twelve Caesars" to remind ourselves that this has been the case for millennia.

Nevertheless, for both of them it seems that the serial compulsive and disposable consumption of the female body serves to reinforce a supremacy of dominance that not all men in power, even the greatest ladies' men, possess. It is a typically rapacious behavior with respect to power that constitutes a confirmation of their egos.

Q. Do you think that there is a common vision of the future between these two leaders who see in the goal of self-sufficiency of their respective countries, (Mussolini with the autarky, exasperated by sanctions and Trump with his Make America Great Again rejecting dependency from foreign manufacturers especially from China) a fundamental characteristic of the new world order?

A. Of all Mussolini's many mistakes, his pursuit of autarky was among the most costly. The idea comported with his vision of a resurgent Italy, strong and independent. But it was a base failure and marked by incompetence, corruption, and inefficiencies.

Trump's economic policies, I think, find a different motivation. It's not so much that he is opposed to trade, or believes that America can prosper without it, but instead that he thinks the trade agreements that his predecessors negotiated are detrimental to America and have cost the United States jobs, money, and prestige. He fancies himself a great deal-maker and promises that he can and will do better.

In Trump's manner of thought, this has two additional benefits: it appeals to his constituency by assuring them that high-paying manufacturing jobs will return, and it negates what his immediate predecessor, Barack Obama, has done. Trump seems determined to undermine everything that Obama did and in fact often mentions Obama policies that he, Trump, claims have failed. It betrays Trump's personal insecurities and his vindictive nature.

But Trump's promises here are much like his promise to have Mexico pay for the barrier wall—empty and mostly counterproductive. He renegotiated NAFTA, gave it a different name, and agreed to virtually the same terms. He blundered into a trade war with China with dire consequences for American exports, especially agricultural goods. (China, I should note, needs to change its trading practices. That country's theft of intellectual property does endanger the world commercial system, and previous American presidents, going back to Reagan, have lamented it but done nothing about it.) And in perhaps his most inane economic decision, Trump withdrew the United States from negotiations for the Trans-Pacific Partnership, thus ceding economic and political influence in the Pacific basin to China.

In addition to his economic policies, Trump has taken other measures to distance the United States from the rest of the world. He has withdrawn from the Paris Accord on the Environment, threatened to reduce or eliminate certain American contributions to the UN and other international organizations (most recently the WHO because of the coronavirus crisis), and criticized NATO members and their leaders.

How do any of these decisions and actions make America great? They don't, of course. But they do appeal to Trump's voters in a sort of perverse way, and they do appeal to him, the deal maker. He seems to sincerely think that others are cheating or deceiving the United States, and he takes it personally, as if he were still building hotels and running casinos and his competitors were taking advantage of him. *Make America Great Again* provides him with the pretext to take measures that demonstrate his independence of thought and appease his supporters. It is, as always, all about him.

Q. Speaking again of similarities of times, it is remarkable that the coronavirus today has caused millions of deaths, just as the Spanish flu did. Do you think that Trump's America and the whole world have lessons to learn from that pandemic, which Mussolini, with a significant image reference in Il Popolo d'Italia, attributed to the "filthy habit of shaking hands"?

A. There is a lesson to learn, and it is the polar opposite of what Trump has done. First, a pandemic is, by definition, an international crisis. It requires international cooperation, not shaming and blaming others. It also involves advice and counsel from authoritative sources, such as epidemiologists and virologists, and not politicians such as Trump attempting to score political points and satisfy personal grudges.

It also requires planning, both for the near and long term. First, contain the virus through testing, isolation, and social distancing and then eliminate it through a vaccine. Then stockpile the needed medical supplies throughout the world for the next pandemic—there is sure to be one—and establish an international agency to oversee and coordinate information and communication.

Will Trump agree to these commonsensical measures? Perhaps, if he can take credit for them. But he likely will lose interest once the crisis has passed. His vision extends only to how he looks in tomorrow's newscasts.

I had never come across Mussolini's quote about "the dirty habit of shaking hands." But here again is another similarity with Trump, a noted germaphobe. Long before the coronavirus took hold, Trump was known to wash his hands after shaking hands or avoiding the practice altogether. In this, as in few other matters, he may have been right.

ROBERT J. CALLAHAN

Bob Callahan was a Foreign Service officer for thirty-two years, ending his career as ambassador to Nicaragua from 2008 to 2011. In addition to other assignments in Latin America (Costa Rica, Honduras, and Bolivia) and Europe (London, Athens, and Rome), he served in Baghdad as the press attaché and embassy spokesman from 2004 to 2005. He also taught national security policy for two years at the National War College and spent three years as a diplomatic fellow at George Washington University, where he taught courses and lectured on foreign policy, public diplomacy, and international relations. He speaks Spanish, Italian, and Greek.

Since his retirement from the Foreign Service Bob has written articles on topics as varied as foreign affairs and education reform for the *Chicago Tribune*, *Washington Post*, *Miami Herald*, and *Cape Cod Times*, among others. He has also led training classes for American diplomats and other Federal government employees assigned abroad and addressed the House Foreign Affairs Committee on the U.S. government's policy toward Nicaragua.

Bob, who was born in Chicago, has a B.A. in modern European history from Loyola University and an M.A. in American history from DePaul

Figure 9.1   Callahan Interview.1. Robert J. Callahan.

University. Before joining the State Department, he was an editor at Loyola University Press. Bob is married to the former Deborah Brown of Worcester, Massachusetts, and they have two adult sons and a granddaughter. Bob and his wife currently reside on Cape Cod.

Interview with Sociologist Franco Ferrarotti

Q. It has been said that, more than the 1930s, the decade of the 1920s, as Mussolini was coming into power is similar to the time preceding Trump's election. What similarities do you see between the two historical periods and what do you think these similarities are driven by?

A. Historical comparisons are difficult to make and are often not very credible. History does not have a manual, it does not proceed on a fixed track, even if there has never been a lack of intellectuals, those self-described station masters who, with a signal disk and a whistle, have presumed to predict the course of history, if not to direct it. Marx liked to say that historical facts occur twice: first as tragedies; then as farces. It is a well-known fact that the arrogance of the learned has no limits. Having said that, I see a profound affinity between the 1920s and our times with respect to "normal" politics, so to speak, and its actual inability to deal with emerging social needs: redistribution of wealth, unemployment and job insecurity, as well as security and social stability. In other words, in both periods, political representation is no longer representative. Respect of formal procedure aside, it is out of step with its voters. Throughout the 1920s, Italy was rife with the rhetoric of "mutilated victory," Futurism and D'Annunzio's followers, all of which were already expressions of pre-Fascism (I speak about this in my book *Futurismo come prefascismo*, [*Futurism as Pre-fascism*], Chieti, Solfanelli 2016). More recently the United States had to address the problems of its "rust belt," had to face the decline of its long-standing industries and the de-qualification of its skilled workers (the working class aristocracy). This created a discontent in those key US states, foolishly forgotten by the Democrats because they were considered safe (see Michigan, Ohio, Indiana, etc.).

Q. Do you see any similarities between Mussolini's personality and Trump's?

A. Certainly. They are two authentic "gamblers." Neither has respect for the truth as a confirmed binding reality shared among individuals. Total self-centeredness. For Trump the philosophical concept of *non-contradiction* is inexistent. He denies in the afternoon what he stated in the morning. Mussolini tried to take advantage of any circumstance. He declared Italy's entry into the war in 1940 thinking that the conflict would last no more than a few weeks. He wanted to earn Italy a place at the peace table.

Between the two, there is of course a great difference in their paths to power. Mussolini had already become director of the *Avanti!*, as a socialist of anarcho-syndicalist origins, when, (perhaps with secret funds from the French security services), he switched to interventionism, founded *Il Popolo d'Italia* and in October 1922 carried out the "March on Rome," comfortably from the sleeping car of a train. Trump is an entirely different story. He entered politics without any political background. It makes me think that, in elaborating the concept of charismatic power, Max Weber has forgotten the type embodied by Trump: the charisma of the robust bank account. Trump is a real estate developer and unscrupulous contractor blessed by luck, at least up to now.

Q. Both Mussolini and Trump, with great foresight with respect to their times understood the power of new technologies, utilizing the not yet wide-spread new mass media as tools for creating political consensus: cinema, newsreels, radio for Mussolini; social networks, television, Fox news channel for Trump. Do these means really influence voters and if so how? And what has been the effect of fake news, that Trump has so shrewdly made popular?

A. No doubt about the propaganda skills of Trump and Mussolini. As I noted in my book *Fascismo di Ritorno* (*Reverse Fascism*), (Rome, Eega Editions for Autonomies and Local Powers, 1973) they feel the pulse of public opinion as soon as it forms. They grasp it and shape it. In particular, they exploit the need, typical of young people, to devote themselves to a cause, The Fascist slogan: *Libro e moschetto fascista perfetto* (*A book and a musket: a perfect Fascist*), was coined for them, to capture the young people's enthusiasm. Even more radical was Nazism with the Hitler-Jugend and its anthem:

"We march for Hitler
Through night and hardship
With the flag of youth
For freedom and bread."

It is the funereal *Sein zum Tode* (*Being toward Death*) of Nazi totalitarianism. The use of lies was an everyday occurrence for Fascism and Nazism: the "perfidious Albion"[1] and the worldwide conspiracy of the Jews, for which the "final solution" was needed, along with the sinister industry of the crime of the crematoriums.

Q. Both Mussolini and Trump have been called serial predators with women. Do you think this characteristic influences their relationship with power? And why is power, dominance, and winning, so important to them?

A. Mussolini's case is textbook: women are used in two senses: a) as a sexual object and "angel of the hearth"; b) but also, paradoxically, as a "reproductive" machine because numbers translate to power. Hitler is sexually more ambiguous. In both, domination over women is a clear sign of feeble personalities who continually need to assert their dominating power because they are insecure of it, and they need continuously to reconfirm it. Trump is just like that. They are all weak personalities who cannot bear the idea of defeat.

Q. Do you think that there is a common vision of the future between these two leaders who see in the goal of self sufficiency of their respective countries, (Mussolini with the autarky, exasperated by sanctions and Trump with his Make America Great Again rejecting dependency from foreign manufacturers especially from China) a fundamental characteristic of the new world order?

A. Trump, in his isolationism, is more consistent and politically firmer than Mussolini. If he were less ignorant, he could refer to the "Monroe doctrine" which, historically, had its own dignity. Mussolini represents the typical isolationism of ragamuffins. With both men, their inadequacy as world leaders shines through. In an era in which technological innovation is becoming progressively available worldwide, rather than govern it, Trump and Mussolini retreated to their respective turfs (although Trump's is a continent!). It is a very dangerous situation: while, as I have said, technological innovation, driven and pushed by multinational companies, possesses a global dimension which blurs, if not actually erases, historical variables generally levelling these out, Trump and Mussolini both pulled back into their national borders in an instinctive motion of self-defense and autarky.

Meanwhile, fake news, has caused the emergence of a sort of "interior colonialism" whereby individual cultures arm themselves against other cultures considered "underdeveloped" and intrusive, if not *non-cultures*. This is in contrast to what we should be doing to face the challenges of this third millennium and that is to develop and experience a concept of "cultural shared tradition" as a first step towards the rediscovery of the fundamental unity of the human family.

This is not a matter of hasty, intellectually irresponsible syncretism, but rather of identifying and focusing on points of convergence to nurture and spread a common awareness that today, and even more so tomorrow, in the nuclear situation of our times when we are faced with unforeseeable deadly and universal risks such as the current pandemic, the choice is clear: talk or perish. It is essential, as never before, to understand that identity and otherness are correlated concepts and daily practices of life. Instead, Trump unleashes an anachronistic "tariff war."

Although they are very different in their family and their professional backgrounds, Trump and Mussolini are alike in the promptness with which they paid their debts to the big economic interests that supported them. Trump increased the federal estate exemption thereby protecting many large estates from taxation; Mussolini abolished the registration of shares, therefore making more it difficult to trace and tax the owners.

Q. *Speaking again of similarities of times, it is remarkable that the coronavirus today has caused millions of deaths, just as the Spanish flu did. Do you think that Trump's America and the whole world have lessons to learn from that pandemic which Mussolini, with a significant image reference in Il Popolo d'Italia, attributed to the "filthy habit of shaking hands"?*

A. There is no doubt that an interesting, but also disturbing, coincidence between World War I, which marked the suicide of Europe, and the current situation has lessons for humanity that go beyond sanitary precautions. The Coronavirus is a hard blow to the illusion of our technical omnipotence. While people were already thinking, in addition to the moon landing, of traveling to Mars and what to do with free time determined by jobless growth, the Coronavirus has brought us back down to earth. It has forced us to rethink profit not only in terms of accounting outcomes, but has also forced us to keep in mind the conditions needed to maintain an eco-systemic balance. The virus is also forcing us to rediscover a sense of our limits and to understand that it is not sufficient to move forward for things to go well. We must also wear a mask and wash our hands. Fascism wanted to abolish the use of the formal pronoun *Lei* (meaning "You") substituting it with the use of the pronoun *Voi*,[2] but was especially obsessed with spitting on the ground. It is well known that, when a secretary entered an office, the spittoon would come out. In the '30s, which some historians have called "the years of consent to Fascism," it is not the clubs and the castor oil that stand out as representations of Fascism but the public places plastered with signs "Do not spit on the ground." A great, witty comedian of the time, Ettore Petrolini, replied with amusement: "Fine. All right. I'll spit in the air."

The current pandemic is a genuine, sudden and unexpected catastrophe. Like all emergencies, it exposes the true social situation, beyond official rhetoric. It is a situation of fearful and cruel inequalities. Trump and Mussolini, in this respect, once again coincide: they are represented respectively by police brutality and the totalitarian state.

Karl Popper and Hannah Arendt have dealt seriously with totalitarianism. Popper saw its roots in Plato, Arendt individuated its main characteristic in mass conformism, keeping in mind Adorno's and Horkheimer's *The Dialectic of Enlightenment*. Personally, I am going to follow another path. Totalitarianism is only achievable today. There were insurmountable technological limits to the perfect realization of it in the past; massive rallies and nightly marches could not be the complete expression of Fascism and Nazism. It is today with the technology available and the ability of widespread control over single individuals that totalitarianism is truly feasible. You cannot control what you do not know, such as those who can retreat into their privacy. Today privacy is over and gone. There is no escape for the individual. Those in power have effective and invasive means to control each and everyone of us. In Italy we have a public agency which guarantees individual rights to privacy, but it is really just a name and not a thing. It is guarantor of nothingness.

FRANCO FERRAROTTI

A Sociologist and multifaceted intellectual; in addition to being among the main protagonists of the institutionalization of sociology in Italy in the '60s, he was a deputy of the Italian Chamber of Deputies and then pursued an academic career culminating in becoming professor emeritus of sociology at the University of Rome *La Sapienza*. He earned a degree in philosophy at

Figure 10.1   Ferrarotti Interview.1. Franco Ferrarotti

the University of Turin in 1949, with a thesis on *La sociologia di Thorstein Veblen (The Sociology of Thorstein Veblen)*; in 1952 he founded with his friend Nicola Abbagnano the *Quaderni di Sociologia (Sociology Notebooks)*; and in 1967, he founded the journal *La critica sociologica* (Sociological Critique) of which he is still editor. Beginning in 1948 and for twelve years he worked closely with Adriano Olivetti and as a representative the *Movimento Comunità* (Community Movement), was elected as an independent deputy to Parliament in the III Legislature (1958–1963). He succeeded Adriano Olivetti in Parliament after his resignation on November 12, 1959. From 1957 to 1962 he was director of the Division of Social Factors in the OECD in Paris. In 1961 he was awarded the first chair of sociology in Italy, at the University of Rome *La Sapienza*, after winning the first competition announced in Italy for this discipline, and today is considered the Dean of Italian Sociology. In 1962 he contributed to the creation of the department of Sociology at the University of Trento, where he was awarded his second chair as professor of sociology. In 1978 he was appointed *directeur d'études* at the *Maison des Sciences de l'Homme* in Paris; he was awarded the Lifetime Achievement Award by the *Accademia Nazionale dei Lincei* in 2001 and was made a Knight of the Grand Cross in 2005. He has lectured in Europe and the United States. Among his many publications are *Il dilemma dei sindacati americani (The dilemma of American trade unions)* (1954); *La sociologia come partecipazione (Sociology as participation)* (1961); *Trattato di sociologia (Treatise on sociology)* (1968); *Roma da capital a periferia* (Rome from capital to periphery) (1970); *Vite di baraccati* (Lives of slum dwellers) (1975); *Storia e storie di vita* (History and life stories) (1981); *Max Weber e il destino della ragione (Max Weber and the destiny of reason)* (1985); *L'Italia in bilico (Italy on the edge)* (1990); *La tentazione dell'oblio* (The Temptation of oblivion)(1993); *L'enigma di Alessandro* (The engima of Alessandro) (2000); *La convivenza delle culture* (The cohabitation of cultures) (2003); *Il senso del luogo* (Sense of place) (2009); *La concreta utopia di Adriano Olivetti* (The tangible utopia of Adriano Olivetti) (2016); *Al santuario con Pavese. Storia di un Amicizia* (At the Sanctuary with Pavese. Story of a Friendship) (2016).

NOTES

1. Albion is an ancient name for Great Britain. It is sometimes used poetically and generally to refer to the island and was used often by Mussolini to refer to Great Britain.

2. Both *Lei* and *Voi* translate as "You." During the Middle Ages *Lei* did not exist in the Italian language. The only two existing forms for "You" were *Tu* (*you* informal) and *Voi* (You formal). *Lei* appears to have entered the Italian language in the 1500s as a very formal form reserved for use with powerful people who deserved respect

and apparently is due to Spanish influence in the Italian peninsula. Mussolini decided to ban the use of *Lei* not only because it was foreign but not "manly" enough; *Lei*, infact is also the Italian word for *she or her*. He imposed the use of *Voi* in formal situations and in those situations where respect had to be shown when addressing a superior, thereby restoring, in his mind, what he thought was the true character of the Italian language.

Bibliography

ARCHIVE AND CONFERENCE PROCEEDINGS

Archivio Centrale Dello Stato Roma Eur sezione Minculpop, Reports, Busta 5 con il titolo *A Complete List of All Subsidies Given to Italian Newspaperman, Artists and Writers 1933–1943.*

Della Seta, Simonetta. *Atti della Conferenza Italia – Israele: Gli ultimi centocinquant'anni.* Gerusalemme, May 16–17, 2011.

VIDEO YOU TUBE

Canali, Mauro. *Claretta tradisce Mussolini con Luciano Antonetti: Il carattere di una donna.* https://www.youtube.com/watch?v=gyJ4Qoe_wxw.

NEWSPAPERS

Barbaro Michael, and Twohey Megan. "Crossing the Line. How Donald Trump Behaved With Women in Private." *New York Times*, May 14, 2016.

Burleigh, Nina. "Trump's Women are Trapped in a Cult of 'Empowerment'." *New Republic*, April 13, 2020.

Draper, Robert. "Is Trump's Campaign Too Small? Or Is Clinton's Too Big?" *New York Times*, July 26, 2016.

Erovcef, Vladimirovic Viktor. "La Russia cos'è?" *La Repubblica*, October 30, 2009.

Fabre, Giorgio. "Mussolni contro Lenin." *Il Manifesto*, January 14, 2018.

Farhi, Paul. "Fox News CEO Roger Ailes, Network in Final Talks on Exit." *Washington Post*, July 19, 2016.

Frassati, Alfredo. "D'Annunzio e i legionary." *La Stampa*, April 13, 1921.

Gentile, Emilio. "Mussolini e Lenin." *Il Sole 24 Ore*, May 4, 1917.

Gray, Emma. "Donald Trump and the Making of a Predatory President." *Huffington Post*, October 26, 2019.

Heer, Jeet. "How the Southern Strategy Made Donald Trump Possible." *The New Republic*, February 18, 2016.

Hook, Janet, and Monica Langley. "How Trump Won and How the GOP Let Him." *Wall Street Journal*, May 5, 2016.

Illing, Sean. "A Political Scientist How Big Data is Transforming Politics. Big Data Makes It Easy for Candidates to Dismiss Their Opponents." *Vox*, March 16, 2017.

Leonhardt, David. "It Isn't Complicated, Trump Encourages Violence." *New York Times*, March 17, 2019.

Maffi, Maffio. "Gli accordi franco italiani." *Corriere della Sera*, January 8, 1935.

Messina, Dino. "I rapporti (economici) segreti tra l'Italia fascista e l'Inghilterra." *Corriere della Sera*, August 1, 2013.

Milbank, Dana. "Donald Trump, America's Modern Mussolini." *Washington Post*, December 8, 2015.

Mussolini, Benito. "Dalla neutralità assoluta alla neutralità attiva ed operante." *Avanti!*, October 18, 1914.

Novelli, Massimo. *La Repubblica*, December 14, 2008.

Page, Clarence. "What the OJ Simpson Trial and Donald Trump Have in Common." *Chicago Tribune*, March 18, 2016.

Raines, Howell. "Why Don't Honest Journalists Take on Roger Ailes and Fox News?" *Washington Post*, March 14, 2010.

Sherbakova Irina. "Vladimir Putin's Russia is Rehabilitating Stalin. We Must Not Let Happen." *The Guardian*, July 10, 2019.

Whithnall, Adam. "Donald Trump's Unsettling Record of Comments about His Daughter Ivanka." *Independent,* October 20, 2016.

Woodrow, Wilson. *Il Popolo d'Italia*, October 1, 1918.

Zakaria, Fareed. "We Once Trusted Too Much in Inevitable Progress. We Got World War I." *Washington Post*, November 8, 2018.

Zakaria, Fareed. "Why Trump Caved on China." *Washington Post*, January 16, 2020.

JOURNALS AND MAGAZINES

Berenson, Tessa. "President Trump's Re-Election Strategy is to Convince America He is the Man to Fix All This. Will It Work?" *Time Magazine*, April 20, 2020.

Blair, Gwenda. "Donald Trump's Funeral Problem." *Politico*, September 1, 2018.

Blum, Jason, McCarthy Tom, and Sherman Gabriel. *The Loudest Voice.* TV Series. Showtime. 2019.

Bobbio, Norberto. "L'ideologia del fascismo." *Quaderni della F.I.A.P.*, n. 14, 1975.

Canella, Mario Francesco. "Rivista di psicologia normale e patologica." In *Organo della Società Italiana di Psicologia*. Bologna: Zanichelli, 1940. 175-318

Entous, Adam. "The Enemy of My Enemy." *The New Yorker*, June 18, 2018.

Fabbri, Dario. "Donald Trump è un incapace: ma nonostante lui gli Stati Uniti restano padroni del mondo." *L'Espresso*, January 18, 2017.

Kruse, Michael. "The Mystery of Mary Trump." *Politico*, November/December, 2017.

Mascaro Lisa and Mary Clare Jalonick "All Roads Lead to Putin: Impeachment Ties Ukraine, Russia" *AP News* (U.S. News), December 7, 2017.

Sheffield, Matthew. "Michael Moore: People Will Vote for Donald Trump as a Giant 'F**k You' and He'll Win." *Salon*, October 26, 2016.

Solotaroff, Paul. "Trump Seriously. On the Trail with the GOP's Tough Guy." *Rolling Stone*, September 9, 2015.

Thompson, Derek. "Who are Donald Trump Supporters, Really?" *The Atlantic*, March 1, 2014.

Tyson, Alec, and Shiva Manian. "Behind Trump's Victory: Divisions by Race, Gender, Education in Pew Research Center Fact Tank News." *The Numbers*, November, 9, 2016.

Woller, Hans. "I rapporti tra Mussolini e Hitler prima del 1933." *Italia Contemporanea*, 1994.

FILM, TV PROGRAMS AND TV SERIES

Bear, Joy. *The View*. ABC TV Show. March 6, 2006.

Blasetti, Alessandro, director. *Vecchia guardia*. Fauno Film S.A. 1934. 91 min.

Blum, Jason, McCarthy Tom, and Sherman Gabriel. *The Loudest Voice*. TV Series. Showtime. 2019.

Caracciolo, Nicola. *Edda Ciano*. Rai3, November 11, 1997.

Cicchino, Enzo Antonio, director. *Propaganda* in *La Grande Storia*, RAI 3, June 4, 2010.

Forzano, Gioacchino, director. *Camicia nera*. Istituto Luce 1932. 93 min.

Istituto Luce. *Il viaggio del Duce in Piemonte*. 1939. 28 min.

Lizzani, Carlo, director. *Mussolini Ultimo Atto*. Prodotto da Enzo Peri, 1974. 135 min.

Moore, Michael. *Fahrenheit 11/9*. Documentary 2018. 120 min.

Mussolini, Benito. *Discorso Ventennale dei Fasci D065804*. Istituto Luce, 1939. 13 min.

"Negli abissi della superpotenza." *Limes*, September 8/18, 2018.

O'Donnel, Norah. "Ivanka Trump Responds to 'Disturbing' Accusations About Her Father." *CBS This Morning*, May 18, 2016.

Paradisi, Umberto, director. *A noi!* Istituto Luce, 1923. 50 min.

Rose, Charlie. *Interview to Steve Bannon in CBS 60 Minutes September 10, 2017*.

Sorkin, Aaron. *The Newsroom*. TV Series. HBO 2012–2014.

The West Wing. TV Series. NBC 1999–2006.

Thomas, Lowell, director. *Mussolini Speaks*. Columbia Pictures, 1933. 74 min.

Todd, Chuck. *Meet the Press*. NBC February 28, 2016

Tyrnauer, Matt. *Where Is My Roy Cohn?* Documentary, Prime Video, 2019. 97 min.

Willimon, Beau. *House of Cards*. TV Series. Netflix. 2013–2018.

Williams, Wendy. *"The Wendy Williams Show."* Fox. February 26, 2013.

Zavoli, Sergio. *Nascita di una dittatura*. Rai 1970.

BOOKS

Alatri, Paolo. *Le origini del fascismo.* Rome: Editori Riuniti, 1971.

Albright, Madeleine, and Bob Woodward. *Fascism a Warning.* New York: Harper Collins, 2018.

Angell, Norman. *The Great Illusion: A Study of the Relation of Military Power in Nations to their Economic and Social Advantage.* New York and London: G.P. Putnam's Sons, 1911.

Appadurai, Arjun. *Modernity at Large: Cultural Dimensions of Globalization.* Minneapolis and London: University of Minnesota Press, 1996.

Arendt, Hannah. *Between Past and Future: Eight Exercises in Political Thought.* New York: Viking Press, 1961.

Arendt, Hannah. *The Human Condition.* Chicago: University of Chicago Press, 1958.

Arnold, Catherine. *Pandemic 1918: Eye Witness Accounts from the Greatest Medical Holocaust in Modern History.* New York: St. Martin Griffin, 2018.

Badiou, Alain. *Trump o del fascismo democratico.* Milan: Meltemi, 2019.

Baima, Bollone Pierluigi. *La psicologia di Mussolini.* Milan: Mondadori, 2007.

Barker, Brian Wiatrowski, Myc. *The Age of Netflix, Critical Essays on Streaming Media, Digital Delivery and Instant Access.* Jefferson: McFarland & Company, 2014.

Benjamin Walter. *Illuminations.* New York: Schocken, 1968.

Bennet, Lance W., Regina G. Lawrence, and Steven Livingstone. *When the Press Fails: Political Power and the New Media from Iraq to Katrina.* Chicago: University of Chicago Press, 2007.

Bhabha, Homi. *The Location of Culture.* New York: Routledge, 1994.

Boczkowski, Pablo J., and Zizi Papachirissi. *Trump and the Media: The Election of Donald Trump and the Great Disruption in the News and the Social Media.* Cambridge: MIT Press, 2018.

Boratto, Ercole. *A spasso col Duce.* Rome: Castelvecchi, 2014.

Burleiugh Nina. *Golden Hancuffs: The Secret History of Trump's Women.* New York: Gallery Books, 2018.

Buser Steven, and Leonard Cruz, eds. *A Clear and Present Danger: Narcissism in the Era of Donald Trump.* Asheville: Chiron Publications, 2016.

Campbell, Joseph W. *Getting it Wrong: Ten of the Greatest Misreported Stories to American Journalism.* Oakland: University of California Press, 2010.

Canali, Mauro. *La scoperta dell'Italia.* Venezia: Marsilio, 2017.

Cassero, Riccardo. *Le veline del Duce.* Milan: Sperling & Kupfer, 2004.

Chomsky, Noam. *Requiem for the American Dream: The 10 Principles of Concentration of Wealth and Power.* New York: Seven Stories, 2017.

Chomsky, Noam, and Edward Herman. *Manufacturing Consent: The Political Economy of the Mass Media.* New York: Pantheon, 2001.

Cicchino, Enzo Antonio. *Il Duce attraverso il Luce.* Milan: Mursia, 2010.

Deakin, Frederick William. *La brutale amicizia.* Turin: Einaudi, 1990.

De Felice, Renzo. *Mussolini il rivoluzionario, 1883–1920.* Turin: Einaudi, 1965.

De Felice, Renzo. *Mussolini il fascista. Vol. I: La conquista del potere, 1921–1925.* Turin: Einaudi, 1966.

De Felice, Renzo. *Mussolini il fascista. Vol. II: L'organizzazione dello stato fascista, 1925–1929.* Turin: Einaudi, 1968.

De Felice, Renzo. *Mussolini il duce. Vol. I: Gli anni del consenso, 1929–1936.* Turin: Einaudi, 1974.

De Felice, Renzo. *Mussolini il duce. Vol. II: Lo Stato totalitario, 1936–1940.* Turin: Einaudi, 1981.

De Felice, Renzo. *Mussolini l'alleato. Vol. I. L'Italia in guerra, 1940–1943. Tomo I: Dalla guerra "breve" alla guerra lunga.* Turin: Einaudi, 1990.

De Felice, Renzo. *Mussolini l'alleato. Vol. II. L'Italia in Guerra, 1940–1943. Tomo II: Crisi e agonia del regime.* Turin: Einaudi, 1990.

De Felice, Renzo. *Mussolini l'alleato. Vol. III. La guerra civile 1943–1945.* Turin: Einaudi, 1997.

Del Boca, Angelo. *Le guerre coloniali del fascismo.* Rome-Bari: Laterza, 1991.

DiMaggio, Anthony. *When Media Goes to War: Hegemonic Discourse, Public Opinion and the Limits of Dissent.* New York: Monthly Review Press, 2009.

El-Faizy, Monique, and Barry Levine. *All the President's Women: Donald Trump and the Making of a Predator.* New York: Hachette Book, 2019.

Erlich, Matthew, and Joe C. Saltzman. *Heroes and Scoundrels: The Image of the Journalist in Popular Culture.* Chicago-Springfield: University of Illinois Press, 2015.

Fallows, James. *Breaking the News: How the Media Undermine American Democracy.* New York: Vintage, 1997.

Franzinelli, Mimmo. *Il duce e le donne.* Milan: Mondadori, 2015.

Fusco, Giancarlo. *Mussolini e le donne.* Palermo: Sellerio, 2006.

Gentile, Emilio. *Mussolini contro Lenin.* Bari: Laterza, 2018.

Giannini, Filippo, and Guido Mussolini. *Benito Mussolini, l'uomo della pace: Uno scudo protettivo: Mussolini, il fascismo e gli ebrei.* Milan: Greco & Greco, 2004.

Gonzalez, Juan, and Joseph Torres. *News for All the People: The Epic Story of Race and the American Media.* London: Verso, 2011

Grandi, Dino. *25 luglio. Quarant'anni dopo, a cura di Renzo De Felice.* Bologna: Il Mulino, 1983.

Grandi, Dino. *L'inevitabile Asse. Memorie raccolte e presentate da Gianfranco Bianchi.* Milan: Jaca Book, 1984.

Grandi, Dino. *La politica estera dell'Italia dal 1929 al 1932.* 2 vol., Rome: Bonacci, 1985.

Grandi, Dino. *Il mio paese. Ricordi autobiografici.* Bologna: Il Mulino, 1985.

Gremmo, Roberto. *Mussolini e il soldo infame.* Biella: Storia Ribelle Edizioni, 2008.

Guspini, Ugo. *L'orecchio del regime: Le intercettazioni telefoniche al tempo del fascismo.* Milan: Mursia, 1973.

Herf, Jeffrey. *Il modernismo reazionario.* Bologna: Il Mulino, 1988.

Hersch, Eitan D. *Hacking the Electorate: How Campaigns Perceive Voters.* New York: Cambridge University Press, 2015.

Hitler, Adolf. *Zweites Buch. Ein Dokument aus dem Jahr 1928, eingeleitet und kommentier-tvon.* Stuttgart: Anstalt Deutsche Verlags, 1961.

Hostert Camaiti, Anna. *Passing: Dissolvere le identità superare le differenze.* Rome: Castelvecchi, 1996.

Hostert Camaiti, Anna. "Introduzione" to Nicholas Mirzoeff. *Introduzione alla cultura visuale.* Milan: Mimesis, 2002/2021.

Hostert Camaiti, Anna. *Metix: Cinema globale e cultura visuale.* Rome: Meltemi, 2004.

Hostert Camaiti, Anna. *Trump non è una fiction. La nuova America raccontata attraverso le serie televisive.* Milan-Udine: Mimesis, 2017.

Ignatiev, Noel. *How the Irish Became White.* New York and London: Routledge, 1995.

Judis, John B. *The Populist Explosion: How the Great Recession Transformed American and European Politics.* New York: Columbia Global Reports, 2016.

Kershaw, Ian. *Il "mito di Hitler". Immagine e realtà nel Terzo Reich.* Turin: Bollati Boringhieri, 1998.

Khalidi Rashid. *The Hundred Year's War on Palestine: A History of Settler Colonialism and Resistance, 1917–2017.* New York: Metropolitan Books, 2020.

Kuby, Erich. *Il tradimento tedesco. Come il Terzo Reich portò l'Italia alla rovina.* Milan: Rizzoli, 1996.

Lau, Lawrence J. *The China U.S. Trade War and Future Economic Relations.* Honk Kong: The Chinese University Press, The Chinese University of Honk Kong, 2019.

Le Bon, Gustave. *Psicologia delle folle.* Milan: TEA Edizioni, 2004.

Leonardi, Gabriele. *Manuale breve di diritto costituzionale.* Milan: Key Editore, 2019.

Lepre, Aurelio. *Mussolini l'Italiano. Il Duce nel mito e nella realtà.* Milan: Mondadori, 1995.

Levitsky, Steve, and Daniel Ziblatt. *How Democracies Die.* New York: Penguin Random House, 2018.

Lozzi, Carlo. *Mussolini-Stalin: storia delle relazioni italo-sovietiche prima e durante il fascismo.* Milan: Edizioni Domus, 1983.

Luce, Edward. *The Retreat of Western Liberalism.* London: Little Brown, 2017.

Lussu, Emilio. *Marcia su Rome e dintorni.* Turin: Einaudi, 2002.

Macciocchi, Maria Antonietta. *La donna nera: consenso femminile e fascismo.* Milan: Feltrinelli, 1976.

McCormick, John. *Machiavellian Democracy.* New York: Cambridge University Press, 2011.

Mirzoeff, Nicholas. *Introduzione alla cultura visuale.* Milan: Meltemi, 2002/2021.

Mirzoeff, Nicholas. *Watching Babylon: The War in Iraq and Global Visual Culture.* New York London: Routledge, 2005.

Mosse, George L. *Le origini culturali del Terzo Reich.* Milan: II Saggiatore, 1994.

Mussolini, Benito. "Fascismo" *Enciclopedia italiana. vol. XIV.* Rome: Eno-Feo, 1932.

Mussolini, Benito. *Vita di Arnaldo.* Milan: Edizioni Il Popolo D'Italia, 1932.

Mussolini, Benito, Edoardo Susmel, and Duilio Susmel. *Opera omnia di Benito Mussolini.* Rome: La Fenice, 1964.

Nolte, Ernst. *Nazionalismo e bolscevismo. La guerra civile europea 1917–1945.* Firenze: Sansoni, 1988.

O'Brien, Timothy L. *Trump Nation: The Art of Being the Donald.* New York: Warner Books, 2005.

Ottaviani, Giancarlo. *Bugie di carta. Come il potere influenza la comunicazione.* Rome: Sovera, 2007.

Padiglione, Gustavo. *Camerati, in camera! Storia seria ma divertente delle case chiuse sotto il fascismo.* Milan: Mursia, 2003.

Pagani, Osvaldo. *L'orgasmo del regime.* Milan: SugarCo, 1976.

Petacci, Claretta. *Mussolini Segreto, Diari 1932–1938.* Milan: Rizzoli, 2009.

Petersen, Jens. *Hitler e Mussolini. La difficile alleanza.* Bari: Laterza, 1975.

Piazzesi, Mario. *Diario di uno squadrista toscano 1919–1922.* Rome: Bonacci, 1980.

Pini, Mario Filippo. *Italia e Cina, 60 anni tra passato e futuro.* Rome: L'Asino d'oro Edizioni, 2011.

Postman, Neil. *Amusing Ourselves to Death: Public Discourse in the Age of Show Business.* New York: Viking, 1985.

Rauti, Pino, and Rutilio Sermonti. *Storia del fascismo: Verso il governo.* Rome: Centro Editoriale Nazionale, 1976.

Renzetti, Giuseppe. *I documenti diplomatici italiani, settima serie, 1922–1935.* Rome: Ministero degli Affari esteri, 1975.

Rogoff, Irit. *Terra Infirma: Geography's Visual Culture.* New York and London: Routledge, 2000.

Rosenbaum, Ron. *Il mistero Hitler.* Milan: Mondadori, 2000.

Roveri, Alessandro. *Le origini del fascismo.* Milan: Feltrinelli, 1974.

Sarfatti, Margherita. *Dux.* Milan: Mondadori, 1926.

Schwartz, Tony, and Donald J. Trump. *The Art of the Deal.* New York: Random House, 1987.

Scott, Alexander, and Larry Karaszewski. *The People v. O.J. Simpson. American Crime Story.* TV Series. FX, 2016.

Scurati, Antonio. *M. L'uomo del secolo.* Milan: Bompiani, 2018.

Sedita, Giovanni. *Gli intellettuali di Mussolini. La Cultura finanziata dal Fascismo.* Firenze: Editrice Le Lettere, 2010.

Sherman, Gabriel. *The Loudest Voice in the Room: How the Brilliant, Bombastic Roger Ailes. Built Foxnews and Divided the Country.* New York: Random House, 2014.

Shirer, William L. *Storia del Terzo Reich.* Turin: Einaudi, 2014.

Snyder, Timothy. *The Road to Unfreedom: Russia, Europe, America.* New York: The Duggans Books, 2018.

Sontag, Susan. *On Photography.* New York: Farrar Strauss and Giroux, 1977.

Sontag, Susan. *Regarding the Pain of Others.* New York: Farrar, Strauss and Giroux, 2003.

Spriano, Paolo. *L'occupazione delle fabbriche.* Turin: Einaudi, 1968.

Stanley, Jason. *How Fascism Works: The Politics of Us and Them.* London: Penguin, 2018.

Steven, Mitchell. *A History of News.* New York: Viking, 1988.

Tamburri, Anthony Julian. *Signing Italian/American Cinema: A More Focused Look.* New York: Ovunque Siamo Press, 2021

Tamburri, Anthony Julian. *The Columbus Affair: Imperatives for an Italian/American Agenda.* New York: Casa Lago Press, 2021.

Tamburri, Anthony Julian. *To Hyphenate or not to Hyphenate: The Italian/American Writer: Or an "Other" American?* Montreal: Guernica, 1991.

Thompkins, Al. *Aim for the Heart: Write, Shoot, Report and Produce for TV and Multimedia.* Washington: CQ Press, 2016.

Thompson, Mark. *Enough Said: What's Gone Wrong with the Language of Politics.* New York: St. Martin Press, 2016.

Trend, David. *Elsewhere in America: The Crisis of Belonging in Contemporary Culture.* New York and London: Routledge, 2016.

Trump, Donald J., and Bill Zanker. *Think Big and Kick Ass in Business and Life.* New York: Harper Collins, 2007.

Turi, Gabriele. *Il fascismo e gli intellettuali.* Bologna: Il Mulino, 1981,

Villari, Lucio. *America Amara: Storie e miti a stelle a strisce.* Rome: Salerno Editrice, 2013,

Weiss, Andrew S. *With Friends Like These: The Kremlin's far Right and Populist connection in Italy and Austria.* Washington: Carnegie Endowment for International Peace, 2020.

Wolff, Michael. *Fire and Fury: Inside the Trump White House.* London: Little Brown Book Group, 2018.

Zelizer, Barbie. *About to Die: How News Images Move the Public.* Oxford and New York: Oxford Press, 2012.

Index

Balbo, Italo; Bianchi, Michele; De Bono, Emilio; De Vecchi, Cesare Maria

Radio, Mussolini's control over, 50, 55n10

Rai (Radio Audizioni Italiane), 55n10

Raines, Howell, 14–15

ras, squadristi: conflicts with Mussolini, 75; leadership role, 32n2; origins of term, 41n4

Rather, Dan, 66–67

Reagan, Ronald, 14

reality television, 24–25

Red Leagues: Fascist violence towards, 32; impact of the *squadristi* on, 49; landowner efforts to combat, 43–44; power/violence of, 27–29, 44

Reich, Robert, 109

Remnick, David, 26

Renzetti, Giuseppe, 99

Repubblica Sociale (Italian Social Republic), 119

Republican Party: acceptance of corruption, 78; cynicism of, 67; early rejection of Trump, 58–59; focus on candidate celebrity, 81; internal divisions, 25, 59, 80–81; obstructionism by, 81; reshaping of, 78; and the Southern strategy, 77–78; Trumpers, xiii–xiv, 33, 53–54, 80–81. *See also* Fox News; Trump, Donald

Res, Barbara, 129

reverse discrimination, 66

Ricci, Renato, 49

Riccio, Vincenzo, 83

Rolling Stone, Solotaroff on Trump's comments about Ivanka, 128

Rome, ancient: Aventine Secession, 55n8; comparison with modern US, 86; the *quadrumviri*, 41

Romney, Mitt, 45

Romualdi, Pino, 119

Roosevelt, Franklin Delano, 107–8, 135

Rose, Charlie, 36

Rosenberg, Ethel and Julius, 39

Rosenstein, Rod, 91

Rossi, Cesare, 37–38

rural Fascism, 57, 65, 70, 82. *See also squadristi*

Russia: relationship with the US, 86; and the Russiagate/Ukraingate investigations of Trump, 91–92

Ryan, Paul, 61–62

Rykov, Aleksej, 90

Salandra, Antonio, 38, 75, 83

Salvemini, Gaetano, 68, 73n8

Salvini, Matteo (*Lega*), 104–5

Sandelli, Fedora, 121–22

Sanders, Bernie, 39

San Gennaro (Saint Janarius), 17, 22n13

Sarfatti, Margherita, 31–32, 37, 118, 120

Sarfetti, Fiammetta, 120

Sarlin, Benny, 81–82

Scherbakova, Irina, 87

Schiff, Adam, 92

Schwartz, Tony, 126

Scozzese, Francesco Ciccotti, 115

Scurati, Antonio, 115–16

September 11, 2001, trauma from, 4–6

serial predation/misogyny: as characteristic of Mussolini's Fascism, xii, 4, 113–15, 135, 141; and Clinton's election loss, 26, 67, 141; and Trump's relationship with women, 122–24, 135

Sessions, Jeff, 39, 91

sexism. *See* misogyny

Sherman, Gabriel, 13

SIAI-Marchetti, 110n5

Simpson, O.J., 24

Sixty Minutes (TV show), Rose interview of Bannon, 36

slogans: Goebbels' use of, 11; Mussolini's use of, 30, 140; Trump's use of, 51, 101, 105

Slovene areas, 8n1, 8n4

70–71; as a germaphobe, 137; hate speech and violent rhetoric, 33; impeachments, 92; inability to show emotion, 126; inconsistency, contradictory behaviors, 33–34, 113; influence of Cohn on, 38; isolationism, 136, 141; lack of policy or ideological commitments, 40–41, 71, 81; lies, manipulative behaviors, 6–7, 68; mastery of social media, 12, 15, 53–54, 58, 63; move to the right, 63; Mussolini as a model for, 5, 103–4; narcissism, 59–60; narrative approach, 24–25; oratorical skills, 26, 29–30, 61, 81; personal vendettas, 78–79; as a political outsider, 61, 66; as a populist, 41, 61, 67, 77; as provocative, challenging, 29–30, 35; relationships with Israel and Palestine, 100; relationship with parents, 124–26; relationship with Putin, 86–88; and the Republican Party, 23, 58–59, 78–80; rewards for personal benefactors, 142; and Russiagate/Ukrainegate, 91–92; as a self-centered gambler, 140; sensitivity to public opinion, 140–41; serial predation/misogyny, 113, 122–24, 128–30; small size of staff, 34–35; understanding impacts of, xii–xiii: use of fear, hatred and violence, x, 39, 51–52, 61, 63–64; use of mockery, 13; use of slogans, 51; victory, and the unpredictability of elections, 46; views on Europe/ NATO, 95. *See also* Republican Party; social media

Trump, Donald Jr., 127
Trump, Fred Jr., 125–26
Trump, Fred Sr., 68, 123, 125–27
Trump, Ivana Zelnickova, 127
Trump, Ivanka, 35, 127–28
Trump, Mary MacLeod, 124–27
Trump, Melania Knaus, 9, 127
Trump, Tiffany, 127

Trump and the Media. The Election of Donald Trump and the Great Disruption in the News and Social Media (Boczkowski and Papachirissi), 12
Trumpers. *See* Republican Party
Trump or Democratic Fascism (Badiou), 3–4
Trump the Modern Mussolini on America (Milbank), 5
Turati, Arturo, 76
2016 US presidential election: campaign staffs, comparison, 34–35; and Comey's pre-election announcement about Clinton, 91; and the coverage of the presidential debates, 12–13; discounting of Trump during early days of, 9; importance of social media, 34, 53, 135; and misogyny, 26, 67; personalism and corruption, 26; press coverage and false equivalences, 67; role of ideology in, 68; and Trump's call for Russian assistance, 88; and voting against versus voting for, 64
2020 US presidential election, Trump's contesting of, 66
Twitter, Trump's use of, 51, 61
Twohey, Megan, 128–29
Tyrnauer, Matt, 39

Ukraine, war in, xiii
"Ukrainegate," 92
United Kingdom, Brexit vote, 66, 96
United States: European view of as fundamental to Western world order, 96; impacts of *Spanish flu*, 1; Italy's strategic importance to, 105; relationship with Soviet Union/ Russia, 86; relations with Israel, 99; views of politicians on, 44
Urban, David, 36
URI—Unione Radiofonica Italiana (Italian Radio Union), 50, 55n10

About the Authors

Anna Camaiti Hostert lives and works between Italy and the United States. She obtained her degree in philosophy from the University of Pisa and her PhD in Italian Literature from the University of Chicago. She has taught in several U.S. and Italian universities. She is a philosopher in the field of political science and her research focuses on Visual Studies. Her other books include: *Passing* (translated in English with the same title), *Sentire il cinema*; *Metix; Trump non è una fiction*; and she edited with A. J. Tamburri a collection of essays on Italian American cinema, *Screening Ethnicity*. She published the collection of short stories *La vita nelle cose*, and in 2021 she collaborated with Stefano Gnasso and Carlotta Ventura on the essay *Pandexit* published by the newspaper *Il sole 24 ore*. She is the co-founder with the late philosopher Mario Perniola of the magazine of Cultural and Aesthetic Studies *Ágalma*. She is also the author of *RAI-Radiotelevisione Italiana* TV program *Metix*. As a journalist she is the co-founder and columnist of the online newspaper *Succedeoggi*.

Enzo Antonio Cicchino has worked as assistant director for the Taviani brothers in the movies *Il prato* and *La Notte di S. Lorenzo* (*The Night of the Shooting Stars*). He is a documentarist and author for *RAI-Radiotelevisione Italiana* of several history programs; among these *Mixer* and *La Grande Storia*. In 1995 he created the website of art, literature, and history www .larchivio.com. He has also published several books which include novels and a theater trilogy. Among his historical essays are *Il Duce attraverso il Luce* in which he explains Mussolini's political strategy through the images of the Istituto Luce (an Italian Film Corporation founded in 1924 by Mussolini, which became his main tool of propaganda), and with Roberto Olivo *Caccia all'oro nazista* and *Correva l'anno della vendetta*. With Roberto Colella, he published *Mussolini/Churchill. Il carteggio.* In 2017, he also authored the historical novel *Invasioni* about immigration. In 2020, he created the TV channel Erodoto Tv on YouTube.

www.ingramcontent.com/pod-product-compliance
Lightning Source LLC
Chambersburg PA
CBHW022317280326
41932CB00010B/1138